Global Financial Warriors

Global
Financial
Warriors

THE UNTOLD STORY OF
INTERNATIONAL FINANCE IN
THE POST-9/11 WORLD

John B. Taylor

W. W. NORTON & COMPANY   New York | London

For information about permission to reproduce selections from this book,
write to Permissions, W. W. Norton & Company, Inc.,
500 Fifth Avenue, New York, NY 10110

Frontispiece photo courtesy of Chris Taylor

Manufacturing by The Haddon Craftsmen, Inc.

Book design by Brooke Koven

Production manager: Amanda Morrison

Library of Congress Cataloging-in-Publication Data

Taylor, John B.

Global financial warriors : the untold story of international finance in the
post-9/11 world / John B. Taylor. — 1st ed.

p.   cm.

Includes bibliographical references and index.

ISBN-13: 978-0-393-06448-3 (hardcover)

ISBN-10: 0-393-06448-4 (hardcover)

1. International finance—History—21st century. 2. International
finance—Political aspects. 3. International finance—Government policy.
I. Title.

HG3881.T39 2007

332'.042—dc22   2006022162

W. W. Norton & Company, Inc.
500 Fifth Avenue, New York, N.Y. 10110

www.wwnorton.com

W. W. Norton & Company Ltd.
Castle House, 75/76 Wells Street, London W1T3QT

1 2 3 4 5 6 7 8 9 0

To George P. Shultz

Poster located in Treasury's North Lobby—a reminder of mission
and teamwork for everyone who entered

This war on terrorism will be fought on a variety of fronts. . . . The front lines will look different from the wars of the past. . . . It is a war that will require the United States to use our influence in a variety of areas in order to win it. ***And one area is financial.***

—PRESIDENT GEORGE W. BUSH,
from the Rose Garden,
The White House, September 24, 2001

Contents

Preface

T his is the behind-the-scenes story of policymaking in international finance in the years following September 11, 2001—the day when the world began to focus more seriously than ever before on the global war on terror. It is a story that I can tell firsthand. At the start of his administration, President Bush appointed me to head the international finance division at the U.S. Treasury and, after Senate confirmation, I was sworn in shortly before the 9/11 attacks. I remained in that position through the spring of 2005. I was responsible for leading 350 finance experts and staff, some working in the main U.S. Treasury Building in Washington, but many others representing us at international financial institutions, such as the World Bank and the International Monetary Fund, or in fifty foreign countries giving advice to finance ministers and central bank governors. I spent time on the ground in difficult areas like Afghanistan, Iraq, Liberia, and Haiti, made a total of 120 visits to foreign countries, and attended over 400 meetings in the White House, experiences that afforded me a unique top to bottom perspective. I was responsible for coordinating U.S. financial policy internationally—largely with my counterparts in the countries of the G7: Britain, Canada, France, Germany, Italy, Japan, and the United States. I also had to coordinate policy internally with the State and Defense Departments. Communication outside of the executive branch—to the Congress, to the financial markets, to voters—was also essential. I gave over two hundred speeches and made another fifty trips to U.S. cities—mostly to New York to talk with people in the financial markets. I testified before committees of the Senate and House of Representatives twenty-five times.

Why focus on the period since 9/11? Very little is publicly known about what happened in global financial policy during this period. It really is an untold story. While many books have been written on 9/11 and the military heroes and political complexities of the war on terror, none has been written about the financial aspects of the war, and there is certainly no shortage of heroes and complexities to write about. Indeed, thousands of well-trained, highly motivated "global financial warriors" have been quietly fighting in many different ways in this war. International goodwill following 9/11 and new war-driven demands for greater accountability led to a long string of actions to combat terrorist financing, financially reconstruct Afghanistan, implement new policies to contain financial crises, make the World Bank and International Monetary Fund more accountable, and prevent a financial collapse in Iraq. For the most part, these policies have been successful. Serious crises that could have happened were averted, and, with a greater degree of accountability, the global financial system is in better shape to confront problems than it was before 9/11.

All wars have an international finance front, and the global war on terror is no different. The international finance front in World War II included the Lend-Lease negotiations with the British and the Russians, the diplomatic effort to use economic warfare to stop trade through neutral countries to Nazi Germany, the currency reforms in postwar Germany, and the creation of the World Bank and the IMF. Robert Skidelsky's *Fighting for Freedom* documents the role of the great British economist John Maynard Keynes in these efforts, and Dean Acheson's *Present at the Creation* tells the story of the days immediately following the attacks on Pearl Harbor when people did "jobs that needed doing." And "no where was this more true than in making and executing plans for economic dealings with friends, enemies, and neutrals all over the world."*

There are essential lessons to be learned from the people and the actions they took during this phase of the global war on terror. The war isn't over; indeed, it is likely to last many years. The financial front will be essential to ultimately winning this war, but the spirit of international cooperation will ebb and flow and new means to motivate and sustain people's efforts will be needed. Like all historical narratives written close in time to real events, this one has the advantage of conveying lessons while they are fresh. Over time, other people will provide different perspectives. In the meantime the war on terror goes on, and the lessons can be applied immediately.

*See Robert Skidelsky, *John Maynard Keynes, Volume 3, Fighting for Freedom 1937–46* (New York: Viking, 2000), and Dean Acheson, *Present at the Creation* (New York: Norton, 1969), p. 39.

Prologue

I used to joke with my wife that if I were ever to write a book about my experience in Washington, I would call it "My Life in the White House Situation Room." I went to hundreds of meetings in this famous room, which serves as a nerve center of our national security network.

The Situation Room, or "Sit Room" for short, is a small conference room with wood-paneled walls in the basement of the West Wing. To get into the room, you go through a secure outer door and then an inner door. You are not supposed to bring your cell phone in as that could affect the tight security, so during meetings there is always a pile of cell phones on a small desk between the outer and inner doors. When you walk through the inner door, you see on the opposite wall a video screen that can be split into several screens with secure communications from hot spots around the world. On the wall to the right are clocks telling you the time in key places around the world, such as Afghanistan and Iraq, and whatever time zone the President is in. In the middle of the room is a rectangular mahogany table surrounded by a dozen black leather chairs; additional chairs line the walls. The chair where the President sits during National Security Council (NSC) meetings is at the head of the table, facing the video screen. The room is so small that there is virtually no space for anything else except a tiny telephone table and coffee stand near the inner door as you walk in. When all the chairs at the table and along the walls are occupied, the room is as cramped as a crowded city bus at rush hour, and it's difficult to squeeze between the chairs to get from one end of the room to the other.

President Bush usually enters through the same inner door as everyone else, though there is also a back door leading to more secure areas with more video screens. For morning meetings, coffee is available. When the President arrives, the other participants, who are almost always there in advance, stand up. Then the President, usually after pouring himself a cup of coffee, sits down and starts the meeting. Inevitably, the topic concerns a matter of grave importance to our national security. Almost always there is a great sense of seriousness. I was never at an NSC meeting where President Bush did not run it in an intelligent, businesslike way, starting and ending on time, encouraging discussion, keeping people at ease, using humor when appropriate, listening carefully, asking penetrating questions, getting to the heart of the matter, making the decisions, and giving the commands.

ONE OF THOSE MORNING MEETINGS WITH THE PRESIDENT

I remember one of those morning meetings particularly well because I had to make a presentation to President Bush and the NSC on our financial plan for Iraq, which had as its number one goal preventing a financial collapse in the country. A financial crisis could cause great hardship and quickly undermine confidence in the coalition or in a post-Saddam government. The plan entailed, among other things, creating a new currency to bolster confidence and establishing a modern central bank to stabilize prices and the exchange rate. We developed the plan with the close cooperation of a coalition of countries, including the British, the Australians, and the Spanish. The plan was significant enough to the war effort that it required the President's approval before we moved ahead.

The meeting took place around 9:15 a.m. on Friday, May 9, 2003. The room was packed. In addition to President Bush, sitting around the table were Vice President Dick Cheney, Secretary of State Colin Powell, Secretary of Defense Donald Rumsfeld, CIA Director George Tenet, National Security Adviser Condoleezza Rice, Chief of Staff Andrew Card, and three four-star generals with keen interest in the success of our plan: Richard Myers, Chairman of the Joint Chiefs; Peter Pace, Vice Chairman of the Joint Chiefs; and Tommy Franks, Commander of CENTCOM, who was in the Situation Room that day in person rather than in his usual position on the video screen.

As the time came for my part of the briefing, I straightened up, shifted to the edge of my seat, and began going through my briefing slides. I reported that our financial experts in Baghdad had already established a close working relationship with the Iraqis and begun paying people in U.S. dollars, but that it was now time to move ahead and create a new currency. The President made it very clear that financial stability should be our key goal, but also that Iraqi workers and pensioners must be paid fairly, quickly, and more, he insisted, than they were paid under Saddam Hussein. He picked up on the key issues relating to these objectives and he asked good questions. "Why has the value of the Iraqi dinar recovered after its initial fall? How are you going to pay pensioners in different parts of the country?" The meeting moved swiftly from a formal presentation to a free-flowing discussion with more questions: "Who is going to design the currency? What about counterfeiting?" Fortunately, I was prepared with answers, and at the end of the meeting the President approved the plan. After his customary, supportive words of encouragement to me and thanks for a "good job," he switched to a much more serious tone. "You've really got your hands full, John," he said, and I was reminded that my job had just shifted from giving a presentation and answering hard questions about the plan to actually carrying out the plan.

I had gained experience preparing and making presentations as an economic adviser in three earlier presidential administrations, but my current job entailed more than being an adviser because I also had responsibility for getting the decisions carried out. Soon I would testify publicly about the plan before Senators Lugar, Biden, and the Senate Foreign Relations Committee. Then I would fly to Baghdad to go over the plan with our finance experts, whom I had already sent on to Iraq. The most important reason for that trip was to get agreement on an expedited starting and ending date for the currency exchange with Ambassador L. Paul "Jerry" Bremer, just appointed by the President to head the Coalition Provisional Authority (CPA) in Iraq.

A Night on the Ground in Baghdad

I recall flying into Baghdad International Airport late on the night of June 15, 2003. It was a short flight on a C-130 military transport plane from Kuwait. As usual in my travels as Under Secretary, I was wearing a dark blue suit, a white shirt and tie, and black street shoes; also as usual, I was carrying all of my clothes in a small garment bag. Most of the other people on the plane were U.S. soldiers and Marines in their camouflage uniforms, including helmets, flak jackets, and brown desert boots. I was traveling with one of our Treasury financial experts, David Nummy, who was returning to Baghdad from leave in the United States after helping to establish contacts with Iraqis in the central bank and finance ministry in the weeks following the fall of Saddam.

My financial team—working at Saddam's old palace in Baghdad—had arranged for a security detail to pick us up at the airport. When David and I walked off the rear of the C-130 onto the tarmac in the dark night, we expected to find the security convoy, but no one was to be seen. So we trudged along with the soldiers and Marines (they put their helmets and flak jackets on) into the makeshift terminal—a large, tentlike structure—to see what was going on. Inside were a young Army dispatcher and about one hundred soldiers sleeping on cots. The dispatcher had no information about our security detail, and unfortunately he could not even place a call directly to our team in downtown Baghdad to find out where the security detail was.

Luckily, David was carrying a satellite phone that he used to communicate with Washington during his first few days in Iraq. We placed a call and got through right away to Washington. When I got my senior adviser, Ramin Toloui, on the phone, I said in a somewhat heated voice, "Hey, Ramin, there's no one here to pick us up and take us downtown. Do you know what's going on?" Ramin seemed relieved to hear my voice and could understand my frustrated tone. He told me that our team in Baghdad had just called him a few minutes ago to say that security conditions on the Baghdad Airport road had suddenly turned for the worse and the security detail could not come until daylight. "But they say there's a place to sleep at the airline terminal," he said.

"Yes, there is," I said. "But first it's not really a terminal. It's a big tent. And second there are plenty of cots lined up in rows that I could sleep on, but every one of them has a soldier lying on it, and I'm not about to kick one of our soldiers out so I can sleep on a cot."

The only thing to do was sleep on the floor. My travel bag came in handy, as I could open it up and use it as a sleeping mat. It gave me a relatively soft place for my hips and shoulders. I then folded up my suit coat for a pillow and went to sleep. When I woke up after several hours of sleep, it was still before dawn, but a number of the cots were now empty—evidently a military transport plane had come in the night. I was able to crawl up on a cot and get a few minutes of more comfortable sleep. But the light brown sand and dust from the floor made a mess out of my dark blue suit. I would be looking pretty grungy at my crucial meeting with Jerry Bremer later that morning.

In the end, my unusual arrival in Baghdad may have been a blessing in disguise. Not many people in Baghdad were wearing suits anyway, so I could take off my jacket and only my blue pants showed the evidence of my mishap. Later my staff told me that making the effort to go to Iraq at that time was important for morale, and my unusual first night added icing to the morale-building cake by demonstrating that I too could put up with a little hardship. They had put up with

much more. And my story reminded our military and political people in Iraq how serious I was about the currency deal. Maybe it was
even a factor in convincing Jerry Bremer to move ahead and set an
early date for the currency exchange, which he fortunately did.

What Was the Idea? And How Did You Do It?

This two-part story—one part about developing policy at the very
top and the other part about implementing policy on the ground—
illustrates many things about policymaking in the area of international finance. It also sets the themes of this book. The first theme is
that you always have to think about policymaking as having these
two essential, but different, ingredients: *developing* policy ideas and
implementing policy ideas. Both require creativity, leadership, and
hard work. For the parts of my life that I have been a professor working in universities and think tanks, I have focused on developing policy ideas. One of my ideas was a guideline for central banks to set
interest rates, which came to be called the "Taylor Rule"; it has been
applied by central banks around the world. But the idea would have
been useless if others had not found ways to implement it. For the
part of my life when I was in charge of international finance in the
U.S. government, I had to find ways to implement the ideas myself.
In fact, having the opportunity to both develop and implement new
ideas at this important time in our history was what made my job so
fascinating and rewarding. In this book I therefore want to address
two questions which I frequently get asked: What was the idea that
you implemented? and How did you do it?

In each chapter, after reviewing the problem we were facing, I lay
out the ideas we used to address the problem and then explain how
we implemented those ideas. Frequently, the pace was hectic, more
hectic than any chapter-by-chapter account can convey, because we
were dealing with many problems at the same time. For example, in
the days prior to my Sit Room briefing, when my staff was preparing
the slides, I was on the other side of the globe, in central Asia meet-

ing with the presidents of Uzbekistan and Kyrgyzstan, who had been helping the United States in the war on terror by allowing our military to establish bases in their countries.

You can learn a lot about ideas and their execution from stories about people doing things, much more than from descriptions of the ideas and the outcome. One real-world practicality that emerges from the stories is that there is a back-and-forth iteration between an idea and its implementation. After we started implementing the currency plan in Iraq, for example, our people on the ground reported back that we needed to print more currency because it was so popular. So we adjusted the plan. But people up and down the chain of command had to be informed to make sure that this was indeed a proper adjustment, that we had the funds to pay for the printing, that it would not cause inflation, and so on.

LEADERSHIP MATTERS: FROM THE TOP TO THE GROUND LEVEL

The two-part story also illustrates that an effective decision-making process needs to be in place in order to move from ideas to their implementation. I have found it useful to imagine a "financial chain of command" with rough analogies to military chains of command, involving people all the way from the President of the United States to the financial experts on the ground in Baghdad. My administrative responsibility in the international finance area was like a link in this chain of command. During the period of the Iraq currency operations, for example, I would report to Treasury Secretary John Snow, who would in turn report to President Bush, much in the same way that General Tommy Franks, Commander of CENTCOM Command during Operation Iraqi Freedom, would report to Defense Secretary Don Rumsfeld, who would in turn report to President Bush. I would then be responsible for developing the currency plan, much as Franks would develop a military plan. I would be responsible for putting together the right team, setting up a task-oriented organizational structure, clarifying the mission, motivating people, making sure they had the tools they needed, and coordinating with the other foreign policy agencies of the U.S. government.

To make this process work, operational decisions are made every day. Orders are given and on-the-ground follow-up is needed to be sure that they are executed. I always advocated a management philosophy in which people should tell their subordinates *what* needs to be done and not *how* to do it. So, in writing the stories in this book, I sometimes had to go back to the people who worked for me—financial warriors like David Nummy and Ramin Toloui—and ask them how they actually did what I told them to do. I have been very pleased to learn much about their resourcefulness and ingenuity; their actions are some of the most fascinating parts of this book.

Decisions also have to be coordinated with finance ministries and central banks in other governments—the British, the Australians, the Spanish, and eventually the Iraqis themselves in the case of the Iraqi currency plan. Though the people in these foreign governments are not in our chain of command, and certainly didn't work for me, we had to motivate and support those financial warriors too. Here a different kind of leadership is needed, the kind usually found in an effective teacher at least as much as in an effective manager. Motivating people who do not work for you becomes paramount, and requires clear articulation of the importance of the problem to be solved, examples of how they can help find the solution, and credit given for figuring out the solution.

International cooperation requires finding the right coalition to work with. The most effective coalition in international finance is usually the G7, whose seven members—France, Germany, Italy, Britain, Canada, Japan, and the United States—represent about half of the world's GDP. My counterparts in the G7 consisted of the top international finance people in the other G7 governments, and together we worked like an operationally oriented executive committee. Every time there was a financial crisis, or a new policy proposal, or reform initiative, we met as a group—usually by conference call—to exchange views from the various capitals and determine what steps to take next. It was important for me to stay on friendly personal terms with each member of this group, and I did so by doing such things as hosting retreats in the summers at my house in Stanford, California. Like me, each of my colleagues in the G7 managed a large staff in their own capital and reported up through their own chains of command to the finance minister and on to the prime minister or the president.

Sometimes, the chain of command undergoes severe stress. On December 6, 2002, just as we were preparing contingency plans for a possible war in Iraq and doing many other things described in this book, Paul O'Neill resigned as Treasury Secretary. He was replaced by John Snow on February 7, 2003. The news of the resignation came without any warning, though not completely as a surprise, given that Secretary O'Neill had become so outspoken in the press and disagreements in the economic team had grown more and more heated. My main objective after I heard the news was to ensure that the transition to a new Secretary was smooth and that this financial chain of command continued to work effectively in this and every other area of our operations. This required keeping everyone focused on the mission that the President had laid out. Preparing informative briefings for John Snow became a high priority; that he is a quick study, experienced in the ways of government, and fully supportive of the President's goals, made the process as smooth as I could possibly have hoped for. But the change did not happen overnight, and I had to deal with plenty of uncertainties as this unusual transition took place.

INTERNATIONAL FINANCE AS THE THIRD PILLAR OF FOREIGN POLICY

Financial issues have always been a third pillar of foreign policy, along with political and military issues. Over two thousand years ago Thucydides wrote how "The Athenians," needing money for a siege, "... sent out twelve ships to collect money from their allies, with Lysicles and four others in command."* In the modern age of globalization the role of finance in foreign policy is even more important,

*Thucydides, *The Peloponnesian War* (Middlesex, Great Britain: Penguin Classics, 1954), p. 171.

and it is growing rapidly. This elevation of financial issues in foreign policy was a focus from the start of the Bush administration; it received crucial support from the White House and in particular from Condi Rice, the President's National Security Adviser during the first four years of the administration. I believe it is one of the reasons why there are so many stories in this book to tell. Ironically, there were occasional press reports about the declining involvement of the U.S. Treasury in international issues. The magazine *International Economy* ran a cover story in its Spring 2003 issue entitled "The Incredible Shrinking U.S. Treasury," with the cover showing the Treasury Building shrunk down to only one tenth the size of the White House.

But the reality was the opposite, a growing, not a shrinking role. In addition to all the foreign policy tasks taken up by Treasury, subtle changes, perhaps only appreciated by insiders, were being made in the interagency bureaucracy. Interagency meetings of the National Security Council have always taken place at different levels in the bureaucracy. In addition to the meetings with the President, like the May 9, 2003, meeting on Iraq, there are NSC *principals committee* meetings, which cabinet members attend but the President does not. Next is the operationally oriented NSC *deputies committee*, "the senior sub-Cabinet interagency forum for consideration of policy issues affecting national security"; during the period of the Iraq currency plan, I served on the deputies committee. Next come numerous policy coordinating committees and working groups. In the first National Security Presidential Directive that President Bush issued in 2001, he placed the Secretary of the Treasury on the NSC principals committee as a regular member for the very first time, along with the Secretary of State and the Secretary of Defense.* Treasury would correspondingly have a regular spot on the deputies committee. The purpose was to give a permanent place at the table for financial issues.

The trend has implications for how we organize and run financial

*National Security Presidential Directive-1, White House, Washington, DC, February 13, 2001, pp. 3–4.

operations in our government. In the past, finance experts have tried to insulate themselves from foreign policy. As George Shultz and Kenneth Dam put it in their book *Economic Policy Behind the Headlines*: "The Treasury and the Federal Reserve Board have always considered this field their special preserve and have seldom welcomed advice from other parts of the executive branch."* To counteract this attitude, I began telling my Treasury staff to be on the lookout for ways that financial ideas could help our foreign policy, creating a different mind-set from that where they only worried that sound economic policy was threatened by foreign policy issues. This sometimes required out-of-the-box thinking and some dead ends, but there were real successes.

Accountability Is Essential

In my experience in government, accountability is essential to getting things done. General George Patton observed long ago in his World War II memoir that "In carrying out a mission, the promulgation of the order represents not over ten percent of your responsibility. The remaining ninety per cent consists in assuring by means of personal supervision on the ground, by yourself and your staff, proper and rigorous execution."† You need concrete action plans, measurable results, bird-dogging, and visits to the front line, as my trip to Baghdad illustrates.

It is not only the people within a U.S. government agency who need to be accountable, it is also the foreign governments that the United States supports through economic assistance or security alliances, and the international organizations to which those governments belong, including global financial institutions like the World Bank and the IMF. The stories of how we endeavored to bring more accountability to these global institutions are key chapters in this book.

*George Shultz and Kenneth Dam, *Economic Policy Behind the Headlines* (New York: Norton, 1977), p. 110.
†George Patton, *War As I Saw It* (Boston: Houghton-Mifflin, 1947), p. 398.

Global Financial Warriors

CHAPTER ONE

The First Shot in
the Global War on Terror

◆

*On September 24, 2001, President Bush issued an executive order freez-
ing terrorist assets. The start of military operations in the war against
the terrorists—Operation Enduring Freedom—would not begin until
two weeks later, on October 7, 2001, in Afghanistan. As President Bush
would later put it in a prime-time news conference in the East Room on
October 11, "The first shot in the war was when we started cutting off
their money, because an al-Qaeda organization can't function without
money."*

I was in a hotel room in Tokyo on September 11 when the first
plane hit the World Trade Center. I had just flown to Japan as
part of a large Treasury delegation that included Secretary Paul
O'Neill and our spokesperson Michele Davis, as well as many
reporters, including Michael Phillips of *The Wall Street Journal*. We
were there to initiate a new bilateral economic agenda designed to
help Japan pull out of its decade-long economic slump. This would
forge part of President Bush's broader policy vision of a renewed
diplomatic engagement with Japan, which he put forth in his very
first meetings with Prime Minister Junichiro Koizumi.

Like most people, I watched the 9/11 tragedy on television. As
soon as I heard the news, I walked down the hall from my room—
where I was discussing the next day's meetings with our financial
attachés—to another room which served as our delegation's control

I

center, where others started gathering. It was already nighttime in Japan, not the brilliant sunny morning it was in Manhattan. I pulled up a desk chair, put its back between my legs, and got very close—it seemed like inches—to the TV screen. When the first tower started collapsing, I looked up from the screen and turned my head to see faces of horror, disbelief, for some reason noticing, and now remembering, Michael Phillips's look of utter shock. No one knew it then but Michael would later do five tours in Iraq embedded with the Third Battalion, Seventh Marines, and would write a moving book, *The Gift of Valor*, about a young Marine corporal who sacrificed his life to save his fellow Marines, a great American hero in what would come to be called the global war on terror.

We immediately canceled our meetings in Japan, and by the next morning—still 9/11 in the United States—we were on a C-17 military jet flying back to America. Unfortunately, only part of the delegation was permitted on that flight, and we had to leave the advance staff as well as Michael and the rest of the press corps behind to catch a later flight.

An Aerial Refueling and a Change in Course

The plane ride back from Japan was eerie. A C-17 is about as long as a DC-10, but when you're inside it seems much bigger and more cavernous—an "echoing belly" is how General Tommy Franks described it—mainly because there is no separation between the passenger and cargo compartments. The huge, nearly windowless compartment is about twelve feet high, designed to hold tanks and other large military equipment rather than just passengers. The only passenger seats are straight-backed canvas jump seats bolted along the metal wall of the fuselage. Unable to lie down or even slouch in those seats, some of us simply spread out on the cold bare metal deck when we wanted to sleep.

To get back faster, we had an aerial refueling over Alaska. It took place at night, though at that latitude and elevation it seemed like perpetual twilight. The gregarious Air Force pilot invited me to watch the refueling from the cockpit, and it was amazing—the most impressive combination of advanced technology, hand-eye coordination, precision teamwork, and raw nerve that I had ever observed.

The rendezvous with the tanker jet had been arranged when the flight plan was put together in Japan. When we got close to the designated time and place, the pilots started looking for the tanker, which was to fly up from a base in Alaska. They first located the tanker plane on radar. Soon after that, they got visual contact. The co-pilot said to me, "See it, sir? It's right out there." But I couldn't see a thing except stars and the twilight at the horizon.

Our plane was to approach the tanker from underneath, and as we got closer, the small speck the pilots could see grew until suddenly there was this huge jet plane only a few feet above us. Our pilot was using a specially designed joystick with a monitoring device consisting of rows of lights that turned red or green depending on whether our plane was coming up at the right position relative to the tanker. It reminded me a lot of a computer game, but this was for real. These two huge jets were zooming through the dark at something like 500 miles per hour, so it was amazing to me, though seemingly routine to those pilots, that the planes were close enough that I could see the faces of the guys in the tanker as they lowered the fuel hose and somehow got it into the opening in our fuel tank. After a while the tank registered full and the hose was pulled back in, the tanker disappeared into the night, and we headed home across Canada. As we flew into the lower 48 there were no commercial flights to be seen. The plane's radar screen was nearly blank.

That remarkable nighttime aerial refueling would mark a watershed for me and my responsibilities. It was the beginning of a much closer cooperation and coordination with the Defense Department and with the U.S. military. It was also the start of many completely new experiences that I could never have expected when I signed up for a job in Treasury. I suppose I could have gotten a little spooked being in that cockpit, but I felt very calm, kind of resigned to a new purpose where I would be forging new teams to handle new tasks and relying on the expertise and experience of others—people like these pilots—as they would be relying on mine. I slept well that night on the steel deck. Months later, when I flew on other military planes—C-130 transports in Afghanistan, Blackhawk helicopters in Iraq—I would always feel just as calm, even at times when it looked like I was in harm's way.

We were not the only financial officials out of the country on 9/11. Fed Chairman Alan Greenspan was in Europe; he too flew back on a military plane. Horst Kohler, the head of the IMF, was in Europe and, after a call from his first deputy, Anne Krueger, we arranged for military transport for him as well. And my colleagues from the Pentagon, Under Secretary Doug Feith and General John Abizaid, were flying back from Moscow. Their plane flew over New York where they could see the smoldering ruins of the World Trade Center. They were already thinking about the new "war on terror."

An Anxious and Resolute Washington

When I got back to Washington, the city was on alert and I felt the high anxiety. DC was a logical place for another attack, and the Secret Service was particularly concerned about security around the White House and the adjacent buildings, which included the Old Executive Office Building and the Treasury Building. My Treasury office windows looked out directly on the East Wing of the White House just across a walkway. My antique desk faced inward away from the windows so visitors would see the White House when they sat facing me on the "partner's chair" in front of my desk. We were so close that on sunny days people had to squint when they faced me because the white facade shone so brightly. Maybe the location of the Treasury Building next to the White House was not so attractive after all, some of my staff thought out loud, as they looked out my windows and noticed the heavily armed Secret Service people on the roof of the White House. The Treasury staff whose offices were on the other side of the building, facing 15th Street, were the most nervous because of the threat of an Oklahoma City–type truck bomb. When they heard that the NSC staff, located in the Old Executive Office

Building on the other side of the White House, had vacated all the offices that faced 17th Street, they asked if they could relocate, too. For some unstated reason the security experts ruled against it.

We resolutely planned for the worst-case scenarios. We made lists of essential jobs that would have to be done if the Treasury was wiped out—running the $30 billion Exchange Stabilization Fund in case we had to intervene in the currency markets was an example. We visited the remote locations that we would live in if the Treasury Building was destroyed, developed plans for continuity of operations and continuity of government, and reviewed the order of succession.

After checking with the Secret Service and other security experts, I decided to cancel the annual meetings of the IMF and World Bank, which had been scheduled to be held in Washington on September 29 and 30. A number of international diplomats were disappointed and criticized this decision, but our intelligence experts expected large groups of protestors, and a meeting with thousands of foreign financial officials, bankers, and press would have severely stretched the already overextended Washington security forces.

A New Urgency

The pace of activity in Treasury and the White House accelerated sharply after 9/11. I was constantly being called to meetings in the White House Sit Room, sometimes twice a day, beating a path that led out of my Treasury office through the guard booth at the East Gate, into the East Wing, though the Mansion, past the Rose Garden, into the West Wing, and down the stairs to the basement where the Sit Room was located. We were concerned about more attacks around the country, perhaps biochemical or even nuclear, and what that might mean for the economy. What about poison in the New York City reservoir system? What about a private plane flying into a nuclear reactor? We had to deal with a host of new international finance issues, including developing financial support packages for Pakistan and other frontline states, which would play an important role in the Afghanistan war.

My staff worked long hours to prepare detailed reports on the international economic impact of the attacks. Countries that were dependent on tourism or in dangerous parts of the world—unfortunately, crisis-prone Turkey was one of them—would be hurt the most, and we went through possible responses. Of course, not everyone was focused on these new issues, and it was very important for me to make sure that our work continued in other areas—the ongoing financial crises, dollar policy, IMF and World Bank reforms, general oversight of these international financial institutions, and so on. I still did not have an Assistant Secretary for International Affairs to delegate and share responsibilities with; Randy Quarles would not be appointed until months later. A lot of valuable staff time was freed up when I decided to cancel the IMF/World Bank meetings, which require an enormous amount of work to write speeches, organize meetings, and prepare briefing books.

But the most intense work was on terrorist financing. President Bush decided right away that disrupting the financing of terrorists would be a very high priority in the new war on terror. Condi Rice, who as Director of the National Security Council managed interagency coordination, made it clear that Treasury would be responsible for this task. As head of Treasury's international division, I would be in charge of the international part of the operation. I knew Condi Rice very well, and this would not be the last time she would make it clear that Treasury should play a big role in the financial aspects of the war on terror. In the first Bush administration, Condi and I worked together on many international issues, such as Poland's economic reform, and we were colleagues at Stanford before returning to Washington in 2001. Of course, I agreed to take on this new task, but I knew little about disrupting the flow of funds; my whole approach to international finance was to *encourage* the flow of funds.

Under U.S. law, the President had the authority to call on U.S. financial institutions to freeze the accounts of terrorists. Before 9/11, that law had not been used very aggressively. As the staff of the 9/11 Commission put it later in their August 2004 *Monograph on Terrorist Financing*: "Terrorist financing was not a priority . . . there was little interagency strategic planning or coordination.... The then-obscure Office of Foreign Assets Control (OFAC), the Treasury organization charged by law with searching out, designating, and freezing Bin Laden assets, lacked comprehensive access to actionable intelligence and was beset by indifference of higher-level Treasury policymakers." (pp. 4 and 6)

An important meeting of such "higher-level Treasury policymakers" was held on Monday, September 17, 2001. Because combating terrorist financing would involve both the international and the domestic enforcement side of Treasury, that meeting included both me and Jimmy Gurule, the Under Secretary with responsibility for OFAC (which everyone pronounced "Oh-fack"). Ken Dam, the Deputy Treasury Secretary, chaired the meeting. Our first priority was to end the indifference of higher-level Treasury policymakers and to stress the high priority of the mission following President Bush's lead. From the start, we all wanted to make it very clear that there were two purposes of the fight against terrorist financing. The first purpose was to *freeze* terrorist assets and thereby disrupt the flow of funds to the terrorists and thwart future terrorist attacks. Once the bank account of a terrorist or a financier of a terrorist was frozen, the terrorists could not withdraw or use the money. The second purpose was to *trace* the flows of terrorist funds and get information about terrorists and their plans, which was also an important means of preventing further attacks.

Combating terrorist financing requires especially tight coordination among many diverse government agencies with expertise in intelligence, law enforcement, financial regulation, and international financial diplomacy. To accomplish this coordination, it was essential to avoid destructive "turf battles" between agencies or departments. Turf battles occur in all organizations, but they are especially prevalent in government and they often undermine sound policy. Making things run well in government requires that one be on the lookout for such battles. I encouraged my staff to share information with other parts of government with this mantra: "Convey information, don't contain information."

Our first step was to designate a list of terrorists and then issue an executive order requiring U.S. financial institutions to freeze any bank account or other asset held by anyone on the list. As soon as the order was issued, the U.S. banks would be notified electronically; they would then scan all their accounts and freeze the designated assets. Hopefully, the first list could be finalized in a few days and the first freeze could occur in a week. Assembling the list of names would be the job of OFAC, working with the intelligence experts in the FBI and CIA, but also checking with the State Department on foreign policy repercussions. Because we wanted to move as fast as possible, the first list would include mainly al-Qaeda and associated terrorist groups. Over time there would be more lists and the total would grow as more and more terrorists were identified.

Turning to the international front, I argued that international coordination was essential to the success of the operation. Without international coordination, terrorists could thwart the effectiveness of a freeze in the United States by moving their money to other countries. No mechanism for coordination existed at the time, so I had to set one up quickly from scratch. In the days following the September 17 meeting, I worked with the banking and financial diplomacy experts on my international staff to do so, but it was essential to integrate fully the international and domestic parts of the operations, which OFAC staff would work on.

THE INTERNATIONAL STRATEGY

In developing the international part of the strategy, I decided to focus on two goals. First, achieve a *very high participation rate* of countries that would join the United States in freezing terrorist assets. If we could get more countries on board, then we would reduce the chance that terrorist funds could slip through the global financial system and we would increase the chance of tracing the money. Second, come as close as possible to a *nearly simultaneous freeze* with many participating countries freezing a terrorist's assets together.

To implement this strategy, we would create a *broad international coalition* by reaching out diplomatically to other countries and develop an *effective monitoring system* to keep track of how countries were doing. The monitoring system was essential for knowing when to exert diplomatic or other pressure on countries that were not cooperating. While high-level foreign officials might readily promise to cooperate with the United States on a phone call, they might find it hard to fulfill that promise in practice. Many countries did not have an executive order–OFAC process in place, as we did in the United States; others had little experience with financial crime enforcement, or had different views from ours about who was, and who was not, a terrorist, or required different standards of proof. Poor countries needed our advice and financial support to start up freezing systems.

I knew that creating a coalition would require starting with the G7 countries and then fanning out to others. So I organized a conference call with my G7 counterparts on September 20 to explain the situation. As the top international finance officials in their own governments, they were all well placed to implement the needed actions. I told my colleagues that combating terrorist financing would be part of the U.S. response to the 9/11 attacks, and that as soon as next week we were going to begin to freeze the assets of certain individual terrorists. I asked them to do the same in their countries and explained, "This will be the first of several freezing operations over the next few weeks and months. If this operation and future operations like it are to be effective, it is essential that we all move together simultaneously. So I am asking you to put in place systems in your governments so that you can join us in this operation. After that we will be in touch with other countries and we would appreciate your cooperation in this outreach process." For concreteness, I requested that they submit action plans for their freezing operations in their own countries as soon as possible; we would do the same. With this input we would then put together a G7 action plan that would be made public and monitored closely. I was pleasantly surprised that they all readily agreed, and even volunteered to help bring other countries on board. I thanked them profusely. It was an excellent start.

Later that same day, President Bush made his famous post-9/11 speech to a joint session of Congress, with Tony Blair and Rudy Giuliani in the gallery. He said explicitly that, as part of the new war on terror, "We will starve terrorists of funding." And I recalled my phone call that morning as he thanked some of our G7 allies so warmly: ". . . on behalf of the American people, I thank the world for its outpouring of support. America will never forget the sounds of our National Anthem playing at Buckingham Palace, on the streets of Paris, and at Berlin's Brandenburg Gate." The spirit of cooperation and support around the world ran deep in those days, and the positive responses I received on the morning conference call reflected that.

FINISHING OUR ACTION PLAN JUST IN TIME

While the G7 call was an excellent start, we still had to create an action plan for the weeks ahead, detailing how the international and domestic parts of the plan were integrated. For example, the international part called for prenotifying other governments about the U.S. lists of names so they could freeze the assets at the same time as the United States. Prenotification had to be closely held and precisely timed. If their names leaked out, the terrorists could move their money just before the announcement. To get the timing right, the plan had to be specific about when and how OFAC would develop the list of names and then pass it on to the international team. Having a written plan with timelines was essential for the success of the new operation.

I wanted the detailed action plan completed before the announcement of the first freeze in the United States, which had now been scheduled for Monday, September 24. I knew that I was asking a lot of our staff and of OFAC staff to have this done so rapidly, but when close of business on Friday, September 21, rolled around, I was very concerned that it had not yet come together. It looked to me like we had a classic turf problem on our hands. The OFAC staff were unaccustomed to sharing information with others in Treasury, perhaps because there had not been international cooperation on the scale we were planning for before, or perhaps because like other intelligence-oriented agencies they were used to keeping their cards close to their vest. In any case, I needed to intervene.

The next morning, a weapon for the battle for turf was dropped into my hands. I got a message that Condi Rice also wanted a detailed action plan, and as soon as possible, not later than the end of the day. As conveyed by Tim Adams, then chief of staff to Paul O'Neill, "the plan should be very action oriented and avoid what might seem to Dr. Rice to be rhetorical promises." This was exactly what I was looking for, too, and the message from the highest levels of the White House would obviously be a stimulus to action. Indeed, when they heard about the message, key OFAC staff agreed to come in that Saturday morning and work with the international staff to put together the plan.

Given the shortage of time, I knew that I would have to be directly involved in writing up the plan. Ramin Toloui, my senior adviser, agreed to help. I had chosen Ramin to be my "right-hand man" when I first joined the Treasury. A former Rhodes scholar, he had an uncanny ability to work rapidly under pressure while making sure no detail fell between the cracks, which was just the skill I needed now. Soon after getting Rice's message, Ramin and I walked through the tunnel to OFAC, which is located across Pennsylvania Avenue from the main Treasury Building. We met with the staff in their windowless conference room. At the start I asked that no one leave until we were finished, and after about four hours of furious work we did finish.

The action plan was drafted on a large paper pad mounted on an easel that everyone in the room could see. Ramin or I would stand by the easel writing down various steps in the plan—notify five thousand U.S. banks, send cables to all U.S. embassies, call the finance minister from the United Arab Emirates, and so on—writing in ambitious dates and getting reaction from the OFAC experts. Sometimes they saw that our sequence of steps was logistically impossible, so we switched them around or adjusted the timelines to give more time for one step or another. When one sheet was filled, we flipped it over and went on to the next. Proceeding in this way we finalized the plan. When it was done, Ramin tore the large paper sheets off the pad and we headed back to my office, where we reduced it to a concise typewritten document, eight pages long. I then sent a memo to Condi Rice with a copy of the action plan complete with timelines. We finished before the end of the day and well before the scheduled start of the action on Monday.

The plan started with the day of the first executive order and went on to the second tier of names in October. It included G7 finance ministers' conference calls and meetings, as well as individual calls to finance ministries outside the G7, such as Switzerland, Saudi Arabia, Kuwait, and Indonesia. It included an emergency meeting of the Financial Action Task Force, an international group set up in 1991 to encourage better anti–money laundering standards and practices. According to the plan, they would develop new "terrorist financing" standards for countries. The plan had an explicit task for the IMF: providing on-the-ground technical assistance to poor countries. We were helped by Colin Powell's diplomatic efforts to have UN Security Council Resolution 1373 passed, calling on member countries to take all necessary actions to "prevent and suppress the financing of terrorist acts." But based on past experiences with compliance of UN resolutions, I knew our direct contact with other finance ministries would be essential.

The integrated action plan was well received in Treasury and the White House. After reading it and getting reactions, Ken Dam sent a memo to me and the domestic Treasury staff stating: "I've asked John to take charge of the execution and the updating of the plan." While I worried that this assignment would not be well received by OFAC, and cause more coordination problems later, I was very happy that the plan was finished in time and we were all ready to go.

LAUNCHING A STRIKE ON THE GLOBAL TERROR NETWORK

On Monday, September 24, 2001, President Bush issued the executive order naming twenty-seven individuals and terrorist organizations, including Al Rashid Trust, a Pakistani-based financial group that provided financial support to al-Qaeda, and the Wafa Humanitarian Organization, an Islamic charity that also funneled money to al-Qaeda. The order instructed U.S. financial institutions to freeze all their assets.

President Bush announced the freeze in the Rose Garden, and his words sent an important message to terrorists and to my team. Listening to him, I realized that a new breed of warriors—global financial warriors—was about to enter the fight against the terrorists. He said: "Today, we have launched a strike on the financial foundation of the global terror network. Make no mistake about it, I've asked our military to be ready for a reason. But the American people must understand this war on terrorism will be fought on a variety of fronts, in different ways. The front lines will look different from the wars of the past. . . . It is a war that is going to take a while. It is a war that will have many fronts. It is a war that will require the United States to use our influence in a variety of areas in order to win it. And one area is financial."

The second list, containing another 39 names, was released on October 12, and by the end of 2001 there would be seven lists and a total of 162 names. For the second list I notified my G7 counterparts in advance of our own announcement. They then handed the information over to their freezing authorities, who told their banks to freeze the assets on the same October 12 release date. This way we simultaneously froze assets with other countries. To emphasize the unusual international cooperation, I issued a statement that day saying, "I am pleased to announce today that all members of the G7 are taking simultaneous action to block assets of terrorist individuals and groups identified by the United States. This is just one example of the unprecedented level of international cooperation we have received to combat the financing of terrorism." This prenotification process was applied in all subsequent listings and would eventually expand beyond the G7, especially in certain key cases where many of the assets were known to be in a particular country. For example, Pakistan froze the assets of Al Rashid Trust very soon after the first executive order went out.

A JAM-PACKED G7 ACTION PLAN TO COMBAT THE FINANCING OF TERRORISM

To formalize the G7 commitments, I recommended a conference call between the G7 finance ministers themselves, in addition to the frequent calls between me and my counterparts. Such a conference call had never occurred before—at least no one we contacted could remember one—so simply having the call would be unprecedented. That conference call took place on September 25 at 8 a.m. Washington time, and it turned out to be a success in that all the ministers gave their full support to the U.S. efforts to freeze assets. A formal statement was issued after the conference call: "Since the attacks, we have all shared our national action plans to block the assets of terrorists. . . . We will integrate these action plans and pursue a comprehensive strategy to disrupt terrorist funding around the world."

We then held a special G7 meeting on October 6 at the Treasury in Washington, at which we integrated the different national action plans and issued a comprehensive G7 action plan. I insisted that we keep the G7 plan to one page, which meant that we cut the useless rhetoric and jam-packed in the actions. As a result, the plan consisted of only 479 words, took just a couple of minutes to read, and could easily be circulated to get support from finance ministers and central bank governors in other countries.

We, the G-7 Finance Ministers, have developed an integrated, comprehensive Action Plan to block the assets of terrorists and their associates. We pledge to work together to deliver real results in combating the scourge of the financing of terrorism.

More vigorous implementation of international sanctions is critical to cut off the financing of terrorism. We are implementing UNSCR 1333 and UNSCR 1373, which call on all States to freeze the funds and financial assets not only of the terrorist Usama bin Laden and his associates, but terrorists all over the world. Each of us will ratify the UN Convention on the Suppression of Terrorist

Financing as soon as possible. We will work within our Governments to consider additional measures and share lists of terrorists as necessary to ensure that the entire network of terrorist financing is addressed.

The Financial Action Task Force (FATF) should play a vital role in fighting the financing of terrorism. At its extraordinary plenary meeting in Washington D.C., FATF should focus on specific measures to combat terrorist financing, including: Issuing special FATF recommendations and revising the FATF 40 Recommendations to take into account the need to fight terrorist financing, including through increased transparency; Issuing special guidance for financial institutions on practices associated with the financing of terrorism that warrant further action on the part of affected institutions; Developing a process to identify jurisdictions that facilitate terrorist financing, and making recommendations for actions to achieve cooperation from such countries.

Enhanced sharing of information among financial intelligence units (FIUs) is also critical to cut off the flow of resources to terrorist organizations and their associates. We call on all countries to establish functional FIUs as soon as possible. The G-7 countries will all join the Egmont Group, which promotes cooperation between national FIUs, and turn around information sharing requests as expeditiously as possible. We also call on the Egmont Group to enhance cooperation among its members, to improve its information exchange with the FIUs in other countries, and to exchange information regarding terrorist financing. We encourage all countries to establish a terrorist asset-tracking center or similar mechanism and to share that information on a cross-border basis.

Financial supervisors and regulators around the world will need to redouble their efforts to strengthen their financial sectors to ensure that they are not abused by terrorists. We welcome the guidance by the Basel Committee on Banking Supervision on customer identification to stop the abuse of the financial system by terrorists and urge that it be incorporated into banks' internal safeguards. We urge the International Monetary Fund to accelerate its efforts, in close rela-

tion with the Financial Stability Forum, to assess the adequacy of supervision in offshore financial centers and provide the necessary technical assistance to strengthen their integrity.

We ask all governments to join us in denying terrorists access to the resources that are needed to carry out evil acts.

I also insisted that we issue progress reports on the action plan during the next year, effectively monitoring each other's actions. The first progress report was finished on schedule on February 9, 2002. The plan and the progress reports made the cooperative effort a success.

"WE'RE TALKING TO EVERYONE UNDER THE SUN"

As planned, we made calls to many finance ministers beyond the G7 asking for their cooperation. They generally agreed with our requests, and I was struck by the warmth and positive attitude expressed in these conversations, especially by ministers in poor countries in Africa or Latin America who had never talked to a high-level U.S. Treasury official before. Treasury spokesperson Michele Davis exclaimed, "We're talking to everyone under the sun," and was promptly quoted by Michael Phillips in an October 1, 2001, *Wall Street Journal* article: "Global Allies Answer U.S. Calls to Freeze Assets of Suspected Terrorist Operations."

Many useful alliances in combating terrorist financing were forged during these first few weeks of phone calls. One was with Sultan Bin Nasser Al-Suwaidi, the governor of the Central Bank of the United Arab Emirates. Appointed governor when he was thirty-eight, Al-Suwaidi had already served for a decade when we talked after 9/11. Though mild-mannered and unassuming, he was a globe-traveling celebrity in the Arab finance world, looking just as savvy in a dark Western suit in DC as in his traditional Arab dress in Dubai. He knew the intricacies of financing Dubai's futuristic skyscrapers as well as he knew the tricks of transferring money from the back alleys of Dubai's gold district to the mountains of Afghanistan. I respected him for his willingness to lead regional initiatives to crack down on illicit money transfers, and I valued his friendship toward me and the United States.

Another important new friend of the United States on the finance front was Shaukat Aziz, then finance minister, later prime minister, of Pakistan. Aziz worked for Citibank before joining the Musharraf government; he knew volumes about the secretive methods of transferring funds in and out of South Asia. He suggested to me that we invite finance ministers from countries where illicit fund flows were likely to be a problem to a G7 meeting. I thought it was a great idea, and I set up such a meeting in Washington in April 2002. Aziz chaired this historical outreach meeting, and useful information about how illicit money is transferred was shared with the G7 ministers, either at that meeting or later through staff contacts set up there.

THE WAR ROOM

In order to follow up and keep track of the commitments in other countries, I created a special terrorist finance unit at Treasury. I had the unit report directly to me, but viewed it as a resource to all of Treasury and insisted that it work closely with the State Department on diplomatic issues. I had people from OFAC and State detailed to the unit.

This new unit came to be called the "War Room" (aka the Task Force on Terrorist Financing). I made it clear to all members of the War Room that their mission was to respond to President Bush's call to make the fight against terrorist financing a significant part of the new war on terror. And I would quote President Bush's words: "I made it clear that part of winning the war against terror would be to cut off these evil people's money; it would be to trace their assets and freeze them . . . and not only do that at home, but *to convince others around the world to join us* in doing so" (italics added).*

*George W. Bush, "We're Making Progress," Remarks at FEMA Headquarters, Washington, DC, October 1, 2001.

The actual War Room was next to my office, and about the same size, but a dozen people along with computers, phone banks, work tables, and copying machines managed to squeeze in. Maps and charts showing progress lined the walls. Visitors to the Treasury were frequently interested in visiting the War Room. I especially recall giving a tour to Jeremy Greenstock, who was then responsible for terrorist financing at the UN and later special British envoy to Iraq. He was most impressed with how rapidly the operation was set up and said he wanted the UN to develop a similar capacity, though it never did. The extraordinary high spirits and enthusiasm of this band of brothers and sisters who worked in the War Room were apparent to every tourist who entered.

The War Room's main task was to get as many countries as possible to freeze terrorist assets simultaneously with the United States. Its main means toward that end was a country-by-country computerized tracking system. The system produced charts and tables showing how many freezes France or China or Saudi Arabia or any other country had joined in; how much they froze; their progress on the items in the G7 Action Plan; and so on. The information came from a variety of sources, including personal contacts and reviews of thousands of incoming embassy cables. Developed in a matter of weeks, it was the only complete tracking system available in the world.

Armed with this tool, the War Room team supported our financial diplomacy strategy, which included a prenotification program for 25 countries, 425 high-level phone calls and meetings with records of pledges and actions to follow up, and 8 joint designations where the United States and another country jointly put forth a list of terrorists. The War Room also developed and implemented international standards, including eight special recommendations on terrorist financing for the Financial Action Task Force. It led the efforts of the IMF and the World Bank to develop a new country assessment framework and provide technical assistance.

What were the results? A total of 172 countries and jurisdictions issued freezing orders, 120 countries passed new laws and regulations on terrorist financing, and 1,400 accounts of terrorists were frozen worldwide. The total value of frozen accounts was about $137 million, much of that in the fall of 2001. But more important than these numbers was how the international effort furthered the second goal: tracing down and identifying terrorists and preventing terrorist attacks.

I always stressed that the War Room should not be permanent, and after two years I integrated the people and their work into the more permanent Treasury organizational structure, some in the international banking office and others in the newly formed Office of Terrorism and Financial Intelligence. Eventually, John Snow would appoint Stuart Levey to replace Jimmy Gurule and have him head up this new office, which would engage directly with intelligence and other enforcement agencies of our government. Over the two years of its existence, twenty-two people served in the War Room. They are some of the global financial warriors that this book heralds.

THE SWIFT PROGRAM

One of the most impressive cases of international cooperation in combating terrorist financing in the months after 9/11 was the development of a new program to obtain information about terrorists. The information was obtained from a global messaging service—called SWIFT—and it was successfully used to identify and track terrorists and their financial supporters. The program was highly classified, and what I am about to say about the program would still be classified were it not for leaks of information and publication of that information by the *New York Times* and other newspapers in June 2006.

SWIFT—formally the Society for Worldwide Interbank Financial Telecommunication—is a Belgian company that operates a messaging system to transmit information related to financial transactions between banks around the world. There is a huge amount of information in SWIFT, and through the program developed at that time, subpoenas were issued to SWIFT to obtain some of that information. Using the information from SWIFT, intelligence experts could then map out terrorist networks and fill in missing links in chains of terrorists. The information was useful for targeting and disrupting terrorist acts. Authorized by such legislation as the International Emergency Economic Powers Act of 1977 (IEEPA), the program was fully legal under U.S. law.

However, the program was not easy to set up internationally. SWIFT is overseen by central banks around the world, including the Bank of England, the European Central Bank, the Bank of Japan, the National Bank of Belgium, and of course the Federal Reserve. Thus international cooperation was essential and, as is typically the case, difficult to achieve. An elaborate system to control access to the SWIFT information was set up. The system required that searches of the database be done on a terrorism-related basis. Independent audits and other protocols were put in place. In the end, international agreement was achieved and maintained well beyond the first start-up months in the fall of 2001. The unique spirit of international cooperation in those early days helped make the agreement possible.

Those of us involved in creating the program in 2001 or in running and using it in the years after 9/11 were dismayed and disappointed when information about the program and how it worked was leaked to newspapers, who then decided to publish the information, even after being asked not to because publication would reduce the effectiveness of the program in tracking terrorists and stopping terrorist acts. The *New York Times* story appeared on June 23, 2006. It was on page one above the fold with the headline BANK DATA SIFTED IN SECRET BY U.S. TO BLOCK TERROR. The lead was, "Under a secret Bush administration program initiated weeks after the Sept. 11 attacks, counterterrorism officials have gained access to financial records from a vast international database and examined banking transactions involving thousands of Americans and others in the United States, according to government and industry officials." After being criticized by Secretary Snow and others in the administration, including President Bush and Vice President Cheney, for publishing the story, editorial executives claimed that it was not such a big deal to publish the story. After all, they argued, the administration was publicly touting its antiterrorist financing successes. But for those of us involved in the program, this is a faulty excuse. It would be like saying, "We all know that the U.S. military has a signal intelligence program; so how could it be harmful to publish information about the sources and methods that underlie this program?" Knowledge of the existence of an intelligence program is far different from knowledge of the techniques used in the program.

QUESTIONS ABOUT COOPERATION

When I tell these success stories, people often ask, "Weren't there examples where countries did not cooperate?" Countries sometimes disagreed over who should be designated as terrorists. On December 4, shortly after Hamas claimed credit for another suicide bombing in Israel, we designated the assets of several Hamas-related organizations for freezing. As I said in a press conference announcing this freeze: "The terrible events in Israel over the weekend underscore the need for prompt action against all terrorist organizations. Hamas has proudly claimed credit for killing scores of people. Hamas also raises money to support the use of terror in other countries around the world. Clearly, Hamas is a terrorist organization of global reach." One of the organizations whose assets were frozen in the United States that day was the Holy Land Foundation, a Texas-based organization posing as a charity but alleged to have funneled over $12 million to Hamas. But a number of our allies in Europe had objections to this freeze, claiming that there were branches of Hamas doing humanitarian work not associated with terror. Despite our protests, fewer countries froze Hamas assets than froze al-Qaeda assets.

International disagreements also arose over the evidence standards, which were never meant to be as strong as "beyond a shadow of a doubt." Sometimes the United States wanted to designate a terrorist and other governments thought the evidence was not strong enough; sometimes it was the other way around, with the United States questioning the evidence. The reality is that decisions about freezing had to be made with incomplete information. On November 7, 2001, the list of terrorists included an international firm, Al-Barakaat, headquartered in Dubai but with branches and affiliates all over the world, including the United States. Our intelligence information indicated that at least some of these branches were associated with the funding of al-Qaeda. Because Al-Barakaat was operating in many other countries, we called on others to join in the freeze, and I did a press briefing explaining our actions. When the 9/11 Commission reviewed the Al-Barakaat case two years later, they found that the evidence of ties to al-Qaeda was not as clear-cut as we had thought and I had indicated in my press briefing.

A few countries could have implemented their freezing operations more quickly in the first few months following 9/11. In Saudi Arabia implementation was slow and incomplete at first, but improved over time, after persistent high-level requests from the United States and after several terrorist incidents in Saudi Arabia. In a highly visible show of cooperation, on March 11, 2002, the United States and Saudi Arabia jointly designated Bosnian and Somalian branches of a powerful Saudi-based charity, Al-Haramain. Information in possession of the United States showed that these branches of Al-Haramain were diverting charitable finds to Usama bin Laden's al-Qaeda. On January 22, 2004, the United States and Saudi Arabia jointly designated branches of Al-Haramain in Pakistan, Indonesia, Kenya, and Tanzania. U.S. intelligence had evidence that Al-Haramain financially assisted the al-Qaeda affiliated terrorist group Jemaah Islamiyah, which bombed the Bali nightclub where 202 people were killed. Employees of Al-Haramain also assisted in the bombings of U.S. embassies in Nairobi and Dar-Es-Salaam, which killed 224 people.

THE HAWALAS: GOING BEYOND THE FORMAL FINANCIAL NETWORKS

Our freezing operation initially focused on the formal financial system, but as terrorist assets were frozen, they began to increase their use of alternative means to move their money around. This required that we learn about alternative ways to transmit funds abroad and try to prevent the use of these alternatives. One of the most important and fascinating alternatives is the *hawala* (meaning "trust" in Hindi) system, which is especially popular for immigrants in the Middle East and South Asia. A hawala provides a means of transmitting value across national borders without any movements of money taking place, which means there is no record or way to trace the transactions.

A hawala can be located anywhere, in a storefront, or in a section of a jewelry store. Suppose a Pakistani cab driver in San Francisco wants to send $1,000 to his mother who lives in Karachi. The cab driver gives the money to a person working at the hawala. The hawala calls or e-mails a contact in Karachi, tells the contact to deliver the $1,000 to the cab driver's mother, and the money is delivered within hours. No money is ever shipped. There are no records. Everything is based on trust. The hawalas usually charge only 1 to 3 percent, much less than formal financial institutions such as Western Union, which often charge 10 to 15 percent to transfer money.

With a larger volume of money transfers going from the United States to Pakistan than in the other direction, at some point the hawala would have to settle with its contact in Pakistan; but this would occur much later and not be related to the individual transactions. For example, if there was a credit in favor of the Pakistani-based hawalas, it could be cleared off the books when some used American cars were shipped to Karachi. If a shipload of one hundred $6,000 used cars was sent to Karachi, but only $5,000 per car was invoiced, the $100,000 difference would be enough to clear the books of many individual transactions.

To make it more difficult for terrorists to use hawalas undetected, we launched a major initiative to require that hawalas register in the United States; and as part of the international effort, we asked other countries to register them, too. Dubai had become one of the world's centers of the hawala transfer system, with many immigrants from Asia working in Dubai using the system to send money back home.

Until 2001, the hawalas did not have to register. Thanks to their central bank governor, Al-Suwaidi, that has now changed.

To publicize the nature of hawalas and our efforts to regulate them, we suggested that Secretary O'Neill visit a hawala in Dubai during a visit to the Middle East in 2002. As with any cabinet member visiting a crowded area in a city, advance and security people went to visit the hawala the day before. When Secretary O'Neill arrived the next day there was no hawala to see; those running it, to avoid unwanted publicity, had removed all evidence during the night.

INTERAGENCY COORDINATION

Though there were coordination problems among intelligence agencies in the financial area before 9/11, many efforts were made to improve the situation and this benefited the work at Treasury. For example, the FBI set up a new "financial review group" to bring together the work of all the field offices. Later renamed the Terrorist Financing Operations Section, its first job was to determine the financing mechanism behind the September 11 attack. The CIA also set up a new section dedicated to terrorist financing. While the work of Treasury focused at that time primarily on freezing assets, the FBI and the CIA were also interested in getting information about terrorists and terrorist operations from the financial system by tracing and linking assets.

There was sometimes a potential conflict between those goals, especially in cases where the intelligence agencies wanted to keep the identity of a terrorist account quiet for a while in order to obtain information, whereas the Treasury wanted to publicize it and disrupt its use. The State Department would also sometimes have a different perspective, as in cases where the potential designation would raise diplomatic concerns if not handled properly. These different perspectives required that we have a good process to resolve such conflicts. In the early days there was an informal process for cooperation between the different agencies. On a Saturday morning I called one of my colleagues in the State Department, Tony Wayne, pleading with him—as he watched his son's football team—to remove objections by State to designate a terrorist. I do not recall whether his son won the game, but I know that State won that phone call.

Starting in March 2002, a more formal NSC Policy Coordinating Committee was set up to handle these disputes. It was chaired by David Aufhauser, Treasury's general counsel. While there were clearly different interests, most felt that the cooperation in the designation process worked well.

AVOIDING COLLATERAL DAMAGE:
AN ISLAMIC FINANCE STRATEGY

One of the lessons learned in the early days of the war against terrorist financing was to avoid giving any impression that we were targeting Islamic banks. In truth, a traditional bank could just as easily be a conduit for terrorist finance as an Islamic bank, and implying otherwise would violate a defining principle of the global war on terror, as conceptualized by the Bush administration, that it was a war against violent extremist Islamists, not against the Islamic faith.

Because little was known about Islamic finance in the United States, we developed a communications strategy that included outreach and education. We suggested that Paul O'Neill visit a new branch of Citibank in Bahrain that specialized in Islamic finance. The fanfare of a cabinet member's visit helped us publicize our position that we had nothing against Islamic finance and gave us a means of explaining to people what Islamic finance was all about.

I stressed that it had two principles. The first is a prohibition against investing funds in firms that produce items that are against the tenets of Islam, such as alcoholic beverages. The second is a prohibition against paying a fixed interest rate. This principle meant that different kinds of financial instruments had to be developed. For example, a variable interest rate would usually conform to Islamic principles.

As part of our education effort we set up a course entitled "Islamic Finance 101" at Treasury to teach bank regulators in the United

States about Islamic finance and made a point of speaking about Islamic finance whenever we had the opportunity. I also created a new position at Treasury called "visiting scholar in Islamic Finance," and was very pleased that Mahmoud El-Gamal, a finance economist at Rice University, agreed to take that position.

A By-Product of the War on Terrorist Finance: A Global Remittance Initiative

It pays to be on the lookout for new initiatives to make government work better while you are serving in government, because you may have a window of opportunity to implement those initiatives. One of the new initiatives that occurred to me was a by-product of the war on terrorist finance. The initiative eventually came to be called the "Global Remittance Initiative."

In the course of working on the transfer of assets by hawalas and other informal methods, we discovered that immigrants in the United States and other countries were sending rapidly increasing amounts of money back home to their families in poor developing countries. Based on data my staff put together, it looked like the amount was an amazing $100 billion annually, and perhaps as much as $150 billion. This dwarfs the development assistance provided by governments of the rich to poor countries. At the same time, we also found that immigrants were paying large fees to send the money through services like Western Union. Because of inefficient payments systems between banks in developing countries and those in developed countries, the fees for bank transfers were also high.

Reducing remittance fees at banks would increase the amount of money actually going to poor countries, and would encourage immigrants to use the formal system. I encouraged our staff to study these remittance flows, and we made reducing the costs of remittances a special goal. We soon found that many people were excited about our work on remittances. As part of a bilateral initiative with Mexico, for example, we joined with the Mexicans in looking for ways to reduce the cost of sending remittances, and we soon saw the costs decline sharply. Much of the reduction came through providing information about the different fees, which encouraged competition among the transfer service providers, and indeed banks like Citibank and Wells Fargo did lower their fees. And we asked the Federal Reserve to work with Mexico to improve the payments system between the countries, which it did. At our suggestion the World Bank also got involved by collecting data on the size of the remittance flows and how they were used.

We encouraged other G7 countries to examine their own remittance flows. In one G7 meeting where the ministers were reporting about their own remittance flows, the finance minister of Russia, who joined us—making it a G8 meeting—surprised everyone by pointing out that remittance flows from Russia to Georgia were huge, amounting to 25 percent of Georgian GDP, similar in size to U.S. remittances to countries in Central America. Eventually the remittance work grew into a Global Remittance Initiative, which President Bush presented at the G8 Summit at Sea Island in Georgia in June 2004 and all agreed to support.

THE TOP GRADE

In December 2005, just four years after the story I tell in this chapter began, a panel of members of the 9/11 Commission issued a "report card" on various security and intelligence aspects of the war on terror.* They were apparently tough graders. They gave many C's and D's and quite a few F's. But the top grade, an A– and the only grade in the A category, was for the efforts described in this chapter—the war against terrorist financing—and they specially mentioned that "The government has made significant strides in using terrorism finance as an intelligence tool."

On of the reasons for this success was the international cooperation we received. In the months after 9/11 I said this was the *best*

---

* 9/11 Public Discourse Project, "Final Report on 9/11 Commission Recommendations," December 5, 2005.

example of international cooperation in the field of international finance since the establishment of the Bretton Woods institutions at the end of World War II. I still hold this view, and it is now shared by outside evaluators. As another report of an Independent Task Force sponsored by the Council on Foreign Relations put it in 2002: "The general willingness of most foreign governments to cooperate with U.S.-led efforts to block the assets of designated persons and businesses with ties to terrorist financing has been welcome and unprecedented." (p. 15) In addition to the thousands of terrorist accounts and the millions of dollars frozen, using international finance and messaging systems to trace and obtain intelligence about terrorists became an effective weapon in pursuing terrorists and preventing attacks. In public policy it is the bad events that do not happen that are frequently the biggest accomplishments.

This cooperation did not occur by accident. The international strategy and its implementation—from President Bush's leadership to the G7 Action Plan to the SWIFT program to the hard work of the dedicated band of experts in the "War Room"—were essential. In the words of the 9/11 Commission's *Monograph on Terrorist Financing*: "It is common to say that the world has changed since September 11, 2001, and this conclusion is particularly apt in describing U.S. counterterrorist efforts regarding financing. The U.S. government focused, for the first time, on terrorist financing and devoted considerable energy and recourses to the problem." (pp. 6–7)

And the implementation of an international strategy was not limited to the war against terrorist finance, as the next chapter in my story tells.

CHAPTER TWO

Financial Reconstruction in Afghanistan

◆

W e began work on a plan for postwar reconstruction in Afghanistan at virtually the same time that we were asked to put together the international plan to combat terrorist financing in the weeks following 9/11. The military intervention in Afghanistan would not begin until October 7, 2001, but by September 21 the military plans were fully developed and Tommy Franks and Don Rumsfeld had presented them to President Bush. The details of these plans and the start date were highly classified and compartmentalized, but that there would be an intervention was very likely. Not planning for the postwar situation, at least on a contingency basis, would have been irresponsible.

As with any military operation, there was uncertainty about how long it would take to defeat the Taliban, and more uncertainty about what would happen after that. A prediction then that in as little as three years Afghanistan would be unified, a new president of Afghanistan would be elected democratically for the first time in history, and 8 million people would vote in that election, would have been derided as being naive and wildly optimistic. But that is exactly what happened. Getting there would require extraordinary planning and execution on all three foreign policy fronts: financial, military, and political. This chapter tells the financial part of the story.

FUND-RAISING STRATEGIES

The postwar reconstruction would require raising funds to pay for it, and that is where our planning started. We had to create another international coalition, similar to the one we created to combat terrorist financing, but this time we would ask countries to put up large sums of their own money rather than freeze terrorists' money. We first reviewed fund-raising operations in previous administrations and considered the key lessons learned. The fund-raising effort in the first Gulf War in 1990–91 was not very relevant, though very large amounts of money were raised, because the funds were primarily used to support the U.S. military operation in Kuwait; once Saddam's troops had been thrown out, Kuwait was quite capable of funding and running itself. Therefore, I asked my staff for a review of fund-raising and reconstruction efforts in West Bank/Gaza following the Oslo accords in 1993, for Bosnia in 1995, and for Kosovo in 1999, though these were much smaller reconstruction tasks than Afghanistan, which has a population of 30 million people compared to 2 to 4 million in these other regions.

Another difference was that Afghanistan was a much poorer country, with an income per capita lower than poor African countries like Chad or Rwanda. In fact, non-governmental organizations (NGOs) were already channeling funds into Afghanistan, and General Franks was concerned that the NGOs would leave with the start of the conflict, causing a humanitarian crisis. Afghanistan's economy was primitive. Years of war had destroyed much of the infrastructure, including the irrigation system that had brought water down from the mountains since ancient times. Traditionally, powerful warlords ruled vast sections of the country and treated their domains as small countries, collecting their own duties at the borders and even printing their own currencies.

I also consulted with financial experts outside the government, especially those with knowledge of Afghanistan, such as Ishaq Nadiri, whom I had known for nearly twenty-five years and always called by his American nickname, Ned. Ned was born and raised in Afghanistan, came to the United States in 1955 when he was nineteen years old, got a PhD at Berkeley, and was now an economics professor at New York University. Ned reminded me—with personal stories of Afghan traders and textile makers—of the tremendous entrepreneurial spirit of the Afghan people. "They need more than financial aid," he said. "They need ideas for creating a private market economy." Ned's wise advice about the private sector rang true to me and his examples of Afghan entrepreneurs stayed with me throughout my involvement with Afghanistan. I tried to pass on this advice to others in our government and our allies every chance I had.

"Economic Incentives for Frontline States"

At the same time that our work on Afghanistan was beginning, I asked two of my top international senior staff, Nancy Lee and Steve Radelet, to prepare a strategy memo on financial assistance to the "frontline states." Frontline states were countries that could help us in the war on terror—by providing intelligence, allowing overflights, enhancing border control, or permitting us to establish anti-terrorist bases of operations. After consulting with State and the White House, we determined that there were thirteen key frontline states, including Pakistan and the central Asian countries of Uzbekistan, Kyrgyzstan, and Tajikistan. Though smaller in scale, these assistance packages would be even more time-sensitive, because we wanted these countries to provide support for our military actions in Afghanistan.

The taxpayers got their money's worth from government employees like Nancy and Steve. Nancy had years of experience at the Treasury maneuvering through the interagency minefields, and she could bring out the best in any team she led. Steve, having recently joined Treasury from Harvard, brought in policy ideas from the outside, and would later take an influential post at a new think tank in Washington, the Center for Global Development. I asked Nancy and Steve to focus on Treasury's areas of responsibility—support from the international financial institutions—but I also asked them to be specific about how these institutions would mesh with direct U.S. support. Most important, I asked them to be sure that any financial assistance we offered these poor countries included incentives to promote economic growth. They finished their joint memo to me on September 25 and called it "Economic Incentives for Frontline States."

Using their ideas and working with the State Department and the National Security Council staff, we quickly put together a financial assistance package for Pakistan to support President Pervez Musharraf's cooperation with us in fighting the Taliban. We worked with Finance Minister Shaukat Aziz on the details of this plan, which included debt relief, loans from the World Bank, and direct support from the United States Agency for International Development (USAID). By linking the support to economic reforms—such as improved budgetary transparency and spending controls—that Aziz wanted to put in place, we helped him prevent others in his government from thwarting the needed reforms. To the credit of Musharraf, Aziz, and the assistance package itself, economic growth in Pakistan rose dramatically in the next few years, increasing from only 2 percent in 2001 to 8 percent by 2005.

One day a few months later, as I was walking through the colonnade next to the Rose Garden on my usual path from Treasury to the West Wing, I saw President Bush and President Musharraf coming out of the Oval Office. President Bush called out to me, "Hey, John, come over, I want to introduce you to President Musharraf." We stopped to talk briefly about how I was working at Treasury and had taken an interest in the financial assistance package for Pakistan. It was President Bush's usual gregarious self, but this time, I am sure, it was also his making sure that Musharraf knew he took seriously the economic reform part of our financial package for Pakistan, and that Treasury was keeping track of the progress.

Moving to Warp Speed

Our review of past fund-raising efforts revealed a number of key steps to follow. First, a *needs assessment* was done, usually by the World Bank staff, which indicated what the goals of financial reconstruction were—schools, roads, financial stability, pro-growth market reforms, and so on—and provided estimates of how much money was required to accomplish these goals. The needs assessment is where most of the economic analysis—both microeconomic and macroeconomic—of postwar reconstruction would take place. To me, it was much like fund-raising at Stanford or any other university: you had to show the donors what their contribution would be used for and that it would be used wisely in order to get them to contribute. Second, a high-level *donors' conference* was held, attended by cabinet and other senior officials, at which countries would pledge certain amounts of funds. If high-level officials attended, it would help generate pressure in their home country for a larger contribution. And third, *coordinating groups* were formed to keep track of how much countries pledged at the conference. Following these steps seemed like a good way to proceed, and had the advantage that prospective donors in the other countries would be familiar with it.

Two things worried me as I contemplated applying these lessons to the Afghanistan case. The fund-raising process frequently took a long time, maybe a year or two for the pledges to take place. The needs assessment could also take a long time; especially if little was known about what was going on in the country, which was certainly the case in Afghanistan. In addition, pledged funds were frequently disbursed very slowly, and there was little accountability at high levels of government about what was actually done with the funds.

We simply could not afford such delays or lack of accountability for results. If the Taliban were thrown out of power quickly, which looked increasingly likely as we formulated our plan, we would have to move equally quickly to set up and support a new government. We would have to do this from scratch in a country that had never been a democracy and had been at war for decades. If the new government failed—and we had no idea at the time what the new government would even look like—slipping back into chaos was a real possibility.

To speed things up and emphasize accountability, I decided that we should do our own needs assessment in the Treasury. Though we had only a fraction of the people that the World Bank could assign to such a task, I knew that this strategy would be helpful to get our own ballpark number. I explained that our assessment would be "preliminary" and that the World Bank staff would be welcome to build on our work. My experience in economic modeling and analysis taught me that if you want to have the ability to make constructive criticism, you have to have your own model and estimates, even if they are simple ones. I have also seen how a small group of focused people can do just as good a job as a large group. And, indeed, the Treasury staff produced a remarkably good economic analysis in a very short period of time. Having our own analysis gave me the additional advantage of being better able to insist that the World Bank's needs assessment be done quickly and expeditiously. We could say that if they took too long, we would just use our assessment. It was our ace in the hole.

To focus on timely results, I also asked that the needs assessment set timelines for various activities, with a special emphasis on what could be done quickly and what could be visible. Any new government in Afghanistan would be stronger against the forces of terrorism and efforts by the Taliban to reassert themselves if it was seen to be delivering what the people needed.

INTERAGENCY COORDINATION: MILITARY, POLITICAL, AND FINANCIAL

I regularly attended meetings on Afghanistan in the White House Sit Room at this time, which was essential to keeping the financial part of our efforts coordinated with our military and political efforts. For a few weeks after the start of Operation Enduring Freedom on

October 7 there was little visible progress on the military front, but by early November we started to get reports that the Northern Alliance, working along with our special forces, was suddenly making a great deal of headway against the Taliban. Paul Wolfowitz of Defense and Richard Armitage of State usually attended these meetings. We heard reports from the military of "dramatic improvements for the Northern Alliance" as they "consolidated control of five provinces," and of "pressure on Herat" in the west. In the north, "the conflict in Konduz remains, but a ring is drawn and Taloqan has been taken." In the south, Taliban strongholds remained and some worried that Kandahar could become a redoubt for the Taliban. But it was clear to me that the progress was good.

There was also good progress on the political front. Richard Haas of the State Department and Zalmay Khalilzad of the NSC staff were working with Lakhdar Brahimi, the UN special envoy to Afghanistan, and planning was underway for the international community to create a new interim government. This planning eventually led to the important December 5 meeting in Bonn, Germany, where agreement was reached by the international community to establish an Afghanistan Interim Authority, which would be the "repository of sovereignty," with specific procedures and functions. One of the functions of the Interim Authority was to call an Emergency Loya Jirga, a "grand council" of tribal and ethnic leaders, in Afghanistan in six months. At that time the Afghans themselves would decide on the next stage of government, called the Transitional Authority. Hamid Karzai was chosen to be the chairman of the Interim Authority; he would also be chosen to lead the Transitional Authority, and eventually be elected president of Afghanistan in the first democratic election in Afghanistan's history. But from the vantage point of the fall of 2001, none of this was known.

With the military intervention going well and with the United States and the United Nations working together on the political side, accelerating the financial side now seemed appropriate. I had been pushing hard on the fund-raising plans, and as far as I was concerned we were ready to go whenever the military and political progress permitted. In fact, we had tentatively scheduled an international donors' conference for November 20 in Washington, and by the time of a November 11 Sit Room meeting all agreed that we should go ahead with the donors' meeting as planned. Armitage and Wolfowitz emphasized the importance of coordination with the security and political sides of the house, not only in Washington but also on the ground with Tommy Franks at CENTCOM. As Armitage put it in his typical tough no-nonsense way, perhaps reflecting years of experience in the Defense Department, including military service in Vietnam, "No one moves anywhere without Frank's approval."

A STATE–TREASURY DISPUTE AND ITS SETTLEMENT

I was pushing things so fast that it became apparent that Treasury was getting out in front of the State Department on the fund-raising planning, which created an interagency dispute about who would be in charge of the fund-raising effort. I thought it was important that we remain in the lead, given our effectiveness with the needs assessment, but the reality is that the State Department has far more capability for organizing conferences and pulling large groups of donors together. This is the classic case where the National Security Council, in its traditional role as coordinator of different government agencies in carrying out our foreign policy, can be of assistance. My staff reported that some in the State Department were proposing that they simply take over the fund-raising and financial reconstruction operation completely. I thought this was a terrible idea given the work that my staff had done and the economic expertise required, and told them so. It was also disturbing that the argument was based on turf, rather than substantively focused on the job we had to do. Fortunately, Treasury, State, and NSC staff eventually came to a sensible compromise: Al Larson, the Under Secretary of State for Economics, and I would co-chair the effort. I had known Al Larson for many years and respected him greatly. We worked together on international trade issues when I was on the President's Council of Economic Advisers and he was in the State Department in the first Bush administration and later when he was Ambassador to the Organization for Economic Cooperation and Development in Paris. I knew we could work together, so I was very pleased with the outcome.

Later, in the fall of 2002, Dov Zakheim, the comptroller at the Defense Department, would become a third member of this fund-raising team, and the three of us—Larson, Taylor, and Zakheim—would lead the effort on fund-raising for both Afghanistan and Iraq. I always welcomed help in fund-raising. It was a tough job, and the more people who could get on the phones or make the quick trip the better. The three of us worked together for nearly three years, and built up a reputation for effective teamwork.

FROM CONSCIOUSNESS-RAISING TO FUND-RAISING

As planned, we held the first big donors' meeting at the State Department on November 20. It was not a fund-raising meeting, but rather a consciousness-raising meeting. We wanted prospective donor countries to come and hear our appeals for Afghanistan's reconstruction and to commit to the fund-raising process. We also wanted to get a commitment from the World Bank to complete the needs assessment in time for the actual dollar pledging, which would take place in Japan in January 2002. Having the actual fund-raising take place in Japan was important because Japan, under Prime Minister Koizumi's leadership, wanted to be a significant player in reconstruction. Colin Powell and Paul O'Neill gave opening addresses, and then Al Larson and I chaired the meeting. After the meeting, Al and I did a press briefing along with our Japanese counterparts—Shotaro Oshima, the deputy foreign minister, and Haruhiko Kuroda, the vice finance minister—who we had been working with on the fund-raising plan.

In his opening remarks, Colin Powell provided the important security and political context: "I wish to thank all of you, the senior representatives of foreign finance and development ministries of key partner countries and international institutions, for traveling all the way to Washington on such short notice. Events on the ground are moving swiftly. My government and our coalition partners are pleased to report that the Taliban is in retreat in most of the country. . . . All of us know that the international community must be prepared to sustain a reconstruction program that will take many, many years. This must be a global effort. . . ." Paul O'Neill then laid out the economic situation: "The facts that we confront in Afghanistan stagger the imagination, with an annual average income less than two hundred dollars per person in a place where one out of six children die before their first birthday, in a place where two-thirds of the population are not literate and where only thirteen percent of the population has access to water. . . ."

Each country participating in the conference then made remarks, all of them supportive. The prime minister of Japan sent a special representative, Sadako Ogata, to focus on humanitarian issues, and she forcefully reminded everyone that this reconstruction effort was part of the global war on terror; that "We have to prevent another hotbed of terrorism"; and that this financial support will "help make a smooth political transition in the country." Andrew Natsios, the administrator of USAID, reminded us not to let our effort to combat terrorist financing inadvertently thwart our reconstruction effort by preventing Afghan expatriates from sending money to their families in Afghanistan.

At the close of the meeting, as prearranged of course, the Japanese announced that they would host a fund-raising conference in Tokyo in January and formally asked the World Bank to finish the needs assessment in time for that meeting. We also announced that Saudi Arabia and the European Union would join with Japan and the United States to form a group of four in planning the next stages of the fund-raising, a diplomatic move to include Europe and an Islamic country. The formal titles of the eight participants—two from each country—were "co-chairs of the Afghanistan Reconstruction Steering Group (ARSG)." Al Larson and I would serve as co-chairs for the United States.

At the closing press conference, I emphasized the need to make a "seamless transition" from humanitarian to reconstruction assistance.

Humanitarian assistance is about the provision of food, blankets, and basic necessities to prevent refugees and other displaced people from starving or freezing to death. Reconstruction assistance is about building schools, roads, and the basic infrastructure of a market economy. Once refugees are resettled, much of the funds going to humanitarian assistance should move to reconstruction assistance, but there is always a tendency for relief agencies to make this transition too slowly. This "seamless transition" concept was a euphemism for getting to the reconstruction side more quickly following humanitarian assistance. I offered examples from agriculture—give seeds to plant for the future as well as food to eat now. In the case of education, getting girls and boys back in school and paying teachers had both a humanitarian component and a reconstruction component in that there would be a payoff later from improved literacy rates.

After the November 20 meeting, things went just about as planned as we moved toward the January meeting in Tokyo. Representatives of the World Bank met in Islamabad, Pakistan, on November 27 to hear from the Afghan people about their needs. They were joined by reconstruction experts from the Asian Development Bank (ADB) and the United Nations Development Program (UNDP), two other international organizations that had agreed to help in the needs assessment. The ADB is similar to the World Bank but focuses only on the Asian countries. Other analogous regional banks cover Africa and Latin America. My oversight at Treasury included these regional development banks as well as the World Bank.

Senior officials met in Brussels on December 20 and 21 to review progress on the needs assessment. There I urged the World Bank and the Asian Development Bank to be more specific about visible projects with timelines in the needs assessment. As the Tokyo conference approached, my fellow co-chairs of the Afghanistan Reconstruction Steering Group—the Saudis, the Japanese, the Europeans—were holding conference calls several times a week on logistical issues, and eventually on actual pledges. We had to have most of the pledges wrapped up in advance of the Tokyo conference to ensure that it was not deemed a failure.

At an NSC principals committee meeting early in January 2002, I reported to Powell, Rumsfeld, Rice, and others on progress toward the Tokyo fund-raising event. The World Bank had completed the needs assessment just in time, obviating the need to play our ace-in-the-hole. Their assessment called for funds in the range of $1.7 billion for one year and $10 billion over five years. The United States was planning to offer about $250 million for the first year, or about 15 percent of the total sought, and then stay with that percentage in later years.

On the political front, things were moving too. At another NSC principals meeting in January, Colin Powell reported that the Afghanistan Interim Authority had taken charge in Kabul and was functioning. Of course, this was not the time for complacency. The remnants of the Taliban were a lethal force that the new Karzai government and the international coalition had to reckon with, and the faster we moved toward reconstruction the better.

At the January Tokyo meeting, the pledges for the first year turned out to be $1.8 billion, surpassing the needs assessment. The United States ended up contributing $297 million for the first year. It was more difficult to measure each country's out-year pledges because of differences in the duration, nature, and degree of commitment, but at the end of the meeting my fellow ARSG co-chairs and I estimated that multiyear pledges totaled $4.5 billion. We then formally established an "implementation group" to monitor countries' delivery on the pledges.

FROM FUND-RAISING TO ACTION-RAISING

My pleasure at having helped to raise $4.5 billion for Afghanistan was short-lived, because I soon had to deal with the huge gap between fund-raising, where pledges take place, and what I came to call "action-raising," or getting visible on-the-ground results, such as building roads, schools, or industrial parks. Within one government this is difficult enough, but when you are working with a group of governments in multilateral foreign assistance efforts, it is even more difficult. While international committees, like the implementation group we formed for Afghanistan, can help, it really requires a single-minded focus. Having come from Stanford's Hoover Institution, I happened to know how Herbert Hoover had single-handedly led the Belgian relief effort in World War I, an effort that saved 8 million Belgians from starvation during the German occupation. Through his contacts, logistical skills, and personal persuasion, he managed to deliver 11 million metric tons of food to the starving Belgians in the period from 1914 to 1917, which required fund-raising from governments and charities and negotiating with the Germans and the British to let thousands of ships sail through the Channel and unload in Belgian ports. A committee could never have made this miracle happen.

For this reason, I had urged the State Department to assign a single point person or special envoy to be in charge of monitoring and coordinating the assistance effort. But others, mainly in the State Department, which would have responsibility for filling such a post, felt that we should give the ARSG's implementation group a chance and see how things worked out.

For the next few months my work on Afghanistan focused on core financial objectives—sound fiscal policy and monetary policy in the new government—and I sent Treasury financial experts to Kabul. David Nummy, who would later work for us in Iraq, went in first to assess the situation, and then Larry Seale went for a much longer period of time. The finance minister of the short-lived Afghanistan Interim Authority was Armin Arsala. I had a long meeting with Arsala and our finance team in Tokyo at the conclusion of the fund-raising meeting. Despite the euphoria of success, I stressed how seriously the United States and other donors were going to take fiscal discipline, budget controls, and transparency on the part of the Afghan government. Good budgeting was essential both from the point of view of future fund-raising and macroeconomic performance, including inflation control. It would be disastrous to run a big deficit, finance it by printing money, and then have an inflation crisis as a result. One easy rule of thumb was to keep the budget fully balanced on a cash basis, allowing absolutely no financing from the central bank, even short term. I knew that Arsala, like all finance ministers, would be under pressure to fund many projects of the Interim Authority; making the U.S. position clear would help him resist those pressures.

Budget management in Afghanistan had been in a very primitive state for years. Revenues consisted of two main sources: (1) customs, and (2) budget support from international governments like the United States. Spending consisted mainly of salaries for government workers, including teachers and the military. Records were kept by hand, and from the start there were complaints about teachers or military personnel not getting paid, which was difficult to trace with such poor records. The finance ministry itself was a chaotic place; literally hundreds of workers hung around the hallways with nothing to do. Larry Seale put together the first budget for the Interim Authority—for the fiscal year from March 2002 to March 2003—on his laptop computer. I asked him to monitor revenues and spending and to give me regular updates on the situation. I wanted to avoid a sudden cash crunch, which would then require inflationary finance or some other drastic measure.

The first signs of a brewing budget crisis came to me in a situation report from Larry Seale on June 9, 2002. "While the approved budget contained a number of features to establish strict budgetary discipline, these features have not yet been 'internalized' by the senior officials of the Afghan Administration," Seale wrote. "Additionally, the run-up to the Loya Jirga has added pressure to accommodate various political interests." Larry then went on to give examples of new spending not in the approved budget, including "payments to several provincial governors to support celebrations of the overthrow of the Soviet Army at the end of April" and a decision to increase the amount of food given out to government workers by 37 percent. Fortunately, the cash crunch was not there yet. I decided that we could wait until after the Emergency Loya Jirga and work with the new Transitional government to establish better controls and get the budget back on track for the rest of the year.

When the Loya Jirga finished successfully on June 13, the Interim government changed to the Transitional government. The fifteen hundred representatives to the Loya Jirga chose Karzai as president and he made new cabinet appointments, including Ashraf Ghani as finance minister. Ghani was an ideal appointment. A true patriot, he was making a sacrifice for his country by serving in this job. He was demanding and did not hesitate to put aside diplomatic niceties if it could move his agenda forward. He had worked for the World Bank and was familiar with the international bureaucracies, and he did not hesitate to criticize them.

With nearly six months having passed since Tokyo, I again made the case for a single coordinator for reconstruction assistance. I raised the issue at an NSC principals meeting on July 9 having received some preliminary support earlier from my deputy colleagues. At this meeting, it was agreed that if I could get support from the other donor governments, then State would appoint such a person. I said that I was traveling to Paris that night for a meeting of the ARSG and would raise the issue. And I did just that. At the meeting on July 10, everyone agreed—the Japanese, the Europeans, and the Saudis—that such a coordinator would be a good idea.

The ARSG meeting in Paris was the first formal meeting between the new finance minister, Ghani, and the donors group. Larry Seale had come to Paris from Kabul with Ghani for this meeting. Even though Larry technically worked for me, he was effectively acting as Ghani's budget adviser. At this meeting, Ghani made it very clear that he would have a real problem balancing the budget, and he would have to resort to inflationary financing if more countries did not provide budget support. He had assumed that such support would come in when the budget was approved. However, very few countries were helping. Rather, they were planning to use the funds pledged in Tokyo to support projects, which frequently meant paying contractors from their own countries to do the work.

Ghani was articulate, candid, and persuasive. He began with an emotional reference to the recent tragic killing of the vice president of Afghanistan. He said that the new government—as he kept emphasizing, the first democratically chosen Afghan head of state—had already delivered on many of the commitments made in Tokyo. It had, for example, approved a budget, forsworn deficit financing, and put in place transparent budget controls with outside experts from firms like KPMG providing verification that the controls were sound. He said he appreciated that the United States had helped set up a special trust fund at the World Bank for the purpose of providing budget support. Countries could disburse funds to the trust fund, which would then disburse funds to the Afghan Ministry of Finance. The trust fund, administered by the World Bank, would provide some due diligence that individual donor governments, especially the small ones, could not provide. In this way, the trust fund gave countries some comfort.

At the same time Ghani was critical, in no uncertain terms, of the donor effort. There were "too many meetings, too many people talking, and too many holes in the budget. Donors need to focus on results and on disbursements to support the budget." Then he asked, not rhetorically, but as if he expected an answer on the spot: "What should I tell Karzai when I return to Kabul?" Because I had studied the budget numbers carefully—having Larry Seale in Kabul was a great help—the facts and the tone of the presentation were not a surprise to me. Ghani was worried about the same things that I was, but it was important that it came from him, as a representative of the Afghan government, rather than from me. I was pleased that he decided to make such a strong appeal, and I supported him enthusiastically at that Paris meeting. I could see that the other ARSG cochairs from Europe, Japan, and Saudi Arabia were uncomfortable with Ghani's demanding approach, but this was very serious. If Karzai could not fund the budget, he would have to resort to inflationary finance, which meant he would lose all credibility with the Afghan people, and which would cause serious damage to the economy.

At the end of the meeting, I summed things up. In addressing Ghani's question, I said that the answer to Karzai should be that the international community will focus on quick disbursements, measurable results, and filling the hole in the operating budget. While all agreed, I would soon learn that obtaining such budget support is one of the most difficult fund-raising tasks, especially when there are doubts about procedures for keeping track of how the funds are spent and worries that they are being illegally skimmed for private use. But it was essential.

After the ARSG meeting, Al Larson and I held a press briefing at the American Embassy in Paris, hoping to bring attention to how the international community was still heavily committed to Afghanistan, and dealing with the tough financial aspects of the reconstruction. But most of the questions were about the recovery of the U.S. economy, the dollar, and the economic situation in Latin America, especially the emerging market crisis in Argentina. I also did a one-on-one with David Ignatius of *The Washington Post*, who was working out of Paris, but he too was more interested in these other issues than in our financial work in Afghanistan. Unfortunately, the media was already losing interest in Afghanistan, and I knew that this would make it even harder for us to maintain momentum.

I was very tired at the end of that long day. As on all my trips to Europe, I had flown across the Atlantic the night before and I had gone immediately to the meeting and then to the press conference. I slept well that evening at the comfortable and elegant residence of the American Ambassador in Paris, Howard Leach, a good friend from California who kindly invited me to come there whenever I was in Paris. I must have stayed there a dozen times, usually in the Ben Franklin bedroom on the second floor, with a breathtaking view of the expansive lawns and garden, right in the middle of the city of Paris, with the Eiffel Tower in the distance.

The next day, I got up early for a flight to Frankfurt and then on to Kiev on a military plane—a McDonnell-Douglas C-9B, which is a lot like a DC-9. That evening I had dinner at the residence of another American ambassador, Carlos Pascual, during which we discussed strategies to encourage political and economic reforms in the Ukraine. The day after that I would meet up with Paul O'Neill for a trip to central Asia, a part of the world I probably would not have gone to were it not for the global war on terror. The purpose was to meet with the leaders of the frontline states of Kyrgyzstan and Uzbekistan—where the U.S. military had set up bases to fight the Taliban and al-Qaeda—and to discuss the economic reforms that accompanied the financial packages the United States and the international financial institutions had provided to them.

By the time I returned to Washington on July 19, I thought that we had made some good progress on Afghanistan. The Loya Girga was held on schedule, the new finance minister had just the right aggressive attitude, and when I reported the news that the ARSG was interested in a reconstruction coordinator, a process was put in place to find the right person. Soon Bill Taylor, who had been coordinating assistance in central and Eastern Europe for the State Department, was chosen. I was disappointed that Bill could not start in Kabul until October, but I was delighted that we finally had a point person.

REVISING THE STRATEGY

Despite this progress, I soon realized that we would have to make some further adjustments. I had agreed to help Ghani by making calls to donors asking for budget support. After making a number of such calls, I telephoned him in Kabul on August 1. The reactions were uniformly negative; Japan was one of the few countries to agree to provide budget support, but even that required a great deal of effort internally in the Japanese government. I told Ghani that we needed to revise the strategy. Three actions in Afghanistan were essential, if we were going to raise any money for his budget.

First, he had to demonstrate to donors that the budget process was transparent and the money was being used with appropriate controls. Second, he had to get more revenues internally; donors were very skeptical that the new Afghan administration was doing enough to get the customs revenues from the warlords. Third, he had to be clear that the budget support was not meant to be permanent, and that the Afghan government's spending was on track to be fully financed by Afghanistan itself by a date certain (four or five years perhaps) without international donor budget support. Yes, spending would increase, but so would revenues, and eventually the lines would cross, taking the budget into the black. With this three-part strategy in place, I would make calls to donors on behalf of Ghani, though I knew it would still be like pulling teeth.

Onto the Financial Front Lines: Kabul, with Stops in Manila, Herat, and Dubai

By the end of August, Ghani and I were still concerned about the international support and decided that I should travel to Afghanistan. Under secretaries of the Treasury rarely visit post-conflict areas, especially those where security is still a problem, and for this reason alone the trip would help bring attention to the problem that we were concerned about—getting support from donors and showing on-the-ground results. It would also give me a chance to reaffirm support for our people working in Afghanistan. We planned the trip for the middle week of September; that way Ghani and I could get to Washington in time for the IMF/World Bank meetings, where there would be another meeting of the ARSG and more fund-raising appeals.

Manila: Because the Asian Development Bank had committed several hundred million dollars for Afghanistan and because I was responsible for oversight of the ADB as part of my job, I decided that I would take the long way around to Afghanistan and stop in Manila, the headquarters of the ADB. It would be an additional show of leadership and demonstrate that the U.S. Treasury considered Afghanistan an extremely high priority. Stopping in Manila would also give me a chance to meet with President Gloria Macapagal-Arroyo and Finance Minister Jose Isidro Camacho of the Philippines to convey our concern that their anti–money laundering and terrorist financing laws were not strong enough to combat the financing of terrorists.

My stop in Manila proved very fortunate. I knew President Tadao Chino of the ADB very well. We served together when I was working on Japanese issues during the first Bush administration, and he was also a Stanford graduate. He took on the ADB job after retiring as the top international official in the Japanese Ministry of Finance. Chino wisely decided after 9/11 that the ADB should play a big role in the reconstruction of Afghanistan. He knew that this would be an opportunity to show the world and the U.S. Congress that the ADB could really step up to the plate. When I arrived in Manila, Chino arranged for me to meet with the team that he had assigned to work on Afghanistan.

ADB had taken on several projects in Afghanistan, but the one I decided to focus on that day was an important project to build a new road from Kandahar to the southeastern town of Spin Boldek on the Pakistan border. USAID had responsibility for the road from Kabul to Kandahar, so by completing the road from Kandahar to Spin Boldek, we would open a key truck route all the way from Kabul to the Pakistan border and thereby to the seaport in Karachi. Since Afghanistan is a landlocked country, good access to the sea would offer a huge economic advantage. I met with the ADB Afghanistan team to get an update on the road, but only a few minutes into our meeting I sensed a distressing lack of urgency. They were still talking about feasibility studies and looking for possible contractors, yet it was already one year since 9/11. I reacted by being as tough and demanding as I could—polite but deadly serious. "This isn't business as usual; we're fighting a war, a war on terror, and if you don't get moving like development banks never have before, we could lose that war. Afghanistan's political situation is delicate; if it went back to the wrong people it could again become a training ground for terrorists."

The ADB staff were stunned by my reaction. They had felt that Treasury's new representative at the ADB, Paul Speltz, had already pushed them (which he did) and now they were finding out that Paul's boss was even worse. Surprised or not, they got the message and agreed to expedite things.

Next, I met over lunch with Chino and his senior staff, where I expressed my sense of urgency again. They knew how unusual it was for an under secretary of the Treasury to visit the ADB—no one could remember it ever having occurred before, other than at one of their big annual conferences. In addition to the work on Afghanistan, we were pursuing a reform agenda at the World Bank and the regional development banks like the ADB, so I went over that agenda, too. After lunch I gave an address to the entire professional staff of the Bank, about three hundred people. I went over our economic development agenda and my particular focus on Afghanistan. And finally I had a one-on-one meeting with President Chino where I would relay the message for a fourth time, though privately, and, speaking to a friend, I felt I could be more candid. Before getting into the substance, we compared notes on U.S.-Japan economic relations and agreed that they had improved greatly. I said how pleased we were that Japan had hosted the donors' conference for Afghanistan, and that an outstanding performance by the ADB in Afghanistan would be of great benefit both to the Bank and to Japan. Japan had always been able to exert a great deal of influence on the ADB. It was a tradition that the president of the ADB would be Japanese, and indeed Chino's successor would be Haruhiko Kuroda, my Japanese G7 counterpart. Chino gave me his assurance that he would take a personal interest in the work in Afghanistan. And indeed, after my visit I began to notice a greatly improved attitude about Afghanistan reconstruction in the ADB.

Kabul: From Manila, I flew to Kabul. There were still no commercial aircraft flying into Afghanistan so I picked up a UN plane in Dubai. Because Afghanistan was still a war zone the plane could not take a typical gradual approach into the Kabul airport, which would have made us an easy target of terrorists with portable surface-to-air missiles. Instead, we approached Kabul airport from directly above, descending in a tight corkscrew pattern with the plane banking sharply as it spiraled to the ground. The spiral landing and the sharp banking gave me a good long look down at a dry, drab brown city spinning around with vast tracks of rubble from years of war. What a contrast to what the young British lieutenant Alexander Burnes found when he first arrived in Kabul in 1832. "Its many gardens, so abundant in fruit-trees and song-birds reminded him of England," wrote Peter Hopkirk in his regional history, *The Great Game: The Struggle for Empire in Central Asia*, which I brought to read on the trip.*

The U.S. ambassador, Robert Finn, met me at the airport and we went to the embassy. The grounds were heavily guarded, with high walls, barbed wire, and sandbags all around. Marines were always stationed in a bunker on top of the embassy building. Going off the premises without security was a serious risk. The accommodations— including the ambassador's "residence"—were makeshift steel trailers, essentially containers like the ones that are loaded directly off trucks onto ships. The containers were all painted white and were put together in a cluster on the embassy grounds. What a contrast to the elegant residence in Paris where I slept two months earlier after meeting with Ashraf Ghani. Two U.S. ambassadors inhabiting two entirely different worlds. Meals were served cafeteria-style for both the military—dressed in desert camouflage with their M-16s or other weapons—and civilians in one of the trailers on the compound.

Soon after I arrived and checked into my container, I was given the customary "country" briefing, where I told the top embassy people the purpose of my visit, and they reviewed the political and security situation. I began by congratulating everyone on how much had been accomplished, before going into my concerns. Anyone had to be impressed with these people. They had been living in very tough and dangerous conditions for months.

That night, Ghani held a dinner for me in the prime minister's building and invited the ambassadors from the G7 and some other countries. It was good Afghan food—grilled lamb, baked flatbread, rice, pilau, melons, grapes, a variety of nuts; no wine, of course. Ghani wanted it to be a working dinner at which he and I as a team would make the same pleas we had made in Paris in July: the government needs budget support and we have to start showing some on-

*Peter Hopkirk, *The Great Game: The Struggle for Empire in Central Asia* (Great Britain: John Murray, 1990), p. 142.

the-ground results. At first I found the ambassadors resistant to both the budget support and the request for measurable results. They said that budget support was impossible for them with so few budget controls in Afghanistan. They said that they were measuring results just fine. It would be hard to convince them otherwise without a great deal of detailed work in the finance ministry or visiting projects. Only the Dutch Ambassador fully agreed with me and with Ghani, who clearly was frustrated with the overall tone of the meeting. In any case, I had made my point and all seemed to hear the message.

At breakfast the next morning, I met with Ghani and all his ministerial colleagues from the Transitional government who had anything to do with economics and finance, including transportation, mining, and industry. Here I got my first earful of complaints about how slowly reconstruction was going. They said they were encouraged by the meeting in Tokyo, but had not seen any results yet.

We then went to the finance ministry. It was still filled with the redundant workers that Larry Seale had written to me about in the summer, standing around, leaning against the walls, or sitting on the floor. These workers were being paid, but over time they would have to find work elsewhere. Interspersed between rooms of Afghan people doing apparently nothing were groups of foreigners. There were contractors from USAID and the British Adam Smith Institute, working on automating the payroll and setting up budget controls. In the old government, everything was done by hand. As I looked over those old records with Ghani and his staff, I saw how time-consuming they were to use.

From the finance ministry we went across the street to meet with the central bank governor, Anwar ul-Haq Ahady. Because of security concerns we did not walk, of course, but rather piled back into our secure vehicles. By this time I had gotten used to seeing people walking around the streets holding AK-47s or M-16s as naturally as umbrellas, but it was strange at first. It was quite common for Afghanis to come into a dinner with such weapons.

There were even more redundant workers at the central bank. Here we had lunch and talked about the plans for introducing a new currency. There were still some logistical issues to be worked out—like getting shredders to destroy the old currency. Currency traders in Kabul were nervous and the currency seemed to be depreciating. Things appeared to be on track, so I offered to meet with some of the traders, and we did so before I left, though I could not go to the currency markets because of a security threat. I gave a TV briefing after leaving the central bank and reported positively on the plans for the new currency.

In order to better appreciate the complaints I was receiving about the lack of results, I visited a couple of projects. One was to rebuild a city park and the other to pack school supplies into boxes to be sent to elementary schools. But the operations were extremely inefficient, more like make-work projects than actual jobs. To me this was really humanitarian assistance rather then reconstruction, in that people were simply given cash to come to work and do something, with little emphasis on actually building things. I had yet to see the seamless transition from humanitarian assistance to reconstruction.

I then met with some Kabul businessmen. As Professor Nadiri had told me, they were eager to start up their businesses. They gave me a list of eight things to do to encourage private enterprise. The number one item was a request to build industrial parks where security and utilities could be provided. No industrial parks existed at that time. I found their argument persuasive and pursued the idea with USAID when I returned to Washington. These did not have to match the industrial parks that a town or city in the United States might build; rather, they would require only the essentials: reliable electricity, water, sanitation, and security. Eventually USAID added several industrial parks to its list of projects. It was one of the concrete things we could do to promote the private sector and therefore had a symbolic and a practical value.

We also visited a girls' school, one of the most inspiring things about this visit. I stopped by a biology class and spoke to the teachers and the students. Under the Taliban these girls were not allowed in school, although some of them risked severe punishment by studying clandestinely with their teachers. And now here they were, in the open, with big smiles, learning biology and a lot of other things. Like the kids in all the other schools I visited while I was Under Secretary, these girls were bright, lively, and appeared eager to learn.

Later that day, I met with President Karzai at the Presidential Palace. I was glad that Karzai was interested in economic and finance issues, and like all the other Afghans I would meet on this trip, he was candid. He said he was disappointed in the lack of visible progress on reconstruction. He said his people did not need humanitarian assistance; they wanted help rebuilding roads and schools. He had not seen the promised "seamless transition." He was worried that humanitarian assistance would make people dependent on the goodwill of others. He was very positive about encouraging the private sector, and phrased this in this dramatic way: "I want Afghanistan to develop like Dubai—with a free market and a vibrant private sector trading with other countries uninhibited by government." I would recount that story many times.

President Karzai was also very worried about the currency exchange. He asked if it should be postponed, and I tried to reassure him that it would work just fine. Having a single currency would be symbolically important in his drive to national unity and it would help with monetary policy. While there were risks that something could go wrong, I recommended that they continue as planned.

Herat: Herat is a small oasis town in the remote desert area of western Afghanistan, about fifty miles east of the Iranian border and fifty miles south of the Turkmenistan border, which used to be the Soviet border. I arrived at Herat airport—not much more than a landing strip on the outskirts of the town—after flying from Kabul in a small turboprop over three hundred miles of dry desolate mountaintops in central Afghanistan. The purpose of this one-day side trip to Herat was to engage in some "financial diplomacy" with Herat's famed powerful warlord, Ismail Khan, who as governor of the border province of Herat controlled a major portion of the customs revenues that would be needed to make the reconstruction plan work.

As the plane approached Herat, I could see how it was the only

patch of greenery in hundreds of miles of parched brown desert terrain. And as the plane landed, I could see the dilapidated mud and
stucco houses on the outskirts of town and the crumbling irrigation
ditches that had fallen into disrepair. After years of war with the
Soviets and persecution from the Taliban, Herat was obviously not
the garden city of the past, though it was not nearly as devastated as
Kabul, much of which had been leveled by years of fighting.

Finance Minister Ghani and Ambassador Finn were also along
on this trip. I had been working closely with Ashraf Ghani for many
months now, but it was in Herat that I came to think of him as the
Alexander Hamilton of this brand-new democracy: he faced many of
the same financial issues as the first U.S. Secretary of the Treasury—
including troubles getting customs revenues out of powerful governors—and he was plausibly as creative, hands-on, and hard-driving.
We also had two financial experts on our team, Larry Seale and Anna
Corfield. Anna had just been assigned to the Afghanistan desk in
Washington. She was off a remarkably productive year helping to
implement the tracking system in our War Room for combating
terrorist financing. I was grateful that Anna had agreed to take on
this new responsibility and apply her results measurement skills to
another part of the financial front in the war on terror.

We were greeted on the tarmac by a long line of officials, each
representing a different branch or a different level of the local government or militia. They were all men, mostly older or middle-aged,
with full beards, sun-worn leathery skin, and many, but not all, in
traditional Afghan dress. Anna, covering her short blond hair with a
scarf, was the only woman on the tarmac. I could sense both wariness
and hope in the men's eyes as they squinted at me through the glar-
ing sun. Each one was eager to shake hands and welcome us. As I
walked through the receiving line, American soldiers and State
Department diplomatic security forces carrying M-16s were there to
guard us, scanning the tarmac and beyond for a possible terrorist or
disgruntled former Taliban. A contingent from Ismail Khan's militia
was also there armed with their own AK-47 automatic rifles. It
occurred to me that "our guys" may have been protecting us from

"his guys," but the truth is the American military and the Herat militia were working together, and had been for months.

After coming to the end of the long line of official handshakes, I was greeted warmly by Ismail Khan, who asked me to ride with him back to his house in town so we could begin our talks informally. His red SUV was already lined up in the convoy, and our security people had no problem with my riding in it. They would follow in several cars, with a pickup truck of Khan's troops in the lead. As the long convoy drove away from the airport and toward the city, I could see that there was an Afghan soldier with an AK-47 posted on either side of the road about every fifteen yards or so. When we approached town, I caught a glimpse of Ismail Khan's house, which turned out to be a huge mansion on a mountainside overlooking the town. There were about twenty large army tanks parked at the entrance.

Khan was surprisingly soft-spoken, given that for many years he had been a mujahideen commander who had fought against both the Soviets and the Taliban. He displayed a calm, lordly air, perhaps befitting the current ruler of the people of Herat. He wore a traditional Afghan turban, a distinctive knee-length white overcoat (a *chapan*) over a flowing white robe, and a large white beard. A number of months after my visit, the *New York Times Magazine* captured Khan's bearded face on the cover. The headline on the cover— "Warlordistan: America promised Afghanistan safety, money, and democracy. But the real power is back in the hands of feudal chiefs like Ismail Khan"—captured a skepticism that was not unusual at the time.

As I sat with Khan in the SUV and started talking with him, I thought how different this scene was from the kind of financial diplomacy that I had imagined I would be doing when I joined the Treasury. This was no plush negotiating room, with high ceilings, huge chandeliers, stuffed chairs, and long tables like those in the corridors of finance in the Western world. Instead, as I looked out over the dashboard from Khan's SUV, I saw the mujahideen in the pickup truck ahead.

I got straight to the point. "To build national unity in Afghanistan, which is needed for the security and prosperity of the country, it is essential that the central government under President Karzai have enough revenues to run the government—to pay teachers, police, provide basic services, and to have an Afghan national army. Now the United States and other donors are supporting Afghanistan big time. I personally have been calling the finance officials in other governments to ask them to put more money into the central budget, but they are reluctant to do this when they hear that the biggest source of money—customs receipts at border towns like Herat—is being siphoned off, and indeed being used to support local governors and prevent national unity."

Khan replied that he was very supportive of President Karzai and national unity in Afghanistan. He also said he had begun to send more of the customs money back to Karzai, though I knew from Ashraf Ghani that the sums were still a small fraction of what he was collecting. Khan then got straight to his point, which was a not-so-subtle rebuttal: "You have to understand that my people are frustrated with what is happening. They have heard that billions of dollars have been raised to help Afghanistan, but they can see so little of it being used in their areas." While this was a viewpoint I would hear many times on this visit and wanted to address, I did not view it as germane to my point about customs and told him so.

The American Embassy had arranged for two roundtable meetings for me in Herat, one at the customshouse and the other with a group of local businessmen. The purpose of the meetings was to emphasize the importance of the customs revenue issue and to ask the people how the reconstruction effort was going. Khan asked if he could take me to those meetings in his SUV and introduce me to his people. We agreed, and after some refreshments at his house we headed out to the customshouse, which was just a few miles out of town.

A two-story structure with perhaps ten rooms, it sat on a grade overlooking a dirt parking lot where several hundred beat-up cars and trucks were impounded. Steps led up to the main door, and as we arrived there were throngs of onlookers, who wanted to come inside and join the meeting with us. I had been told there would be about ten or fifteen people, but when I walked into the room, I realized it was really going to be a large, "town hall" style meeting, with me on the hot seat answering questions. About two hundred people were packed in and seating was arranged theater-style; many people stood along the walls or sat on the floor. It was one tough-looking crowd, men who could easily have been guerrilla fighters just months before. Next to the meeting room was a small storage room that was used to store seized opium and Khan was anxious to show me this. When I peeked inside, I saw about twenty-five large bags of opium and other drugs. Khan told me that the bags were going to be destroyed, but who knew for sure.

After making a brief introduction, Khan opened the meeting to the floor. Many hands shot up and soon I was hearing the same points Khan had made on the ride from the airport, though with much more emotion and passion, even anger. One said, "All those UN people do is drive around in big Toyota Land Cruisers. I thought the money was for building roads and schools. I haven't seen anything like that yet." Another said, "We were told that there was going to be support for alternative crops to poppy growing, but we haven't seen that yet either." When things grew unruly Khan got up and sternly quieted them down, explaining that I was only trying to help by raising money in the first place and that I was there to see how it was being used. I said a few words about the reason I was there—customs should be going to the national government—and promised to look into the reasons they had not seen many results on the ground yet.

Then we went back into town for the roundtable with business people. This too was really a town hall meeting, packed to the brim with several hundred business people wearing traditional Afghan clothing and asking many of the same kinds of questions. This time I asked them about their businesses and how the economy was doing since the Taliban left. Their answers were upbeat, and they followed up with questions of their own about market access for Afghan textiles in the United States.

Before heading back to Khan's house for supper, we visited the famous Blue Mosque, some Afghan rug shops, and a glass shop with its own glass-blowing facility. The shopowner's hands and feet were terribly crippled, his bones broken by the Taliban. He said he was looking forward—"God and the Khan willing"—to going back to exporting his glass again now that Afghanistan was free. I said that I knew at least the Khan was willing and he didn't disagree.

During supper, a large Afghan feast, I again raised the customs issue and Khan agreed to do more. I said that the United States would stay in touch with Ashraf Ghani to see how things went. I also said I heard his message about showing real results, and I would report back to Washington and the other governments. After supper we went out on the terrace overlooking the town of Herat and the desert in the distance. The view reminded me of what Salt Lake City must have looked like one hundred years ago when the Mormons came and said, "This is the place." I explained all of this to Khan and said that in a few years Herat could be a modern prosperous city like Salt Lake City. He seemed to appreciate my show of confidence and optimism. On the way back to the airport—Khan and his militia continued to escort me—I asked him how he was able to assemble such a large army. He answered simply: "For most of my life I have been fighting for the people of Afghanistan. I fought the Russians. I fought the Taliban. I was thrown in jail and tortured. I have made many good friends over the years."

The visit to Herat illustrates many of the difficulties we faced in implementing our financial reconstruction plans in Afghanistan. Getting the warlords to relinquish some of their power was not easy, neither was showing on-the-ground results. But I had made the case. And simply coming this far was significant. We could have raised the money for reconstruction and then sat back, but to get things done we had to go to the front lines to talk with the people. I shared the concerns of the people I heard at those town hall meetings, and I would use these examples back in Washington to make the case for some corrections in our strategy, to focus even more on results, and to move from fund-raising to action-raising with our allies in the G7 and elsewhere.

What about Ismail Khan? Over time there was an increase in customs revenue from Herat, but progress was slow, and as much as a year later Khan would still be the reputed warlord of Herat. But the power structure was changing, and eventually our strategy paid off. By 2004, Khan had been persuaded to give up control of Herat and his militia, which was being recruited for the new Afghan National Army. He was offered a cabinet post in Kabul, and though he turned it down at first, he eventually accepted the position of energy minister in December 2004.

On returning to Kabul that evening, I met with the in-country representatives of the international donors. Ghani and I made many of the same points we made with the ambassadors two nights before, but this time I felt the response was more forthcoming. Perhaps our pleas had finally begun to circulate and were making a difference. Before leaving Kabul the next day, Ghani and I held a press conference at which I praised him for the progress he and President Karzai were making in the finance area. It was picked up well by the news media, but the Ghani-Taylor teamwork had not finished yet.

Dubai: We were scheduled to leave Afghanistan at the same time so that we could both be in Washington for the ARSG meeting. I suggested that we stop in Dubai and meet with UAE finance minister Sheikh Hamdan and Minister of State for Finance Mohammed Kharbash. Kharbash acted a bit like a chief operations officer for the Sheikh and did much of the international work for the finance ministry. I knew him well, but I thought it would also be important to visit with the minister, a member of the royal family and Ghani's counterpart. I had spoken with Kharbash many times about supporting Afghanistan, so I thought a joint visit where Ghani would speak for himself would be helpful.

MOST OF THE 1,000-mile flight path from the crumbling mud stucco buildings of Kabul to the futurist skyscrapers of Dubai traverses the arid mountains of Afghanistan and Baluchistan, a vast tribal region that spans the Iran-Pakistan border. When the flight path reaches the Gulf of Oman on the Baluchistan shore, it veers west, crosses the sharp point of the Arabian Peninsula, and extends a few miles into the Persian Gulf. Once there, it turns 180 degrees and gradually approaches Dubai International Airport. From the window of a plane, an almost science-fiction city rises on the double edge of the Gulf and the desert. The Burj al Arab Hotel, built in the shape of a wind-blown spinnaker sail, stands nearly as tall as the Empire State Building, an imaginary boat heading home. A man-made island in the shape of a palm tree blooms off the coast—extending two miles out to sea, with room for hundreds of luxury villas with spacious gardens and swimming pools.

After our plane landed and we were greeted by U.S. Embassy officials, Ghani and I were driven out to meet with the Sheikh at one of the several royal palaces. The meeting room was a large hall with chairs along the walls. The Sheikh sat facing out from the wall and we sat by his side. He asked that I sit next to him, with Ghani further down. For much of the meeting, the Sheikh focused on U.S.-UAE issues, including the UAE's ongoing cooperation in combating terrorist financing and the impact of the economic recovery in the United States on the region. It was only after a considerable time that I could shift the topic to Afghanistan. Ghani made his usual compelling case for support, and eventually the Sheikh said he would be supportive, providing no numbers but asking Ghani to work with Kharbash on details.

After meeting with the Sheikh, the central bank governor, Al-Suwaidi, hosted a huge banquet for Ghani and me, to which he had invited bankers and other businessmen. One of the most helpful and cooperative central bankers I dealt with, Suwaidi was always responsive to our requests in the area of terrorist financing, including the efforts to regulate hawalas. Even more than at the meeting with the Sheikh, U.S.-UAE issues dominated the discussion at dinner, and I had to keep steering the conversation back to Ghani and Afghanistan. Ghani was impressive in his presentations. Gradually one could see people in this very rich country grow interested in their poor neighbor just a two-hour plane ride away but on the other side of the Persian Gulf and a vast desert.

A New Interest in Metrics

The trip to Afghanistan, perhaps the first by an under secretary of Treasury to a war zone, was very successful, and I wrote trip reports for those working on Afghanistan in Treasury, State, and the NSC. But I thought it was also important to report my findings to a broader audience outside of government. When I was invited to speak to the Council on Foreign Relations on September 24, 2002, I decided to focus on Afghanistan. I called my speech "Making Reconstruction Work in Afghanistan," and Anna Corfield and I spent several days working on the message and some simple visual aids. I began by reviewing the amazing progress that the Afghan people had made, but I also called for a change in emphasis from fund-raising to action-raising if we were really going to be successful. I tried hard to convey the importance of metrics and measuring results, and I urged donors, including the United States, to follow this approach.

To illustrate how to set timelines and goals for the number of kilometers of roads built in different sections of the country, I showed a map of the roads in Afghanistan. The map illustrated which countries and international institutions were responsible for different sections: the road from Kabul to Kandahar was marked for the United States; the road from Kandahar to Spin Boldek was marked for the ADB; and so on. My call for action and my illustrations seemed to be well received, and from that date on I would use that map again and again, constantly having my staff update it with new information. I would then explain how the same concept could be used to measure reconstruction efforts in other countries. (Using the map of Afghanistan as an example, I had a map drawn up for Haiti to guide the reconstruction there after President Aristide was ousted in February 2004.)

Around this same time, the NSC started using metrics in earnest to measure progress on U.S.-funded reconstruction in Afghanistan. Measuring results was something President Bush always emphasized. Steve Hadley, the Deputy National Security Adviser, led the

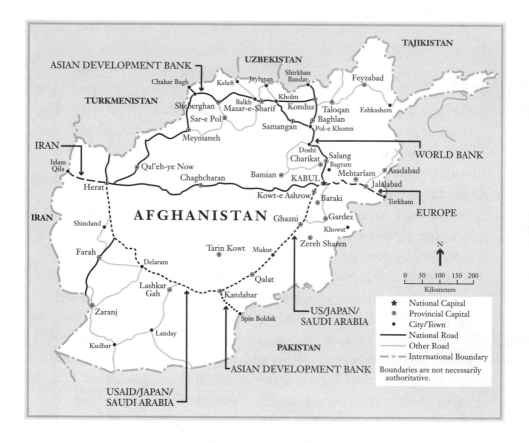

measurable results system for Afghanistan. He insisted on good metrics, but there is no question that we were all following President Bush's leadership. The NSC became more and more interested in measuring results in Afghanistan, and we created more and more detailed checklists and timelines. To handle this increased emphasis on results at the operational level, the NSC deputies committee started meeting once a week just on Afghanistan, which meant that Iraq and other pressing issues would have to be considered at other meetings. An Afghanistan Interagency Operations Group (AIOG) was formed to bring different agencies together on a daily basis and prepare metrics for the weekly NSC meeting. I am sure that this emphasis on metrics was one of the reasons that progress in Afghanistan continued even as another part of the global war on terror would absorb more and more of our time.

Something else very important happened around that time, and it too had President Bush's leadership all over it. USAID had contracted with the Louis Berger Group, an American firm, to be the lead contractor for the construction of the Kabul-to-Kandahar road. Hoping to move things ahead more rapidly, President Bush asked USAID to complete the project in eleven months—starting construction in January 2003 and finishing the first layer suitable for driving by the end of December that year. Additional layers of asphalt would be laid later. The paving was finished on schedule and in record time when compared to other road projects sponsored by international development agencies, whether in Afghanistan or elsewhere. At the ceremony commemorating the completion of the road, Andrew Natsios, head of USAID, said: "The construction of this road that we are about to dedicate is the direct result of a commitment made by President George Bush . . . last fall in Washington. Since that time, President Bush has maintained a deep personal interest in the progress of this road and ensured that we had the necessary funding and support to fulfill his pledge to have the highway open by the end of this year. Under his direction and leadership, an extraordinary and diverse group of people, working under the most difficult circumstances, have joined together to complete this historic task and deliver on his pledge."

Back to Afghanistan

I returned to Afghanistan again in June 2003 to assess progress on revenue collection and check out private sector progress, such as the industrial parks program. Unfortunately, the latter was not going well, but it was not the donors' fault. The Afghans were arguing about what kind of business would get access to the parks. While I was dismayed by the resulting delay, I reminded myself that I was just seeing democracy at work.

On this trip I flew down from Kabul by Chinook helicopter, with a Blackhawk providing cover, to the town of Gardez where one of our new outposts called provincial reconstruction teams (PRTs) was

located. PRTs were set up in dangerous remote areas, where non-
government organizations will not usually go, to provide reconstruction assistance, such as building schools or houses. The Gardez PRT,
reminiscent of a small fort in a Wild West movie, was heavily guarded
and the people inside were much safer than they were on the outside.
Gardez is in an area bordering on the parts of Pakistan where al-
Qaeda and remnants of the Taliban hideout, and they would occasionally make raids and then retreat back behind the border. I was
there to examine whether the PRTs helped foster reconstruction,
and also to assess whether PRTs could be of help in customs collection as they were in so many other civil affairs tasks. After returning
to Kabul, I concluded that a PRT in another less dangerous border
area in the north or west would more likely be of assistance. The soldiers in the Gardez PRT had enough to do providing security for
small reconstruction projects and training Afghan troops.

When I left Kabul, our plane, a C-130, sensed a missile attack
despite the corkscrew flight path the crew was taking out of the city.
The plane automatically sent out hot flares as a distraction to any
possible heat-seeking missile. Our flight that day had been held up a
few hours because of reports that an Australian C-130 had just been
shot down elsewhere in Afghanistan.

STAYING THE COURSE

Throughout the rest of 2003, financial reconstruction in Iraq would
occupy much of my time; but my focus on Afghanistan did not diminish. I remained very concerned, especially about providing for budget
support and getting visible results, perhaps because I was in government at the time of 9/11 or perhaps because I traveled there several
times and personally felt the U.S. commitment. That we were there
for the long term was always a given throughout the government,
even when other difficult issues arose, including the Iraq war, which
would require an even bigger reconstruction effort. To emphasize
that Afghanistan would remain a high priority, I included Afghanistan along with Iraq in our dedicated financial reconstruction task

force under the unwavering direction of Larry McDonald, a highly organized and reliable member of the Treasury staff.

An NSC meeting with President Bush on one Wednesday morning, December 10, 2003, offers a good example of how we stayed the course. The President had seen intelligence reports that there was a shortfall in the Afghan operating budget and he wanted to hear more about it, especially in light of the upcoming elections in Afghanistan in 2004. I got the request for a special briefing for the President on Monday evening and had a chance to review the issue with Larry Seale on the phone from Kabul and then discuss it with John Snow on Tuesday. We prepared a two-page handout for the meeting with the President at which John Snow and I would do the briefing; Cheney, Rumsfeld, Wolfowitz, Powell, and Rice were there, among others. The budget shortfall issue was, of course, one that I had faced continuously since the summer of 2002, when Larry Seale first alerted me to the problem.

The handout first reviewed the progress made thus far: The first full budget—fiscal year 2002–03—had come in exactly as planned. Expenditures were $349 million, domestic revenue was $132 million, and donor funds were $232 million, leaving $15 million extra. Now we were in the middle of the 2003–04 budget. The handout explained how expenditures were planned for $550 million, domestic revenues $200 million, and donor budget support at $350 million. As in the previous year, we were working hard on the revenue side, asking donors for budget support and working to increase domestic revenues, largely through customs. It was tough work, but we were on track: with the year about half over, domestic revenues were $91 million and donors' funds for budget support were $291 million, so at $382 million we were well over halfway to the $550 million goal.

The problem would be with us for a while and Treasury would continue to work on it. The President asked what the full potential for customs revenue was, suspecting that it was probably much higher than what was currently coming in. If the actual funds got closer to the potential, it would reduce—maybe even eliminate—the budget support needed from donors. I explained that recent efforts to get more funds from the provinces—especially Herat—were paying off, which indicated that we could get even more with a concentrated effort. The President was eager to push this effort further and asked for more intelligence on the potential for increased revenue.

Zal Khalilzad, who President Bush promoted from the NSC staff to replace Robert Finn as Ambassador, was on the video from Kabul during that meeting. Zal would always have one of those "Join or Die" snake flags designed by Benjamin Franklin behind him when he spoke from Kabul, symbolic of how the warlords of Afghanistan would have to join to support the whole country or Afghanistan would die. While we discussed the budget in Washington, Zal had pressed the mute button on his speaker controls in Kabul. When it was his turn to speak he forgot to press the mute release, and we could only see his mouth moving without any sound. President Bush told him to press the speaker button, but apparently all Zal heard was the word "button." He quickly looked down at his shirt. As Zal pointed quizzically at his shirt like a Chaplinesque character in a silent movie, the whole Sit Room broke into uncontrollable laughter, until it dawned on Zal what the problem was. He pressed the speaker button, was heard in Washington, and went on to report on how the new constitutional Loya Jirga was going and his efforts to help bring the different parties together. That we could be relaxed and have a good laugh was characteristic of the way that President Bush kept things calm even in the most intense situations.

PUSHING FURTHER: THE GREAT ACCELERATION

Although we had made good progress on the budget, we decided around this time to initiate yet another diplomatic effort, this time to work along with our allies to *accelerate* funding further. As Zal reported, the constitutional Loya Jirga was going well and it looked like it would finish in January 2004, resulting in a new constitution and scheduled presidential elections in the summer or fall of 2004. In anticipation of this election, it was more important than ever to get funds disbursed and have a visible impact. We made many calls and put together a G7 action plan. Donor fatigue was becoming a problem; within the U.S. government, fund-raising fatigue was setting in. Even turf-conscious people who thought fund-raising was their job seemed to tire of it, but we plugged away. I published an op-ed in the *Financial Times* on November 28, 2003, making the appeal: "When the [Afghan] people go to the polls next June, will they have seen improvements in their lives? Will they feel that the transitional government and the international community have met their commitments? Will they feel that the progress has met their expectations? We want the answer to be Yes."

I returned to Afghanistan for the third time on February 16, 2004, to push the acceleration effort. Zal Khalilzad suggested that I meet with the G7 ambassadors to Afghanistan to make the case, and he agreed to set up the meeting. We met over dinner in a private restaurant; the pleasant venue itself was a small sign that the private sector was growing. My appeal to the G7 ambassadors was simply that they too should accelerate the disbursements of funds and start to follow the results measurement system that we were using in the United States. I was pleased that they seemed to share our view about the need for acceleration.

On this trip I again looked into the customs collection issue, which remained important to the budget and therefore to fund-raising. On the afternoon of February 17 we flew up to northern Afghanistan to visit another provincial reconstruction team. This one was operated by the German military in the town of Konduz, near the northern border. My hope was that this PRT could play a role in helping with revenue collection, perhaps simply by training border police and providing security to customs officials. The PRT's commander was not encouraging, however. He was reluctant to dilute his mission, though to me it was as big a part of the mission as the small building projects.

We had a little trouble getting back from Konduz, which had repercussions for my next mission, to northern Iraq, and illustrated how interconnected all our operations were. The Konduz airport was merely an abandoned landing strip with an old unused terminal.

There were no commercial flights; in fact, there were almost no flights at all. When our C-130 pilot landed and handed us off to the German military, we arranged that the plane would return late that evening to pick us up so we could fly to Erbil in northern Iraq. I was scheduled to meet with the Kurdistan branch of the Iraqi Central Bank. The airport was only about two miles out of town, but the road was so bad that it took about half an hour to get there. So, after visiting the PRT and having a wonderful German dinner with our hosts, we headed back on the bumpy ride to the airport. When we got to the airport that night we could hear our plane's engines above the clouds, but the crew radioed to the Germans that they could not land because there were no runway lights. The German military drove their SUVs out on the runway and provided makeshift lights, but the C-130 pilots were not given permission to land with this unusual arrangement. We had to drive back to the PRT and wait until daylight.

Despite the logistic difficulties, the PRT visit had some payoffs. During a visit by Karzai and Ghani to Washington in June 2004, Karzai himself pushed the idea of using PRTs to help with the revenues issue in a meeting with Secretary Snow and me. Having been to two PRTs in Afghanistan, I felt that there were some possibilities, but I knew the military's reluctance. I arranged for Doug Feith of the Defense Department to meet with Ghani and me, and the meeting took place in my Washington office on July 12. Feith said he would look into the matter. I followed it up by going to CENTCOM in Tampa in August to explain the situation to the military leadership directly. In the end, Feith recommended that Lieutenant-General David Barno, whom I had met in Afghanistan, add customs collection to the border police work that the military was planning. It was not exactly using the PRTs, but it was very close; more important, a resolution to the persistent customs collection problem was finally taking place.

EIGHT MILLION people voted in the Afghan presidential election on October 9, 2004. Karzai won with 55 percent of the vote. After the votes were counted (it took three weeks), President Bush said: "I congratulate President Karzai on his election victory. . . . Through this simple act of voting, the Afghan people declared to the world their determination to move beyond a brutal legacy of oppression, terror, and fear to a future of hope, democracy, and freedom. The large turnout by Afghan women, who made up 40 percent of all voters, confirms that there is a vital role for women in the politics of a nation proud of its Islamic heritage."

This election also represented a victory in another battle in the global war on terror. A democratic government would reduce the chances that Afghanistan would again become a sanctuary for terrorists. This foreign policy success would not have been possible without the political element: the international support from the coalition countries for the Bonn and Loya Jirga process. It would not have been possible without the military element: the Coalition Forces driving out the Taliban and then training the Afghan National Army and providing security.

And as the stories in this chapter illustrate, it would not have been possible without the financial element: the expedited fundraising, the focus on budget support from donors, the insistence on a sound budget without inflationary finance from the central bank, the warlord strategy, the customs strategy, the measurable results framework both within the United States and internationally, and the reform-minded dedication of the finance officials in the new Afghanistan government. To be sure, there is still much to do, but the key lesson thus far is that continued relentless commitment to results, up and down the financial chain of command from the President to the global financial warriors on the front lines, is essential.

CHAPTER THREE

Avoiding Global Financial Contagion

◆

Not only did the 9/11 attacks and the possibility of subsequent attacks threaten an already fragile global economy in 2001; they also threatened to pull our financial warriors away from the never-ending job of preventing and mitigating international financial crises. As a manager, I made it a top priority to prevent this from happening. We had to proceed simultaneously with both our anti-financial crisis agenda and our anti-terrorist agenda.

The attacks of 9/11 hit at a bad time for the global economy. The United States was in the middle of a recession, and the entire world economy was experiencing its most significant downturn in a decade. The collapse of stock prices in the United States and Europe that began the previous year shocked investor confidence, and the rash of corporate scandals left investors in a near-panicky mood. Production was falling in Europe and Japan as well as the United States.

The fallout for emerging market economies was huge. Francisco "Paco" Gil-Diaz, the finance minister of Mexico, visited the Treasury soon after I came on board in 2001 to talk firsthand about the downturn's effects on his country. He and his team sat around the big mahogany table in my office bemoaning the worsening economic situation in Mexico, pointing to production and employment charts with lines plummeting like spilt coffee pouring off the edge of my table. "John, I know you did research back at Stanford about how economies are connected, but look at these charts and you can see that connection before your very eyes. The U.S. recession is causing a lot of grief in Mexico." Paco is a straight-talking, reform-minded economist, who studied at the University of Chicago; he has good free market instincts. He and his whole finance ministry would turn out to be key collaborators of ours in IMF reforms over the next two years. But now he was more concerned about the current economic mess than about reforms.

Conditions were even worse in other emerging market economies—such as Turkey and Argentina—where financial crises from the 1990s were persisting. There was a danger that, as in the 1990s, the financial crises of 2001 could spread like wildfire, and the fragile world economy seemed like a tinderbox. Reflecting the continuing high risks to investors, emerging market countries had to pay a burdensome 10 percentage point "risk premium" on average on their government debt.

I spent a lot of time studying the grim-looking charts and tables of statistics. One of those tables looked like this:

1996	1997	1998	1999	2000
234	119	69	59	1

The number that was shrinking—really bursting like a bubble— from triple to double and then to single digits was the amount of private capital flowing to these emerging market countries, in billions of dollars. This row of numbers appeared in the IMF's *World Economic Outlook* (or *WEO*), produced during the summer of 2001 and published just after 9/11. The funds to finance emerging market countries were drying up, and the IMF economists predicted it would get worse. They estimated that in 2001 capital flows would "turn negative for the first time since the mid-1980s."

Risks of financial contagion—so apparent after the Russian financial crisis of 1998—were still on everyone's mind. "Financial contagion" refers to the effect of a financial crisis in one country on the financial markets—interest rates, stock prices, and currencies—in other countries. Because many people often asked me about how contagion worked, I created some charts that I eventually produced as a small laminated bookmark to hand out. I figured that even if people did not digest the charts right away, they might use the bookmark in a book they were reading and think about the charts later. Years earlier I had used a similar technique to explain monetary policy to people, printing the Taylor rule for interest rates on the back of my business card.

Here is what one side of the bookmark looked like (see right):

The charts show the difference between interest rates in emerging market countries in three regions of the world and the interest rate on U.S. Treasury securities. EMBI refers to the Emerging Market Bond Index prepared by JP Morgan, which bond traders and financial analysts use to gauge developments in emerging markets. The EMBI is measured in basis points, which means that when the charts on the bookmark show 900, interest rates are 9 percentage points higher in that part of the world than in the United States. The crisis in Russia

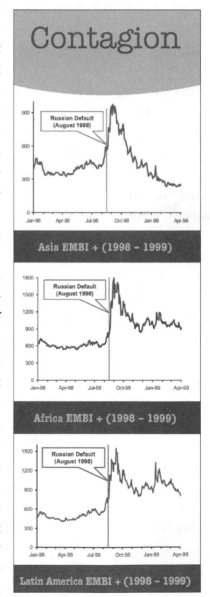

is marked by a vertical line indicating the day that Russia defaulted on its debt: Monday, August 17, 1998. Look at how interest rates skyrocketed all over the world, even in geographically distant regions like Asia, Africa, and Latin America. This is what is known as contagion, and these higher interest rates caused damage in these other regions.

At the time of the Russian default, the Federal Reserve was so concerned about the impact of the global financial crisis on the U.S. economy that it sharply cut its overnight interest rate. The minutes of the Fed's September 1998 policy meeting nicely sum up the situation at the time: "The intensification and further spread of turmoil in international financial markets, notably since the outbreak of a financial crisis in Russia in mid-August, had spilled over into U.S. financial markets. . . . It was clear that the contagious effects of international economic and financial turmoil had markedly increased the downside threat to the domestic expansion." In 2001, with the U.S. economy in recession, and with the additional blow of 9/11, you had to be concerned about another contagion event coming from the emerging markets.

A particular concern was the financial crisis in Argentina. *The Economist* wrote in its July 21, 2001, issue that

> *There are some eerie parallels between 1998 and today. In July three years ago, Russia was facing deep fiscal problems. . . . [This year] Argentina [is] also in deep fiscal trouble. By mid-summer 1998, Russia was having trouble selling domestic debt; reserves were falling and overnight interest rates were soaring. Argentina had similar problems last week. In mid-August 1998, Russia was forced to devalue and default. . . . This set off a chain reaction of panic across the globe. This "contagion" between seemingly unrelated financial markets and assets caused (in President Clinton's words) "the most dangerous financial crisis in 50 years."*

The story of the Argentina crisis is as complicated as a Dostoyevsky novel. Different people hold different views about what happened and why. As Standard & Poor's wrote in their review of the crisis on April 12, 2002, it "has proven long, cumbersome, and complex to track given the numerous conflicts, measures, counter-measures, announcements, denials, contradictory actions, and ambiguous regulatory frameworks that characterize the country's operating environment." The people at the IMF's independent evaluation office have written their own review, but many of the decisions were made within the U.S. government and the other governments of the G7. Adding to the complexity, the passage of time—the knowledge of how events turned out—has altered views and changed how one can interpret past conditions, making it difficult to portray accurately what the world looked like to policymakers and other players at the time the decisions were being made.

REVIEWING THE STATE OF PLAY

On the evening of August 2, 2001, around a month before the 9/11 terrorist attacks, I was on a commercial aircraft about to take off from Washington's Dulles Airport; I was thinking about my arrival in Buenos Aires the next morning and the scheduled two days of meetings with the president, the finance minister, the central bank governor, private bankers, economists, and the press. I was embarking on a special mission to investigate firsthand the economic crisis in the country and to deliver a message on behalf of the United States. As President Bush later described that mission to the press at a briefing in Crawford, Texas, on August 13: ". . . we sent John Taylor down there, and he met with President de la Rua, had a very good visit. He delivered our administration's message, which is they've got to implement the reforms that they recently passed through their legislature."

I had twenty-one people working on Argentina at the time, organized into teams of experts: a legal team, a debt team, a monetary policy team, a financial market team, and so on. With such a large number of experts I could have taken a big delegation with me to Argentina, but I wanted it to be a low-key, fact-finding and message-delivering trip, without a lot of press attention. I brought only one person, our Argentine desk officer, Natan Epstein, a bright young numbers-savvy PhD in economics, who had been working tirelessly with me on the Argentine financial crisis throughout the summer. Natan was so plugged in with the Argentines that he received daily reports from the central bank at the same time the central bank governor did.

From the minute the plane left Dulles Airport, I reviewed my thick "Argentina briefing book" prepared by our Treasury experts. A briefing book—something my staff prepared for every trip I made— is like a playbook for a football game; it reviews the recent record, gives a sketch of each person you might meet up with, lists talking points for how to approach them, and how to respond to whatever they might do. The state of play in Argentina was very dire. In a deep recession, amazingly one that had lasted for three years, Argentina's real GDP already was down by 9 percent. Crippling general strikes, protests, and even riots in the streets of Buenos Aires and other cities were becoming commonplace as unemployment rose to 17 percent.

The problem, in my view and that of the Treasury team, was that Argentina had drifted away from the beneficial pro-market reforms instituted in the early 1990s. Government spending was outstripping the low revenue growth, causing government debt to rise, increasing the risk that Argentina would be unable to pay its creditors and would *default* on the debt. As a result interest rates rose, holding back investment and economic growth, which in turn further reduced investor confidence. The growing debt and the declining confidence raised doubts about the government's ability to maintain the popular "convertibility law," which kept the peso fixed one-to-one with the dollar. Thus, a *devaluation* of the peso increasingly looked like a possibility.

To try to address these problems, Argentina, under the leadership of newly elected President Fernando de la Rua, and the IMF had initiated a reform program in March 2000. The IMF had been active in Argentina for much of the 1990s, so this latest initiative was almost an extension of previous programs, though technically it was new. As part of the new program, the IMF agreed to provide $7.2 billion in loans to Argentina with the aim of tiding the country over until economic growth picked up; in turn, Argentina was to enact government spending controls and budget reforms.

But government spending continued to increase and economic growth did not pick up. The crisis deepened, and only a few months later, in November 2000, the Argentines had to ask the IMF for additional loans. One of the last acts of the Clinton administration in the international finance arena was to sign off on these loans, which amounted to another $6.5 billion, bringing the total to $13.7 billion. The IMF board formally approved the increase on January 12, 2001.

Signs of renewed economic growth still failed to materialize, the crisis continued to deepen, and for the next few months and into the fall of 2001 the Argentine government proposed one fix after another to improve the situation. Early in March, President de la Rua changed finance ministers, replacing Jose Luis Machinea with Ricardo Lopes Murphy. This occurred just as I was joining the Treasury and I looked forward to calling Lopes Murphy to congratulate him. Before I could call, he too was replaced; his mistake was that he tried to do what he was supposed to do. When he announced much-needed plans to control government spending growth, he was greeted with protests and threats of another general strike. In response, on March 20, President de la Rua appointed a new finance minister, Domingo Cavallo, who as finance minister in the early 1990s had been responsible for many of the pro-market reforms. Very well known in Argentina and in the international community, Cavallo was a charismatic figure, exuding determination to turn things around in his country, and for a while investor confidence did increase. In my view, Domingo Cavallo was sincere in his efforts to help his country; but over time, as he introduced new ideas in rapid fashion, his dogged determination was often seen as impetuousness.

On Saturday, April 14, Cavallo announced an unusual alteration in the exchange rate system in Argentina. Under this alteration, if, in the future, the dollar significantly strengthened against the euro, the government would let the peso automatically depreciate against the dollar. His aim was to prevent the price of Argentina's exports from rising to uncompetitive levels in the event that the dollar rose much further against the euro. On the day Cavallo made that announcement, I got a worried call on my cell phone from Stan Fischer, the first deputy managing director of the IMF; we agreed that the modification was not a good idea. It would reduce confidence in the government's commitment to the fixed exchange rate and it was potentially confusing to most people. But it was too late; the decision had been made.

The following Saturday, April 21, Cavallo called me to review the overall economic situation. He explained that the markets had misinterpreted his new exchange rate announcement, and I replied that this was probably because it was a complex proposal. He also mentioned that he was planning a voluntary exchange of government bonds to spread some debt payments further into the future, and thereby relieve short-term pressures. He expressed concern that American economists were "publicly saying we should more aggressively restructure our debt; I am not worried, but the bankers are worried about these statements and that drives bond prices down." And he complained that the Argentine Central Bank was not lowering reserve requirements, which would increase the money supply and, in his view, stimulate the economy. This revealed a troublesome dispute with the central bank, which would not inspire confidence. On April 26, the central bank governor was fired.

Cavallo traveled to Washington on April 28 and visited with the top management at the IMF, as well as with Paul O'Neill and me at the Treasury. The Argentine budget deficit was already coming in higher than planned and he had come to pledge to all of us that, as the new finance minister, he would make the necessary adjustments. He said that he would not be asking for more loans. Instead, he was working on the debt exchange that he had mentioned on the phone with me, now referring to it as the "mega-swap." The proposal called for private investors to voluntarily swap their Argentine bonds for new bonds, which would require lower interest payments during the next year.

The mega-swap was completed on June 3, but after a short positive reaction in the markets, confidence waned again because the swap did not change the fundamental financial situation. Short-term payments had gone down, but to compensate investors, future payments had to go up by an even greater amount, causing the total present value of the debt to rise. This too was not good for confidence.

Then, in yet another bold move—viewed as one of desperation by some analysts—on July 11, President de la Rua and Minister Cavallo announced a new "zero deficit plan," which would require by law that the government budget be balanced. While a balanced budget would certainly have a great positive impact on the debt situation, it was clear to all involved that it would be very difficult to implement: To bring spending down to match revenues and balance the budget, they would have to cut the same government programs that they had found impossible to cut just a few months earlier. As a result, the plan did not restore confidence. In fact, it may have reduced confidence. The announcement that the government would no longer run a deficit signaled to many Argentines that their government could no longer get any credit in the private markets, which was essentially the truth. Fearing default on the government debt, more and more people began to withdraw their deposits from the banks that were holding much of this debt. A run on the banking system had begun.

On July 21, Secretary O'Neill was quoted in *The Economist* as saying: "They've [i.e., the Argentines] been off and on in trouble for 70 years or more. They don't have any export industry to speak of at all. And they like it that way. Nobody forced them to be what they are." Economist Michael Gavin of UBS Warburg wrote in his newsletter that the statement was "Amazing. Astonishing. Appalling. Afrightening." The concern of Gavin and other analysts was that such statements could reduce market confidence in Argentina, but by this time the fundamentals of the situation were more telling than statements by public officials.

BUENOS AIRES

By the time the pilot announced that we would soon land in Buenos Aires, I had finished my briefing book and slept for several hours. Before the plane landed, I wanted to reread a memo from my staff I'd received back on June 4, the week I was sworn in. It contained a photocopy of twenty pages from Chrystia Freeland's book *Sale of the Century*, which tells the story of the Russian default in August 1998. Most relevant to me, it featured a visit to Moscow by a predecessor of mine, Treasury Under Secretary David Lipton. The twenty pages described how David had traveled to Russia on August 13, 1998, just four days before the crisis-spreading Russian default, "to tell his old friends that Uncle Sam thought the game might be up," and that the large $23 billion IMF loan package, pushed through and heralded by the United States only one month earlier, was not working. Freeland relates how David met with Russia's thirty-five-year-old prime minister, Sergei Kiriyenko, and its thirty-four-year old finance minister, Mikhail Zadornov, on that two-day trip. She describes how David told them the grim news and how they received it.* I could not help but draw some lessons for my own trip. The suddenness of turning from "full support" to "the game is up" in thirty days left little time for the markets to adjust to or anticipate the Russian default. Could this sudden policy reversal have been the reason for the global meltdown illustrated on my bookmark? Whatever the answer, to me the story was a warning not to change policy too abruptly, or at least to signal your policy intentions enough in advance to allow the markets to adjust gradually.

My arrival in Buenos Aires was not the low-key event I had hoped for. Throngs of news reporters and cameramen were waiting to greet me. Security people quickly rushed me through the airport

---

*Chrystia Freeland, *Sale of the Century* (New York: Crown Business, 2000), pp. 301–303.

and escorted me to a waiting car, which sped off as reporters shouted questions and the cameramen ran alongside, pointing their cameras through the windows. The media would dog me at every step of the trip, even setting up a stakeout at the entrance to the palatial American Ambassador's residence where I was to have meetings with the bankers and economists. Getting in and out of the central bank would prove particularly difficult. Located in the old part of town, the narrow streets meant that reporters were pushed right up to the front door.

Riding downtown from the airport, I glanced at the Argentine newspapers, which were already running stories about my arrival, complete with photos and cartoons. Here is a political cartoon that appeared in *La Nación* on the morning of my arrival:

President de la Rua is standing behind Finance Minister Cavallo, pointing to me: I am wearing a Superman suit and holding money to hand out. I was not able to think much about it at the time, but something was wrong with this picture. The government of a major emerging market country had apparently become economically dependent on the decisions of an under secretary of Treasury from the United States.

My first meeting was with Cavallo. It started with an hour-long one-on-one in his office, and then continued for two more hours with him and his staff. Cavallo felt that it was important for me to perceive the current situation within the longer history of Argentina. He told me how he and President Carlos Menem had introduced significant economic reforms—privatization, ending hyperinflation, trade liberalization—that resulted in 4 to 5 percent growth per year. But in the late 1990s these reforms went off track as President Menem's administration was plagued with corruption scandals; now President de la Rua was trying to return Argentina to a reform agenda.

He spoke passionately about the importance of trust and credibility in economic policy, and how the reforms he introduced in the early 1990s were meant to bring such trust and credibility to Argentina. Default and devaluation were unthinkable in his view because they would destroy the country's credibility for a very long time. Cavallo felt that with the support of additional funds from the IMF, he could get over the current problem and the reforms would take hold. Of course, I realized that this moving story was meant to persuade me of the merits of additional funds; but as I listened, and asked questions, I could see that Cavallo didn't even want to hear the words "debt restructuring," let alone take charge of such an undertaking and make it work.

I then went to visit the central bank governor, Roque Maccarone. We met in the boardroom of the bank, a splendid Greek Revival building. When I arrived, a crowd of reporters swarmed between my car and the front entrance. With the help of security people I pushed right through them, aiming for the archway where BANCO CENTRAL DE LA REPÚBLICA ARGENTINA was carved in the stone above the door.

For weeks I had been studying the same money statistics as Maccarone, so he had little to add about the data, which showed deposits in the banks declining precipitously as people withdrew their money—obvious evidence of a bank run. But it is one thing to look at data on a bank run and quite another to be in charge of a banking system during a bank run. So I was anxious to get his "on-the-ground" views. Like most bank runs in history, this one was caused by doubts by depositors that their money was safe in the banks. They wanted to get their money out while the getting was good. In Maccarone's view, the run was set off by President de la Rua's announcement in July that the country no longer had access to credit and would have to run a zero deficit. People reasoned that a government default must be around the corner and that the banks would be left holding a lot of worthless government debt, unable to pay their depositors. Better to take the money out of the banks before the default. Like Cavallo, he told me that they could stop the run with additional loans from the IMF to back the deposits.

My meeting with President de la Rua took place at the Casa Rosada, the huge pink presidential mansion, built in 1873 on the Plaza de Mayo. It was from the balcony of the Casa Rosada that Madonna sang "Don't Cry for Me, Argentina" in the movie *Evita*. The plaza had for many years been the scene of massive protests. In 1955, a military aircraft trying to overthrow President Juan Perón bombed the square, killing three hundred people. When I arrived, there were still signs of more recent protests related to the ongoing financial crisis, including a general strike on July 20, which I was told was the seventh general strike since de la Rua became president. Temporary steel barriers surrounded the building and were opened to let my car and the security vehicles through. (Protests would flare up again later in the year, leading to more violence, injuries, and even several deaths.)

The president's office was on the second floor of this grand building, and getting there required that I walk up an imposing flight of steps. Colorful palace guards, dressed in their formal blue and red uniforms, were stationed at various points. When I arrived at the president's much more modest office, I was surprised that he wanted to meet with me alone. It was very unusual for an economic official of a foreign country to meet with the president of a country without the finance minister and other cabinet ministers present.

De la Rua spoke in general terms about his desire to restore economic growth to Argentina as in the early 1990s. He said there was no need for bilateral money from the United States, but they needed the additional support from the IMF to overcome the deposit run. He emphasized that he was very serious about the zero deficit law and that he had strong political support to implement it. I asked whether the protests, strikes, and demonstrations would affect implementing the law and he replied that the silent majority was very supportive.

At the end of the meeting, he thanked me for coming. He said he appreciated the support of President Bush, who had called him recently. He told me that my visit was already helpful, and that I was a man on whom the future of his country depended.

Finally, I had separate meetings with bankers, business leaders, and economists at the American Ambassador's residence. All present stressed how important it was for the IMF to add more loans to the program again, just as it had done the previous January. At the dinner that evening, the bankers stressed more than anyone the urgency of providing more funds.

Throughout my visit, everyone bolstered the case for additional money by saying that the entire region would be badly damaged by a default in Argentina. Indeed, this was a view shared by many politicians in the region, most of whom issued a call for the United States and the IMF to support Argentina at this crucial time.

My last meeting before leaving was with Domingo Cavallo, back in his office. At this meeting he gave me a short written description of the request he was making to the IMF. It called for supplemental funds equal to $8 billion. He asked that the United States support this loan, but he too did not ask for bilateral support. The nature of the request—its large size, having come directly from the president of an important country, its regional implications—meant that the decision about whether to support the request would be made further up the U. S. financial chain of command.

AN ASSESSMENT

On the flight back to the United States I relaxed for a while, even watched the movie, and then outlined my assessment of the situation. First, the Argentine debt was very likely unsustainable. The private sector debt swap did not work and the zero budget deficit law would be very difficult to implement. Argentina was facing a long-term insolvency problem, not a short-term liquidity problem. No onetime infusion of funds, even in the tens of billions, was going to eliminate the insolvency problem unless the nation made the necessary policy adjustments. The IMF would soon have to stop increasing its loans to Argentina. In fact, it probably should not have increased the loans at the end of 2000, or perhaps not even started the new program in Argentina in the spring of 2000. In addition, there was no "plan B" in place to restructure the debt or deal with the exchange rate if the IMF stopped lending. It was highly unlikely that the Argentine economic team would embrace such a plan without a lot more time and pressure from abroad; this presented a serious problem because they would have to be the people to make a plan B work.

If the IMF did not support the Argentine request for additional funds now, there was a high probability of a sudden default, a continuing run on the banks, an abandonment of the fixed exchange rate, and more social unrest and general strikes. It could be a Russian crisis all over again. However, if the IMF did provide the additional funds now, it would give Argentina a little—but very little—breathing room, by stopping the bank run for a while. But the bailout itself could not cure the insolvency. Argentina would likely be back to the IMF in a less than a year, asking for even more funds.

GENERAL OBJECTIVES

The essential task, in my view, was to mitigate the global impact of Argentina's highly likely default. One of the reasons the Russian default had spread was that the international community changed policies quickly with little warning; hence the default was unanticipated until very close to its actual date. If the international community could somehow signal its intentions and move more gradually this time, we could reduce the chances of contagion. In my view, there was nothing automatic about contagion. If investors discriminated between countries based on their policies, there was no reason that a default in Argentina would have to spread to countries that had little connection with that nation. Of course, a meltdown in Argentina would have impacts on Uruguay, because the financial connections between the two countries were very close.

Our resulting strategy to deal with contagion comprised three parts: First, try to change policy gradually, or at least try to signal the policy changes in advance so that markets could anticipate and adjust to the news. This would not be easy because if we said yes to Argentina's funding request now, but indicated that it was the last time, we had to be sure that our government, or the other G7 governments, would not change the position the next time. Second, help countries like Uruguay that were following good policies but were clearly affected by the crisis in Argentina. Third, do research on, and speak publicly about, the causes of contagion. I hired Kristin Forbes, an expert on financial contagion from the MIT Business School, to join the Treasury and do just this research. By bolstering my arguments with her data and research, I would frequently try to make the case that contagion was not inevitable.

It was also very important to try to mitigate the impact of a default on Argentina, but the Argentine government's reluctance to think about an alternative made that very difficult. I thought that "dollarization"—the complete replacement of the Argentine peso with the U.S. dollar—as El Salvador and Ecuador had recently done, would mitigate the impact of a default. I explored various ways that the United States could assist with this. We could also hasten a recovery after the default by working with the creditors, the IMF, and Argentina to design a good recovery program. We should work with the Argentine government to help the people of Argentina just as we would work with any ally in difficulty, but additional IMF lending had to end at some point. I personally hoped that Argentina could, after a default, start a new chapter of reform without IMF involvement.

THE AUGUST AUGMENTATION

Now that the Argentines' $8 billion request was before us, we had to make a decision, hopefully one that would follow these general objectives. A large number of meetings were held on this subject—too many to describe individually—at all levels in the G7, at the IMF, and within the U.S. government. They started as soon as I got back and lasted right up until August 21, when the decision was finally made. There were literally hundreds of phone calls, and everyone had a chance to weigh in on a complicated and always fluid situation. As the G7 and the United States deliberated, the IMF was negotiating with Argentina. Horst Kohler, Stan Fischer, and Domingo Cavallo would summarize the negotiations to us as they progressed, but not always painting the same picture, of course. One day I got a call from Kohler while I was on the phone with Fischer, and at the same time Domingo Cavallo was trying to get through to me too. It was a good thing that our phones had a lot of lines.

One of the first G7 conference calls took place on August 8, soon after I returned from Argentina. I began by giving an overview of my recent trip, keeping pretty close to the summary I worked out on the plane but stressing the urgency of making a decision quickly, certainly in the next two weeks. Stan Fischer reported that indeed Cavallo had requested another $8 billion in support. Stan seemed to be leaning in favor of offering such support, assuming that he could obtain specific commitments to implement the zero deficit law. As always in this kind of situation, people were reluctant to reveal their views early on. Given that my government itself had not decided on its position, I was clearly not equipped to present the definitive U.S. view at this time and neither were the other G7 players. Stan did mention that even with the augmentation, the chance of making it through without a debt write-down was not high, maybe about 50 or 60 percent. The augmentation would likely only buy a few months, in his view. The most striking information conveyed in this call was that Brazil and other Latin American governments were lobbying all the G7 governments to augment the loans just as Argentina had requested. This kind of political pressure was probably going to influence the final decision.

Another G7 call occurred one week later, on August 14. By now it was clear that the situation was more urgent. Stan Fischer was beginning to make the case for additional funds more explicitly, though candidly admitting that it had only a fifty-fifty chance of success, and that it would buy only a few months. By now, others were leaning more toward support as well.

This being the vacation month of August, many of the meetings within the U.S. government took place through conference calls. It was clear to me from the way the various calls were going that the United States would ultimately decide to go ahead with the augmentation. For example, Secretary Colin Powell was concerned that saying no to Argentina's request could lead to an even larger request later. Bob Zoellick, then the U.S. Trade Representative, whose trade agenda intersected with these finance issues, said that we needed a fully worked out plan B, with the IMF and Argentina fully on board, if we were to say no to this augmentation. Lawrence Lindsey, then the head of the National Economic Council, agreed with Zoellick. Condi Rice worried that saying no would make us seem removed and it was important to stay involved with the region. In contrast, Glenn Hubbard, then chair of the Council of Economic Advisers, thought that we should simply say no now and let them default and devalue. Although a final decision would not be made until the weekend of August 18–19, it seemed inevitable that we and most of the G7 were going to argue for augmentation. The only question was whether we could tie it in with some form of debt restructuring, or at least with a commitment from Argentina to start working on a plan B.

In the end the augmentation, announced by the IMF on August 21, did provide such a condition. The $8 billion would be divided into two parts: $5 billion—to be disbursed immediately—would be devoted to stopping the bank run, and $3 billion—to be disbursed later—would go toward some kind of debt restructuring. Using the

$3 billion this way was novel, and like most novel ideas, some criticized it. Many people pointed out that $3 billion was not enough to make much difference in a voluntary restructuring. They were correct; but tying the $3 billion to a debt restructuring had the advantage of strongly signaling that this was in fact the final augmentation, and that if Argentina could not make the necessary policy adjustments, it was time to move ahead with plan B. Many proposals for a restructuring were circulating around the academic and policy community at the time, and it was just a matter of choosing one and implementing it.

QUIET BEFORE THE "NOT SO PERFECT" STORM

The augmentation quieted things down in Argentina. Most important, the bank run stopped. Only a few weeks later, the 9/11 attacks hit and I recall being very thankful that we had followed this approach. If there were a global financial crisis on top of 9/11, it would have been more than a perfect storm. However, it was clear that Argentina's debt situation was not sustainable. We could still hope for orderly restructuring, but default and devaluation remained a likely possibility. During the fall, we held several NSC principals committee meetings to confirm that all agencies were in agreement that there would be no more augmentations of the current IMF program. There was also interagency agreement that we would abide by the IMF decisions as it enforced the current program and would withhold more disbursements if the program was off track.

By mid-October, Argentina finally indicated that it was ready to restructure its debt. I first got the news at an October 18 dinner meeting in New York City with Bill McDonough, president of the New York Fed; Jacob Frenkel, an economist and former governor of the Bank of Israel, who had become an adviser to Cavallo; and Cavallo himself. It was at this meeting that Cavallo first began to discuss Argentina's effort to restructure. On October 28, Cavallo announced his new plan, in which he would request that Argentina's creditors reduce their contracted debt payments by $4 billion per year; but by now even this amount would not be enough to solve the debt problem. Soon thereafter, on November 6, Standard & Poor's reduced Argentina's sovereign credit rating to SD ("selective default," the lowest possible rating other than "complete default"), citing Argentina's implementation of a "distressed debt exchange." Once the word was out about the S&P decision, people again began to withdraw funds from Argentina's banks. On December 1, Cavallo imposed a limit on withdrawals from bank accounts at $1,000 per month, a very unpopular decision.

By this time it was also clear that the zero deficit plan was not being fulfilled, and that Argentina's deficit was larger than was promised in the IMF program. On December 5, the IMF announced that it would not disburse any more funds to Argentina. I was regularly talking to Daniel Marx, the finance secretary under Cavallo at the time. He called me after the IMF announcement to say that the situation in Buenos Aires was getting "ugly, very ugly." Central bank reserves were falling. The default and the devaluation seemed near.

Cavallo made one last effort to stem the tide. Just before the end I got a call from Jacob Frenkel, who was on the line with Cavallo in Buenos Aires. Frenkel reported that the Argentines were now willing to call for a debt restructuring significantly deeper than before. They were also willing to dollarize. Cavallo said the legislature would pass the budget cuts during the first week of January 2002. But Cavallo would not last as finance minister until January. The riots and the protests grew, finally forcing de la Rua and Cavallo to resign on December 20. It was left to the new president, Rodriguez Saa, to default on the debt, which he did on December 24. Another new president, Eduardo Dualde, then ended the fixed exchange rate on January 6, 2002, and the peso depreciated sharply. The job of restructuring the debt and reengaging with the creditors would not be taken on until after Nestor Kirchner was elected president in May 2003.

WHERE DID ALL THE CONTAGION GO?

How did the Argentine default affect the global financial markets?
When people asked me that question, I would show them the flipside
of the bookmark mentioned earlier.
Here is what the flip side looks like:

You can see that there was very
little global impact of the default.
The charts are arranged in the
same way as those showing the
contagion after the Russian default
on page 72. The date of the Argentine default is marked by the vertical line at December 24, 2001.
Unlike the Russian default, there is
no big jump in the wiggly line
showing the interest rate around
the world. In fact there is no jump
at all, meaning the Argentine
default had very little impact on
other emerging markets. Also,
unlike the Russian default, there
was nothing that "spilled over into
U.S. financial markets" as the Fed
had described the contagion in
1998, and no special action by the
Federal Reserve was required.

I was again thankful. We did
not have the most dangerous financial crisis in fifty years. Our strategy of moving gradually and trying
to signal intentions, which we
hoped would let markets adjust

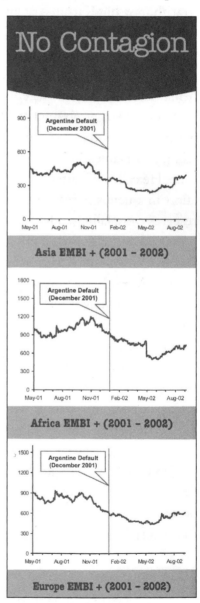

over time to contain the global contagion, had worked. As always in economics, it is difficult to prove that any one factor influences another. The drop in contagion in comparison with 1998 may also have been due to more discriminating investors, but I always thought that our strategy was an essential part of the story.

WORKING WITH THE NEW TEAM TO HELP ARGENTINA RECOVER

Of course, this lack of contagion did not make the people of Argentina feel any better. The three-year-old recession deepened in 2002, with the decline in GDP greater than in the three previous years. I made sure that our staff did everything we could to help the Argentines recover from the default and the devaluation. I called the new finance minister, Jorge Remes-Lenicov, on January 12. He was the fourth finance minister in the past year. I told him that we would try to assemble a group of central bankers to help them set up a new monetary policy now that the country had a flexible exchange rate. He was very interested in the plan.

Then I called Arminio Fraga, the central bank governor of Brazil and a former student of mine at Princeton, to see if he could lend a hand. I also spoke to Guillermo Ortiz, the central bank governor of Mexico, who had been a student with me at Stanford years ago. David Dodge and Carlos Masad, the central bank governors of Canada and Chile, respectively, agreed to help. In this way I put together a team of central bank governors from our hemisphere—all of whom conducted policy with a flexible exchange rate—to advise the Argentine Central Bank. On January 17, Mario Blejer, an old acquaintance of mine, was appointed as Argentina's new central bank governor, and he was happy to have the support. Thanks to Blejer, the inflation rate did not return to double digits as many feared it would after the huge depreciation of the currency. And with money growth increasing by enough to finance a strong recovery, Argentina rebounded from the slump with amazing speed. As time passed, I would keep in touch with the monetary policy officials. (After John

Snow replaced Paul O'Neill as Treasury Secretary early in 2003, he made a special effort to reach out to Argentina and approved of the approach we were taking.)

In April 2002, Remes-Lenicov resigned as finance minister, and was replaced by Roberto Lavagna. I called Lavagna as soon as he was appointed.

"Congratulations, Minister Lavagna," I said.

"Thanks for calling, but I am not sure congratulations are in order. It's a very difficult job."

"But it's really good that you're willing to make a difference for your country. We're anxious to hear what the plans are. What about the exchange rate?"

"I have convinced people here that it is a mistake to go back to a fixed or pegged exchange rate. Rather, we will continue with the floatation, though with some intervention."

Lavagna stayed on as finance minister for the next three years, and I worked closely with him as he dealt with the IMF. There were two more IMF programs, a short one taking them up to the May 2003 election and a longer one to last through the debt restructuring. Relations between the IMF and Argentina were always tense, and the negotiations would sometimes break down over personal issues. From time to time I had to negotiate with Lavagna on behalf of the IMF, an arrangement that both the Argentines and the IMF seemed to appreciate.

Two Principles of Engagement and the Debt Negotiations

In designing the short program, I stressed the principle that the IMF should not overprescribe to Argentina, but rather focus on a small number of policy targets, especially those regarding money growth and the deficit, and hold Argentina to these firmly. By following good monetary and fiscal policy, I was convinced that Argentina could rebound quickly from the depths it hit after the default. Some critics complained that the short program was weak because it did not have a lot of conditions, but I thought it was strong because the conditions were targeted to the recovery and we were firm about Argentina meeting them.

In designing the longer program, during which the debt restructuring would take place, I stressed another principle: that neither the United States nor the IMF should take sides as Argentina negotiated with its creditors. There was a lot of pressure on us to take sides, usually the side of the creditors, but we resisted this pressure. One common argument for taking the side of the creditors was that if Argentina negotiated too hard and got too good a deal, investors would not want to lend to Argentina or to other emerging market countries again. But my view was that letting Argentina and its creditors work it out on their own would be best for the market, reasoning that the possibility of intervention simply raises uncertainty about debt negotiations. One subtle way that people would try to get us to intervene was by asking us to agree to set a high target for Argentina's budget surplus. With a high surplus, Argentina would have more left over to pay to its creditors. We insisted that the longer IMF program must not have a specific surplus target, and although some other G7 members complained—especially Italy, where many bondholders resided—the program did not have a specific target. I discussed this issue many times with John Snow, and he was on board with our approach to both the short and the longer IMF programs.

The debt negotiation was not easy. It took two years. Hundreds of thousands of people around the world owned Argentine bonds. Many were small investors in Europe. In some cases, financial experts—for example, the former German central banker Hans Teitmeyer and the Carnegie Mellon economist Adam Lerrick—organized groups of these creditors and negotiated on their behalf, showing that the negotiation could work well without the IMF intervening. Many creditors complained that Argentina did not negotiate fairly and would never budge from its original position, but Adam Lerrick showed afterwards that both sides compromised to get the final deal.

I suggested many times to Lavagna that Argentina pay back the

IMF as soon as possible. That way they would not have to worry about the IMF overprescribing, and, quite frankly, they would then not be able to use the IMF as an excuse. We all had to admit that the IMF engagement with Argentina did not have a good record, so I felt that Argentina had to start taking responsibility for itself. For this reason, I was delighted when Argentina decided to pay back the IMF in 2005. While there is still a great need for economic reform in Argentina, as in many other countries, it does not need to have an IMF program to make the tough reform decisions.

HELPING THE URUGUAYANS HELP THEMSELVES

Our strategy to combat contagion also required that we assist countries that were following good policies but were hit directly by a nearby crisis. This required a huge effort in the spring and summer of 2002 as Uruguay was indeed hit hard by the crisis in Argentina. Uruguay had a solid record of implementing market-oriented economic policies when the crisis in Argentina caused a run on the Uruguayan banking system. It did not have a debt problem before the Argentine crisis, but the depreciation of the Argentine peso caused a depreciation of the Uruguayan peso, which dramatically raised the cost of making debt payments in dollars. I was in close contact with the Uruguayan government and President Jorge Batlle about the situation during the first half of 2002. Uruguay borrowed from the IMF during this period with the aim of building reserves in the financial system and bolstering public confidence that the government's finances were being put on a more sustainable footing.

By the early summer it became clear that these measures were not enough to stop the bank run. We needed to stabilize the situation and prevent a breakdown in the payments system that would compound the damage already done to Uruguay's economy. However, it looked like the IMF was not willing to provide any additional assistance to Uruguay without an immediate and massive restructuring of the Uruguayan debt. This did not seem consistent with our anti-contagion policy. The Uruguayans came to us and asked us to look into the situation. As in the case of Argentina, I assembled a team at the Treasury covering every aspect—fiscal and debt, monetary, banking, legal, and IMF issues. We held a series of intensive meetings with Uruguayan officials to develop a strategy for confronting the bank run decisively. For the entire weekend of July 27–28 we met with the Uruguayans in my Treasury office, developing a plan to support the banking system.

Uruguay's banking system was dominated by dollar deposits, which meant that the central bank could not print money to satisfy the increased demand for deposit withdrawals. When depositors saw that the central bank's foreign reserves totaled less than the amount of dollar deposits in the system, they rushed to get their money out before the banks ran out of dollars. In our talks with the Uruguayans that weekend, we agreed that the only way to convince people to keep their money in the banks was to back deposits dollar-for-dollar. Backing all deposits in the system was not viable because Uruguay would have had to borrow an immense amount. Going line-by-line through the various categories of deposits, we worked with the Uruguay team to develop a plan to fully back dollar checking and savings deposits while rescheduling the time deposits—increasing the time before people could cash these time deposits in.

To finance the deposit guarantee plan, we persuaded the IMF to mobilize additional funds. As well as rescheduling time deposits, the Uruguayan government would take strong measures to suspend the operations of four private domestic banks. The U.S. Treasury provided a short-term, $1.5 billion loan from the Exchange Stabilization Fund to the government of Uruguay to provide a bridge to the disbursement of funds from the IMF.

The IMF package and bridge loan were a success. The rapid provision of financial support bolstered confidence and enabled Uruguay to reopen the banks without a resumption of the bank run. The bridge loan from the U.S. Treasury was repaid in just four days.

The Uruguayans followed through on their commitments to keep their economic policies on track. With the return of stability, they successfully executed a debt exchange in May 2003. They embraced fiscal policies aimed at bringing down debt levels, and the government increased the key budget balance from a deficit of 1.2 percent of GDP in 2001 to a surplus of 3.6 percent of GDP in 2004. As the government proceeded with financial sector reforms, confidence improved. By 2004, bank deposits recovered to about 80 percent of their pre-crisis level and Uruguay's economy grew 12 percent in 2004.

President Batlle visited Washington in the spring of 2003, and in a meeting on April 23 in the Oval Office he reviewed his country's crisis. Sitting next to President Bush, he told the President and the entire group: "We were down and out. You reached way down, and then picked us up," dramatically illustrating by reaching his hand down to the floor of the Oval Office and then raising it over his head. Later that day, President Batlle visited me in the Treasury to thank me personally, and later still he would award me with their national medal, the Uruguayan equivalent of the Medal of Freedom.

At about the time of President Batlle's visit, it became clear to me that we were moving away from the serious financial crises that had been such a problem in the 1990s and into the first two years of the Bush administration. In a speech to the Council of Americas in New York later that spring, I went out on a limb and noted this very promising change. I reported that spreads were down and capital flows were up. As it turned out, economic growth in Latin America did pick up sharply to 5.6 percent in 2004.

Our strategy of funding countries that help themselves and saying no to others who go off track was brought out nicely by President Bush in a meeting in the Oval Office with another Latin American leader, President Nicanor Duarte of Paraguay. The meeting took place on September 26, 2003, and I was there because issues relating to the international financial institutions were expected to arise. During the meeting, President Duarte asked President Bush for some help with IMF support, and President Bush said: "That's why John Taylor is here. He is not here simply to sit and listen. He is our man on the IMF. We would like to help you, but you—and I don't want to lecture here—have to help yourself. The IMF can't help you if you are not following the right policy. Some countries come around and ask us for help with the IMF, but they don't do anything themselves. I don't like that. So Taylor is tough. He will help you help yourself and do the good policies which I know you will."

I visited Argentina again in April 2004. I met with President Kirchner in the Casa Rosada, in the same office where I saw President de la Rua in August 2001. It was a good, cordial meeting. The president said with unmistakable satisfaction that the Argentine economy was still ripping along. I told him I was concerned about the sustainability of this growth if Argentina did not implement economic reforms, such as fiscal reforms that would reduce overspending by the provincial governments. He explained to me in great detail about the complex fiscal relations between the central government and the provinces in Argentina, drawing on his experience as governor of Santa Cruz province for a dozen years. I wished him the best of luck in implementing these reforms.

Happily, this time there were no political cartoons of me and the Argentine president and finance minister.

CHAPTER FOUR

New Rules for the International Monetary Fund

◆

We at Treasury should view the post–September 11 period much as our predecessors at Treasury viewed the post–World War II period. They thought it was imperative to create new international financial institutions in part to help prevent another war. We should think it is imperative to reform these same international financial institutions in part to help prevent future acts of terror.

—JBT's speech to the Bankers Association for Finance and Trade, February 7, 2002

The International Monetary Fund was created in July 1944 at a conference of international finance officials held in Bretton Woods, New Hampshire, right in the middle of World War II. The main objective of the IMF, in the founders' view, was to avert or resolve financial crises by providing funds to countries to help them finance temporarily large trade deficits. The loans would enable countries to avoid instituting harmful economic policies—such as high tariffs or currency devaluations—which would reduce imports but also stifle economic growth. Such policies were in good part responsible for the terrible economic conditions leading up to World War II.

The United States and Great Britain led this reform of the international monetary system, but disagreed about how to design the IMF and about how much power it should have. Historians have brought these technical disagreements to life by portraying them as a battle between two economists: John Maynard Keynes, who was consulting for the British Treasury, and Harry Dexter White, who was chief international economist for the U.S. Treasury. Keynes wanted an institution that would operate like a global central bank, issuing its own international money, and that would therefore wield considerable power. White argued for a less powerful institution. Rather than a global central bank, he proposed an institution that could lend only the amount that the United States and other large countries lent to it. In the end, the Bretton Woods conferees agreed to the U.S. plan rather than the British plan; or, more personally put, the White plan won and the Keynes plan lost. The personal part of the story has continued to attract interest both because of Keynes's prominence and because White was later identified as a spy for the Soviet Union.

Soon after 9/11 the United States began preparations for another significant reform of the international financial system. As with the establishment of the IMF, the objective was to avert or resolve financial crises, an objective that took on a new urgency in the post-9/11 world. Preventing crises would help prevent the hardship, poverty, and disillusionment with market-based democracies that financial collapses could bring about. But rather than create a new IMF, or abolish the old one, this reform would give the existing IMF new rules to follow. Just as during World War II, there were significant disagreements about how to achieve these objectives. And, in an eerie parallel with World War II, journalists personalized the differences as a battle between two economists, this time Anne Krueger, the first deputy director of the IMF, and me. Krueger and Taylor were "at logger heads about how to best reform the international financial system," *The Economist* wrote on April 6, 2002, noting the irony that "until recently both were colleagues at Stanford's Hoover Institution." As in 1944, the question of how much power the IMF should have was central, and on this issue the U.S. Treasury ended up on the same side that it was sixty years earlier, reluctant to give too much power to an international financial institution.

Despite this disagreement, the international community came together, and after many setbacks, agreed on a reform package, and then implemented it so rapidly that everyone, even a most optimistic backer like me, was surprised. As Simon Kennedy, the veteran financial reporter from *Bloomberg News*, wrote on September 27, 2002, the reform "would amount to one of the biggest changes to the international financial system since the gold standard was dropped in 1971."

HELL-BENT FOR REFORM

During the 1990s, the frequency and severity of financial crises in emerging markets increased markedly. A review by the consulting firm McKinsey in 2002 found that the 1990s experienced 60 percent more crises than the 1980s. The Mexican financial crisis of 1994 was the first serious emerging market crisis of the 1990s; fifteen more serious crises throughout Latin America, Asia, and Russia followed. Treasury Secretary Robert Rubin, Deputy Secretary Larry Summers, and Fed Chairman Alan Greenspan appeared together on the cover of the February 15, 1999, issue of *Time* as the men who had dealt with the crises, but many of those crises persisted into 2001 when the 9/11 attacks hit. Such crises, and widespread criticism and controversy about the IMF's attempts to resolve them, brought about calls for reform from across the political spectrum and around the world. On the positive side, the crises did cause a number of emerging market countries to begin making improvements in their economic policy—especially monetary policy. Many central banks reformed their monetary policy by placing much greater emphasis on keeping inflation low and by introducing a more flexible exchange rate.

But a number of policymakers and economists, myself included, thought that the IMF also needed reform. Indeed, before I came into the Bush administration I became very concerned with how the IMF was responding to the crisis in Russia, where it supported an economic plan the government publicly admitted lying about, or in Indonesia, where it insisted on so many loan conditions that the program was guaranteed to fail. I began to think that no IMF would be better than the one we had, and I said so in a TV interview in 1998. It was on a show produced by the Hoover Institution called *Uncommon Knowledge*, hosted by Peter Robinson, a former speechwriter for Ronald Reagan who drafted the famous line: "Mr. Gorbachev, tear down this Wall." The show was filmed on December 15, 1998, and it aired on a number of public television stations soon after two former Treasury secretaries, George Shultz and William Simon, and former Citibank chairman Walter Wriston wrote a *Wall Street Journal* piece maintaining that "The IMF is ineffective, unnecessary, and obsolete." That George Shultz had also served as Secretary of State made the piece even more noteworthy.

Peter opened the show by saying, "No less a figure than former Secretary of State George Shultz has called for the International Monetary Fund to be abolished," and then continued, "The IMF, a useful thing to have on this earth? John?"

"I agree it should be abolished. I'd like to do it," I said.

Peter, recognizing that this might be interesting after all, interjected in surprise, "It should be abolished?" And I went on, "It should be abolished, I agree. And I'd like to do it slowly in a way that takes some of the talents there and uses it in a more effective way. There's a lot of highly skilled people there and if they can be doing things in another venue it would be very appropriate."

"Slowly, skillfully, wrap it up and shut it down."

"Right."

Three years later, this short exchange became the subject of a *Washington Post* story by Paul Blustein, with the headline: TAYLOR ADVOCATED KILLING IMF. The story appeared on February 8, 2001, as soon as rumors started circulating that President Bush might nominate me to serve in the Treasury international position where I could actually do something to reform the IMF. It's the kind of story that gets into the media echo chamber and is repeated again and again. And it was.

When President Bush did nominate me, *The Economist* noted on March 5, 2001, that the "under-secretary for international affairs—a key post—is John Taylor, a highly respected economist who said two years ago that he favoured abolition of the IMF."

In my confirmation hearing, Senator Max Baucas of Montana raised the question: "I read somewhere that you at one time advocated abolition of the IMF. . . . I wonder if you could expand on that, please." And, recognizing that I needed to get confirmed if I were to implement any reform, I replied: "I do not think that is how I would put it at this time. That was several years ago. . . . [The IMF] can be reformed."

When Argentina requested additional aid from the IMF in the summer of 2001, *Bloomberg News* noted on August 10 that "In a 1998 television appearance, economist John Taylor said that the International Monetary Fund should be abolished. . . . Today, Argentina brings its request for as much as $9 billion more in IMF aid to Washington, and Taylor—now the U.S. Treasury's top international official—will strongly influence whether the country gets the aid. Taylor's disdain for bailouts is going to be tested. . . ."

THE PROBLEM

What exactly was the problem that required reform of the IMF? Many of the crises in the 1990s occurred as a result of a country's debt getting too high, which made it difficult for the country to pay interest and principal on its debt. Most often the debt consisted of bonds sold to private investors in other countries—mainly the United States, Japan, and Europe—and most of the debt was in U.S. dollars. As a result, the interest and principal on the bonds had to be paid in dollars, rather than in the national currency of the country. The seed of many debt crises was a country spending much more than it was taking in, and thereby having to borrow from abroad. But a common way for a country to move from an economic problem to an economic crisis was through a large depreciation of the exchange rate, which made the foreign debt denominated in dollars much larger and harder to pay. In Mexico's 1994 crisis, the peso lost half of its value against the dollar in two weeks in December 1994, so Mexico had to find twice as many pesos to pay interest and principal on each dollar of debt that it owed. Sharply cutting government spending or raising taxes to make these payments did not look feasible and could cause a recession.

Once a country got into this situation, it seemed to have no choice but to borrow even more money and use this money to pay its creditors, or, alternatively, default on its loans, something that no government ever wanted to do. But who would lend new money to a country in such a shaky situation when default seemed imminent? Borrowing more money from the private sector was unlikely. This is where the IMF came in. If the country could get a large influx of loans from the IMF, it could use these funds to pay its private sector creditors, which would hopefully tide the country over to better times. Many refer to such a large influx of loans from the IMF as a "bailout," and though it has pejorative connotations, the description is really quite apt. The IMF would effectively be bailing out the bondholders and the country from the financial mess. In the case of the Mexican financial crisis, the IMF made loans and the United States topped off the loans by lending directly to Mexico from the Treasury's Exchange Stabilization Fund, creating a huge bailout package of $50 billion.

Even if the IMF loans prevented the default and the country eventually got back on its feet—as happened in Mexico—the emergency lending operation created destructive disincentives for other countries, or even the same country, in the future. For example, the president of an emerging market country, observing such IMF bailouts and recognizing the possibility of future bailouts, might avoid or delay making politically unpopular budget adjustments and thereby let the debt get too high. Or the finance minister of the country might be less concerned about the risks of borrowing too much in a foreign currency. The government also might not build up its own foreign reserves, which it could use to pay interest or principal on foreign debt in an emergency. Investors too might come to expect a possible bailout in the future, and thus be willing to lend to a country they would not otherwise consider. The reformers were concerned about these disincentive effects, which they called "moral hazard." Some economists tried to find evidence of moral hazard or estimate its size by studying the markets for debt, but that proved difficult because many other forces impact these markets. As a theoretical matter, moral hazard must exist, but it is very difficult to determine how large it is.

AN UNPREDICTABLE PROCESS

The bailout process had an even more serious problem than moral hazard. The problem was created by *uncertainty* about the bailout process itself, and in particular whether the IMF and its major shareholders had the political support at home and the technical ability to engage in such rescue attempts in a given situation. Critics argued that the bailouts merely rescued Wall Street investors while the people in the countries were harmed anyway because, as in Mexico, there was still a sharp recession even with a bailout. The criticism grew intense when the United States chose to top off IMF loans to increase the size of the rescue package, as it did in the case of Mexico. The unprecedented magnitude of that bailout brought an avalanche of criticism from Republicans in the Congress and elsewhere, which Robert Rubin has thoroughly documented in his book *In an Uncertain World*. Bailouts also raised the ire of the international community, especially central banks like the Bundesbank in Germany and the Bank of England, which put much emphasis on the moral hazard problem.

Democrats also criticized the situation. Joe Stiglitz, a former economic adviser to President Clinton and a recent Nobel Prize winner, argued in the April 2002 issue of *Project Syndicate* that "The big bailout strategies, associated with the Clinton-era IMF of Michel Camdessus, Stanley Fischer, Larry Summers, and Robert Rubin failed abysmally. An alternative is demanded." And finally there were the foreign policy implications of any bailout decision, which brought in many other actors in the U.S. government—State, Defense, the CIA—and in the governments of the other IMF shareholders. Bailing out a strategic ally might be the preferred strategy of the foreign affairs ministry, even if it didn't make sense to the finance ministry. This made the bailout decision even more complex and the outcome more uncertain.

All this uncertainty rendered it difficult for investors and emerging market countries to assess what the IMF and its shareholders would do in a crisis. The decisions about whether to support an IMF bailout were not purely economic and financial. Would the U.S. Congress exert pressure against bailouts by the administration—say by reducing funding for the international financial institutions or by passing legislation restricting use of the Treasury's Exchange Stabilization Fund? Or would political pressures from the State Department or the White House to support a strategic ally lead to another bailout? The personalities of the players in Treasury, in State, and in the White House all became part of the calculation. So did the perceived relative power of the Treasury versus State versus the White House staff.

For private investors, this lack of predictability added even more risk when deciding whether to put their funds in emerging markets. The uncertainty probably added to contagion fears as well. With little to go on, every bailout decision had big implications for the likelihood of future bailout decisions. Russia's sudden default in 1998, for example, signaled to investors that the United States would be less likely to support future IMF bailouts, subsequently raising risks in other emerging markets, which caused investors to withdraw from those markets.

Indeed, in the late 1990s, the continuing emerging market crises and the uncertainty about the response of the IMF led to a sharp reduction in the flow of investor funds to emerging markets. Net private capital flows averaged more than $150 billion per year to emerging markets from 1992 to 1997, but then fell off sharply to less than $50 billion per year in 1998–2000. Guillermo Calvo, perhaps the world's greatest academic expert on emerging market crises, called such a sharp drop-off a "sudden stop."

Solving the problem would require that the IMF and its shareholders provide more clarity about the process and be more systematic about whether it would say yes or no to a country's bailout request. It would have to institutionalize this more systematic approach in some way, perhaps by amending the rules and regulations under which the IMF would agree to an exceptionally large bailout. Of course, one way to reduce uncertainty about what the IMF would do would be to remove it from the picture entirely; but I was looking for a less extreme option.

RULES VERSUS DISCRETION

My thinking on IMF reform was heavily influenced by my research and experience in central banking over the years. Modern monetary theory and policy—as it has developed in the past twenty-five years—argued strongly for clarity and predictability in monetary policy decisions by central banks. If a central bank followed clear-cut principles when it made its interest rate decisions, the markets would react more efficiently and smoothly to the decision. This would lower risk and increase economic stability. My research showed that some of the principles for setting interest rates could be expressed in a simple formula, which economists call the Taylor Rule. This emphasis on clarity was in marked contrast to earlier views that encouraged a mystique surrounding how monetary policy decisions were made. The fact that economic performance improved greatly when monetary policy became more predictable and systemically focused on a clear goal of price stability is one of the major achievements of economics in the twentieth century.

Applying these ideas on monetary policy to the International Monetary Fund would not be easy. It would require placing some limits on IMF bailouts, with clearly stated criteria for when those limits might be exceeded. The IMF and its shareholders would have to be transparent about what these limits and criteria were. In practice, it would require saying no to bailout requests in some well-defined circumstances.

And applying the limits in actual cases would be the most difficult part of all, for in reality policymakers would be under heavy pressure to provide a bailout in a given situation even if they had agreed earlier not to provide such a bailout in those same circumstances. Policymakers with responsibility for the international financial system would be reluctant to say no and let the country default. They would argue that a sudden default could be very harmful to the country and possibly to the rest of the world. For example, if private banks held a large portion of the government's debt, the fear that banks themselves might go down with a government default could cause a run on deposits and a curtailment of business loans that would adversely affect the economy. Further, a sudden default could cause global contagion as did the Russian default. So, simply agreeing to limits on IMF lending would not be credible, because policymakers would ignore the limits in the heat of the crisis. Economists call this problem "time inconsistency," and it was one of the reasons that monetary economists argued for rules rather than discretion in central banking. Getting limits passed—and thereby instituting some rules versus discretion at the IMF—would require dealing with or mitigating time inconsistency pressures. This in turn would require a more orderly process for debt restructuring and a reduction in the likelihood of contagion.

During the late 1990s, there was a great deal of debate going on in the G7 about putting limits on exceptionally large IMF loans. On one side of this debate were the British, especially the Bank of England, which under Governor Eddie George proved the most outspoken. This side wanted to put limits on a country's access to large IMF loans. On the other side was the United States. Lawrence Summers and Alan Greenspan sent a letter to Eddie George on July 24, 2000, laying out the reasons why they thought strict limits on lending to a country were not appropriate. They argued that each crisis was different and that there was little need to constrain policy decisions with strict limits. Of course, no one was talking about limits that were so strict they would never ever be exceeded in any circumstance. The debate was whether you could be specific about the circumstances that would permit the IMF to exceed the limits.

When the Bush administration came into office, I thought it unwise to change directions instantaneously; but I did look for opportunities to take some immediate actions that would signal a change, in particular, that we wanted to move in the direction of the "rules" or "limits" camp. For example, I stressed, as a principle, that the United States and other individual governments should not "top up" the lending of the IMF during a specific bailout operation with their own loans. The idea was that *total* IMF funds are limited by the total amount that United States and other countries have already agreed to put into the IMF. Thus, the IMF faced an *overall* budget limit when deciding how much to loan to countries, but not a specific limit on a loan to each country. I had discussed this concept with Alan Greenspan over lunch soon after I arrived, and since it was a milder concept of limits than he had previously objected to, he was supportive. When we had to make a quick decision about the IMF's request for a $10 billion loan from the Treasury's Exchange Stabilization Fund for Turkey, we said no and emphasized the "no topping up" principle. For the most part, I believe we have stuck to this principle. The only time the Exchange Stabilization Fund made a loan while I was Under Secretary was for a four-day bridge loan for Uruguay in 2002, and even in this case the U.S. loan didn't increase the total size of the package.

The "limits" debate continued in the G7 during the first few months of the Bush administration. The issue came up in my first face-to-face meeting with all my G7 counterparts in June 2001. The meeting was held at the sprawling Palazzo del Ministero delle Finanze in Rome, and we had to follow signs saying "Environmental Conference" to the meeting rooms so we would be incognito, not exactly the best example of transparency. (The practice was soon dropped.) I wanted to signal at this meeting that the new administration in Washington was going to lean toward the limits camp, stating that our first principle was the presumption that the IMF should provide the support to a country without bilateral topping up from governments. My British counterpart, Gus O'Donnell, was willing to accept this idea as a first step, but complained that it was a weak concept of limits, much less binding than the limit on individual countries that he was still advocating. He was right, of course, but it moved the ball in the right direction. I also stressed, as a second principle, that we would show some aversion to strong-arming private banks to get them to agree to lend more to a country during an IMF bailout, a tactic sometimes called "bailing in." I felt that a good rules-based system would say what the IMF policy was and then let the private sector make its own decisions without G7 arm-twisting. There was no way that we could develop a transparent ruleslike procedure for such coercion, and it was hard to hold the private sector to any such agreement anyway. And I worried that a private bank might expect a quid pro quo for such an agreement at some point in the future.

When the G7 finance ministers and central bank governors met in Washington in October 2001, their main focus was on completing the new G7 Action Plan to combat terrorist financing, but the "limits" issue came up, too. Eddie George was again calling for limits on large-scale lending to countries, and Alan Greenspan continued to show much skepticism. The only kind of limit that would work in practice would be zero, Greenspan argued, for all other limits would be too hard to define, enforce, and adhere to. Though he was not advocating it, Greenspan's zero limit would imply shutting down the IMF, at least in this sphere of business. But there was a general sense in the discussion at that meeting—the first G7 meeting in the post-9/11 world—that the time for debate was over and we had to find a way forward in resolving the limits issue. In addition, I believe that the continuing crisis in Argentina, which had again required more funds from the IMF in August, convinced everyone of the need for reform.

To move things forward, we would have to find a way to deal with the high costs of default. If policymakers were to be able to say no in the face of the country having to stop making payments on its debt, the country would need a more orderly procedure for restructuring that debt and coming to new terms with its creditors. Business firms in the United States or other countries traditionally restructure

their debt with creditors through the help of a bankruptcy procedure. The judge in a bankruptcy court is responsible for making the
tough decisions about who has to sacrifice more, the firm or its creditors. Yet there was no similar regular process in the case of international debt of sovereign governments, and for this reason the default
was always viewed with great uncertainty and even fear, which created more incentives for a bailout. In other words, *a rules-based
reform of the IMF was inseparably linked to a reform of the process for sovereign debt restructuring.*

The Opening Bell on Debt Restructuring Reform

I had discussed the limits issue with Paul O'Neill many times. He
supported the "overall limit" principle, the "avoid coercion of the
private sector" principle, and the general notion of limiting IMF
bailouts. He was also familiar with the debt restructuring problem
and how it related to limits. On September 18, 2001, Paul and I had
breakfast with IMF head Horst Kohler and first deputy director
Anne Krueger. We had a good discussion about the restructuring
problem. We all agreed that this was something that the IMF, the
Treasury, everyone should be working on. Two days later, on September 20, O'Neill went public with the issue in congressional testimony, referring to his breakfast meeting with the IMF: "as recently
as Monday morning I had breakfast with Horst Kohler from the IMF
and said to him: 'I think now is the time that we need to take the
action that's been talked about for years that's never been done, we
need an agreement on international bankruptcy law so that we can
work with governments that in effect need to go through a Chapter
11 reorganization instead of socializing the costs of bad decisions.'"

Now that the Secretary of the Treasury had publicly endorsed the
need for a reform of sovereign debt restructuring, it would be part of
a broader effort to reform the IMF. Even though our staff was
already going all-out with terrorist financing and financial reconstruction in Afghanistan, I asked our experts to go to work. This was
a hot topic, involving international law, economic theory, and practi-

cal knowledge about financial markets, both domestic and international. Nearly everyone wanted to be involved. I asked Randy Quarles, who was then the U.S. executive director of the IMF, to be the coordinator. Given his legal experience at Davis Polk in New York and his position at the IMF, he was ideal. Treasury's top lawyer, David Aufhauser, and domestic finance head, Peter Fisher, also played active roles, working together with Randy Quarles as a team in typical post-9/11 fashion. We sought the opinion of the New York legal and financial communities, and from the emerging markets countries. Lee Buchheit, of Cleary Gottlieb in New York, was particularly helpful, coming to Treasury so often that he seemed to be on the staff.

COLLECTIVE ACTION CLAUSES

From the start, I was looking for a solution that did not require a new international body, like a new world bankruptcy court. This was the disposition of virtually anyone who had financial market experience, such as Peter Fisher, who had run the trading desk at the New York Fed, and people currently in the private sector. For a bankruptcy court to work internationally, it would have to have the power to tell sovereign borrowers and international creditors how much to lower their claims, analogous to the power a bankruptcy court has over firms and creditors in a single country. How would this power over sovereign governments be enforced? Did we really want to hand over such power to an international body, whether the IMF or a new court? I didn't think so, and even if I did, it was highly unlikely that the U.S. Congress would agree to approve such a powerful international bureaucracy.

This reasoning led us to focus on a decentralized approach, which would rely more on the private sector than on government. We thought this approach would be a better reform and have a much better chance of being implemented. The type of decentralized reform that appealed to our Treasury team had similarities to one put forth in 1996 in the Rey Report issued by the G10, which included the G7 countries plus Sweden, Switzerland, Belgium, and Holland. (In the Gn world, the ns do not always add up.) New clauses—called collective action clauses, or CACs—would be added to a country's bonds. The clauses would describe how the country would work with its creditors to restructure its debt, if it ever needed to do so. A bond being a contract between the borrower and the lender, we could implement the reform simply by encouraging borrowing countries (and their investment bankers and lawyers) to include these clauses in their bond contracts. We began to refer to the proposal as "contract-based" since no laws would be required to implement it, unlike the IMF's proposals. In deciding to take the contract-based approach, I was influenced by the ideas of a number of academic economists, most significantly Barry Eichengreen of Berkeley, who had done research on such bond clauses and was a strong advocate of the approach.

In the meantime, the IMF was busy working away on its own plan. I was in contact with Anne Krueger and told her that Treasury thought the decentralized method would work and had the advantage that it could actually be implemented. I did not tell Anne not to work on the centralized approach if she and the IMF staff were seriously convinced of its merits. Then, on November 26, 2001, Krueger gave a speech in which she outlined IMF thinking. She put forth a proposal to create a bankruptcy court with the IMF having the powerful role of determining when a country should go into a restructuring and by how much the country and its creditors should cut the value of the debt. The IMF called its proposal the Sovereign Debt Restructuring Mechanism, and most people latched on to the acronym SDRM. I was not enthused about the SDRM, and thought that we, in the Bush administration, were coming up with a better strategy. I briefed Paul O'Neill on December 15 about our approach, and he approved it. On February 14, 2002, I went up to Capitol Hill to testify before the Joint Economic Committee of Congress on the approach, and O'Neill included it in his congressional testimony of February 28. There was no secret about which way the Bush administration was going, and by early March we were ready for a more formal rollout.

On March 14, I sent a one-page memo entitled "Next Steps on Sovereign Debt Restructuring" to Paul O'Neill, which stated: ". . . as you know we have already signaled our preference for a decentralized, contract-based approach, in which emerging countries would be required or encouraged to put new clauses in their debt contracts. The purpose of these clauses would be to make restructuring more systematic and predictable. Our preference for this contract-based approach was indicated in congressional testimony (yours and mine) as well as in Randy's statements at the IMF Executive Board and the G-7 experts group in which he participates. The reaction to our approach . . . has generally been positive." I suggested that I use an upcoming April 2 speech at a conference at the Institute for International Economics in Washington to propose our plan formally, and that it would be "a good time to definitively describe our position." I then attached a comprehensive analysis by Treasury staff, which gave the pros and cons of different types of clauses. O'Neill agreed that the April 2 speech would be a good time and place to start the rollout.

On March 22, the influential international financier Bill Rhodes of Citibank wrote an op-ed in the *Financial Times* arguing against the Sovereign Debt Restructuring Mechanism. His reaction was not surprising, but it did begin to catalyze private sector opposition to the IMF's proposal. Partly in reaction to the criticism from people like Rhodes, the IMF began to modify its proposal and Anne Krueger decided to unveil the modification at the same conference where I was to unveil the Bush administration's proposal, though one day earlier, on April 1.

Although the new IMF proposal was an improvement on the original proposal—for example, it called for a newly created panel rather than the IMF to serve as the effective bankruptcy court—it still would require a powerful centralized body and would be hard to implement. I still felt our clause proposal made the most sense. So, when April 2 came and I was to speak, we put forth our proposal as planned.

THE ROLLOUT AND THE INITIAL REACTIONS

My April 2 speech, entitled "Sovereign Debt Restructuring: A U.S. Perspective," was meant to be a persuasive call for action. I knew that this would be the first shot in a lengthy, uphill battle of reform. "It is clear that reform of this process is long overdue," I began. "There has been much useful study and discussion since the mid-1990s when problems with the process became apparent, including the 1996 Rey Report of the G-10. . . . But the time for study and discussion of options should be ending. The time for action is here."

The proposal was purposely not overly prescriptive, because part of the idea behind decentralization was that people in the private sector should work together, within the broad parameters that I indicated, to come up with a good set of clauses. I also emphasized that the proposal was different from the simpler collective action clause proposals put forth in 1996; these had more "bells and whistles" and were designed to do things that a centralized bankruptcy court might do without actually having the court. I insisted that the speech use regular English, without the legal jargon and complexities we used as we developed the plan at Treasury. I substantially rewrote the initial draft, explaining in my own words what the new clauses would do, and getting pushback from our lawyers about how my informal language could have ambiguous legal meaning. I knew that the subject was arcane and thought that the clear expression and communication of our ideas to non-experts was going to be as important for the implementation as the ideas themselves.

I argued that you could divide collective action clauses into three types: (1) a *majority action* clause, which would allow for a percentage of bondholders less than 100 percent to change the financial terms of the bond; (2) an *engagement* clause, which would describe the process through which the debtors and the creditors came together and how they would be represented; and (3) an *initiation* clause, which would describe how the sovereign government would initiate the restructuring, and whether there would be a period during which payments were deferred temporarily. The names of the latter two clauses were my own, not the lawyers', and I was surprised that they came to be used widely in the legal discussion in the months ahead.

I warned that it might be necessary to provide some carrots to emerging market countries to get them to change. One carrot might be lower interest rates on IMF borrowing for those countries that used the clauses, but I was hoping that such inducements would not be needed. Regarding the IMF proposal, I said that study of it should continue but hoped that this study would not interfere with the implementation of the collective action clauses as soon as possible.

Our rollout plan called for me to go to New York City for an early breakfast meeting the next morning, April 3, to explain our proposal to key investors and bankers. Bill McDonough, the president of the New York Fed, whose advisory board I sat on before joining the Treasury, hosted the breakfast in the elegant president's dining room. The meeting included investors from the "buy side" and investment bankers from the "sell side." McDonough was a smooth facilitator, good at bringing people together, and he had a very able chief of emerging markets, Terry Checki, to help. Back in August 1998, McDonough had called bankers together to help resolve the serious crisis that arose when the hedge fund Long Term Capital Management was hit by heavy trading losses following the contagion from the Russian default and was on the verge of collapse. This collapse threatened to bring other financial institutions down with it, and Bill, with the help of Peter Fisher, facilitated a cooperative effort among the banks in which they provided short-term loans to the ailing hedge fund and halted the market implosion.

In my breakfast meeting I was also calling on the private sector to do something, but the group that had to cooperate went well beyond bankers; it included investors, traders, lawyers, and finance ministers and central bankers in the emerging market countries. The task was less immediate, but more complex. It would entail shifting the emerging country debt market to a new equilibrium, one where the price would reflect bond contracts with the new clauses. The templates used by the lawyers would have to change. The investment bankers would have to change their pitch to investors. In emerging market countries, the finance ministry would have to explain the change to its people, and risk being criticized. So I was very pleased that our proposal was generally well received by most of the key players that first morning. And it was followed up by public statements of support from the financial community. On April 9, Charles Dallara, managing director of the International Institute for Finance, a trade association of international banks, put out a very positive statement of support, saying: "Inclusion of collective action clauses in new bond contracts would facilitate debt restructurings over the medium term." That endorsement was significant, for, as Martin Crutsinger explained in an AP story on April 9, 2002, the "key endorsement Tuesday from an organization representing major international banks . . . represents a major policy reversal for the world's large financial institutions."

The news from Washington on the morning of April 3 was not so good. *The Washington Post* ran a story by Paul Blustein about my speech with the headline: IMF CRISIS PLAN TORPEDOED: TREASURY OFFICIAL REJECTS PROPOSAL A DAY AFTER IT IS ADVANCED. Despite our rollout plan, the news was not Treasury's new proposal, but rather that I was attacking Anne Krueger's proposal. "Taylor's speech was especially remarkable because Krueger was picked for her job by the Bush administration, and the evening before, she had presented the same audience with a modified version of her plan that was aimed at dealing with some of the concerns raised by Treasury," Blustein wrote. He did describe aspects of our plan, mentioning that "critics scoffed that the idea has been advocated for years by financial experts to little effect," and quoting President Clinton's former adviser Daniel Tarullo, who said, "little is likely to be achieved." Aside from these light jabs, however, the article emphasized the personal conflict between me and Anne and the institutional conflict between the Bush administration and the IMF. The personal conflict was the news that got into the press echo chamber this time.

The next day, *The Washington Post* editorial page took up the same themes: "... on Tuesday, John Taylor ... declared that the whole idea of a bankruptcy court was a non-starter. The alternative Mr. Taylor hinted at ... seems like a long shot; bond issuers have shrunk from doing that in the past and are unlikely to feel different in the future." This editorial was entitled "Mr. O'Neill Climbs Down," and personally attacked the Secretary for allowing himself to be undercut in his supposed support for the IMF plan by his department and by me in particular. The *Financial Times* joined the chorus with an editorial entitled "Bankrupt US Veto," and *The Economist* criticized me for our decentralized approach, saying, "ever suspicious of government meddling, Mr. Taylor is unwilling to mandate anything at all."

Some writers portrayed the alleged fight between me and Krueger as evidence that the administration was not exercising the tight control over the IMF that Summers and Rubin supposedly exercised when Stanley Fischer was the number two there. They contrasted the fight between me and Krueger to the warm relations between Summers and Fischer.

Of course there were differences of opinion between the Treasury and the IMF, but the idea that Anne Krueger and I were having some kind of personal feud was ludicrous. At the White House Correspondents' Dinner that April, reporters told us that they expected a food fight or some other altercation when Anne and I were seated at the same table. But the reality was that we remained very good friends. We played golf together at the IMF's Bretton Woods golf course in Maryland just as we played golf at Stanford's course in California years before. As former academics it seemed natural to have differences of opinion on professional issues and still remain friends.

Nevertheless, we had to deal with a perception problem. O'Neill argued that it was best to let these differences of opinion play out in public, to have a good debate in the press, despite the fact that the media was focusing more on the personalities in the debate than the substance. In fact, there were some supporters of the IMF plan outside the IMF. Joe Stiglitz, for example, in the same April 2002 *Project Syndicate* article in which he criticized Summers and Rubin, wrote: "Taylor is a distinguished macro-economist but he has paid little attention either to recent developments in economic theory or experiences in economic policy in the arena of bankruptcy. Collective action clauses are important but they are not enough."

Others, myself included, argued that we should simply end the debate now, be candid that we could not support the SDRM, and that it had no chance even if we did support it. The truth was, with the emerging market countries, the bankers, and the investors so adamant in their objections to the SDRM, there was no way that it was going to be implemented. If we kept supporting the SDRM, we might even lose the nascent support we were getting for the collective action clause approach.

On April 5, Paul O'Neill and I went over to the West Wing office of White House economic adviser Larry Lindsey to discuss what we were hearing in the press and to make sure everyone understood the issues and was in agreement. Larry passed around a copy of *The Washington Post* editorial, and O'Neill and I described our position. It was not true that O'Neill had climbed down from the IMF's proposal, or that it was a better proposal. Rather, the Treasury staff had the better proposal and one that seemed much more likely to be put into practice. At the close of the meeting, O'Neill made the decision that we should continue to push hard for collective action clauses, but we should also encourage more work and discussion on the SDRM. Even though I disagreed with the decision, that became the operative policy in the administration, and I followed it. After the meeting in Lindsey's office, we circulated a one-page set of talking points stating that "we intend to move ahead expeditiously to implement the contract-based approach" and that "the IMF will continue to develop an alternative statutory approach." That would require a little backpedaling from the more negative tone of my speech, and I asked Randy Quarles to make the subtle adjustment in a short press briefing.

Pushing Ahead with Multilateral Backing

After hitting this rough patch, I suppose it would have been easy to get discouraged, to walk away; but most of the criticism in the press was personal rather than substantive, not to mention inaccurate. I had confidence in the economic principles on which our proposal was based, and I knew that we were on the right track even though things looked bleak. I remained optimistic with our staff and we continued to press on.

The next step was to get the G7 members on board to support our position on collective action clauses. There was still an ongoing dispute within the G7 on the issue of setting limits on the size of IMF "bailout" packages. To regain the momentum, it would be essential for our reform effort to get agreement to push forward aggressively in favor of the collective action clauses at the next G7 meeting on April 20 in Washington. On Thursday, April 11, Paul O'Neill and I were scheduled to meet in London with Chancellor of the Exchequer Gordon Brown and his top international official, Gus O'Donnell, my G7 counterpart. O'Neill was on his way back from a European tour and I was coming back from a visit to Moscow to further a U.S.-Russian banking initiative. We were to have dinner at Number 11 Downing Street, the chancellor's residence next to Number 10. We made a breakthrough at that dinner, because O'Neill told Brown that the United States would support some limits on the size of IMF bailouts if the British would support moving ahead immediately on the collective action clauses, and Brown readily agreed. This was a change in position for the United States, but the idea that collective action clauses and clearer limits went hand-in-hand had become the essence of our reform effort. Once Brown and O'Neill agreed, it was up to me and Gus O'Donnell to get the rest of the G7 on board. I recommended that we draft an action plan—similar in concept to the successful Action Plan for Combating Terrorist Financing of the previous fall—that would contain the new agreement, get approval by our G7 counterparts, and release it at the upcoming G7 meeting.

Gus and I agreed that I would return to Washington and draft such an action plan over the weekend. I would call our Canadian counterpart, Jonathan Fried, to say that we had a real opportunity for a successful meeting the following week if we could come together on the IMF reform issue, including limits on exceptional access. I told Gus that it would be best if Jonathan sent the action plan to our counterparts with no explicit attribution to my authorship. Knowing that this emerged as a U.S.-British agreement would not help get the others on board. On Sunday, April 14, I got up early, wrote up a draft, talked with Fried by phone, and sent him my draft. Jonathan made some useful edits but kept to the main message, thereby bringing Canada into the agreement with the Americans and the British. Jonathan then sent around his "Canadian" draft on Monday, which gave the rest of the G7 members a week to comment and sign on to it. As in the case of the Action Plan for Combating Terrorist Financing, I urged that we keep it to one page.

On Thursday, April 18, Paul and I had breakfast with Alan Greenspan and went over the action plan. Alan agreed to the language about limiting exceptional access to IMF loans, even though that was a change in position for him, because the limits were now tied in with the collective action clauses. One of the objections to limits had been that they would be ignored in the heat of a default crisis. The collective action clauses, by providing for an orderly restructuring, would lower that heat.

By Friday, the rest of the G7 had signed on to the action plan. The final version was pretty close to what I had written the previous Sunday, based on the American-British agreement reached in London. One thing we could not agree on was the title, so after a long debate I proposed we not have a title, and that carried the day. The final 488-word April 20, 2002, G7 Action Plan read:

> *We, the G-7 Finance Ministers and Central Bank Governors, have today adopted an integrated Action Plan to increase predictability and reduce uncertainty about official policy actions in the emerging markets. The Action Plan is part of an overall endeavor whereby the sovereign debt of all countries would ultimately be investment grade, a rating that every country could eventually achieve with the right policies. The Action Plan would help prevent financial crises and better resolve them when they occur, thereby creating the conditions for sustained growth of private investment in emerging markets and*

helping raise living standards of the people in emerging market countries. We pledge to work together to carry out this Action Plan. The plan comprises the following elements that are complementary and reinforce each other.

We will work with emerging market countries and their creditors to implement a market-oriented approach to the sovereign debt restructuring process in which new contingency clauses would be incorporated into debt contracts. These new clauses should describe as precisely as possible what would happen in the event of a sovereign debt restructuring. The clauses should include super-majority decision-making by creditors; a process by which a sovereign would initiate a restructuring or rescheduling—including a cooling-off, or standstill, period; and a description of how creditors would engage with borrowers. Within these parameters, we will work with borrowers and creditors to make the clauses as effective as possible, examining such issues as aggregation, new private lending, and treatment of existing debt. We will also work with the International Monetary Fund on incentives for countries with IMF programs to adopt such clauses. With this market-oriented approach to the sovereign debt restructuring process, we are prepared to limit official sector lending to normal access levels except when circumstances justify an exception. It is becoming clearer that official sector support is being limited. Limiting official sector lending and developing private sector lending are essential parts of our Action Plan.

We will work with the IMF to improve the quality, transparency, and predictability of official decision-making as a key means of crisis prevention. Specific actions include a more pre-emptive analysis of debt sustainability using market-based measures of credit-worthiness, a consideration of a greater degree of independence between the surveillance or analysis role and the lending role at the IMF, and a clarification of the lending into arrears policy of the IMF.

We support further work by the IMF on proposed approaches to sovereign debt restructuring that may require new international treaties, changes in national legislation, or amendments of the Articles of Agreement of the IMF. Since these changes would take time, this work should not delay the expeditious implementation of the approach described above; indeed, this work is complementary.

We emphasize that this Action Plan should increase the incentives for governments to pay their debts in full and on time. These incentives, which include the benefit of continued market access at reasonable interest rates, should remain.

The action plan gave us momentum that lasted from April through the summer and into the fall of 2002, a period during which people would start writing down actual clauses. I asked a number of Wall Street lawyers and investment bankers to work together on this. To stimulate thinking, the G10 put together an experts group to work on "model clauses." Randy Quarles was asked to head up that group, and I thought it was very good for him to do so. By this time, Randy had left his position at the IMF and joined me in the front office of Treasury's international division as Assistant Secretary, someone who I could confidently share responsibilities like this with. My main concern was that the G10 group would be too prescriptive, and we would lose the chance for the private sector and the borrowing countries to develop the clauses on their own. Randy as chair could keep that from happening.

Struggling to Move a Large, Disparate Group

The lawyers and the bankers remained generally supportive of the clauses, but they were not able to agree on draft clauses as I had hoped. Differences of opinion seemed to grow as the experts moved from general principles to specific language. People did draft sample clauses, but they could not agree on which to choose. We appealed to people's own or public service interests rather than create any carrots or sticks, but I began to worry that we might need to apply some financial incentives to motivate them.

As the summer of 2002 drew to a close, I decided that a meeting of senior people from the governments and the private sector could help break the impasse. I hosted a meeting in the Treasury's ornate historic Cash Room on the evening of September 26. I invited investors, bankers, private sector finance experts, representatives from emerging market countries, and the top international finance officials from the G7 countries to discuss the reform. I hoped that the group could issue a press statement endorsing particular collective action clauses. I spoke to the head of the bankers' trade association, Charles Dallara, on the phone from Manila, where I was trying to expedite support from the Asian Development Bank for Afghanistan, and asked him for his support.

The meeting was unusual because both the private sector and high-level public officials from the G7 and emerging market countries were in the same room. Most official multilateral meetings like this excluded the private sector. Among others attending were Bill Rhodes, vice chair of Citibank and Mohamed El-Erian, who managed $8 million of emerging market debt for the investment fund, Pimco. That a meeting like this was needed reflected the unusual nature of the reform. It was not in any one individual's interest to make the change. The investment bankers and the lawyers saw it as a costly change in their template for issuing bonds. Borrowing countries thought that the clauses would raise their borrowing costs. Yet viewed from a global perspective, the clauses would have a beneficial effect—a positive externality—by reducing the chance of financial crises. Each participant would get only a small fraction of that large global gain.

In the end we did not get agreement at that meeting on any formal written statement, despite a lot of hard work. There were some heated moments caused largely by the private sector's disappointed expectation that the official sector—especially the United States—would simply kill the SDRM, which they continued to despise. Although I was personally against the SDRM, under current U.S. policy I could not say anything more than that we wanted to go ahead with the clauses now and still study the SDRM. The other representatives from the G7 were equally unwilling to come out against the SDRM. As a result, we appeared heavy-handed and obstinate in the eyes of the private sector. Although the meeting was at times acrimonious, I did not hear anyone actually come out and say that the clauses in principle were a bad idea. While there was still disagreement about the details, I felt I could accurately give an upbeat assessment of the participants' support of the collective action clause reform. Accordingly, Simon Kennedy wrote in *Bloomberg News* on September 27, 2002, that "'There was unanimous support . . .' Taylor told a group of reporters. 'I anticipate it happening in the next few months.'"

The next day, *Bloomberg News* ran a story that raised serious questions about whether any such reform was ever going to take place, let alone in the next few months. The story, entitled "Mexico Rejects Debt Workout Proposal in U.S. Setback," reported that Mexico's finance minister rejected the reform plan and Brazil's central bank governor Arminio Fraga was "skeptical" of it, concluding that "That reaction undercuts Taylor's claim yesterday. . . ." I was surprised and disappointed with this reported reaction from two of the most important people from two of the most important emerging market countries. It was another setback—not the first time, not the last. But I continued to be optimistic.

A New Approach

That fall, we tried to break the logjam with a different approach. We started a concerted but less public effort to persuade individual emerging market governments to "just say yes" and issue bonds with collective action clauses of their own choosing, hopefully not too far from the general principles I had outlined in my April 2 speech. By moving first, that country might serve as a catalyst for other countries. Later on, the clauses could be modified or perhaps made part of a common approach.

Draft clauses had already been written, so it was just a matter of choosing one. I set up a small team at Treasury to keep track of our diplomatic effort, and modeled it after the War Room I had set up to bring the international community together to combat terrorist finance. We drafted talking points to put in any bilateral meeting with any officials in the Treasury. I called finance ministers in emerging markets and met with them when I could. The country that we spoke to most often was Mexico. I developed a particularly close friendship with my Mexican counterpart Agustin Carstens, who had an apartment in the same Watergate Building as me. We met with small countries as well as large countries. I recall a meeting over breakfast in the Watergate Hotel with the finance minister and the central bank governor of Costa Rica where I made the case for the new clauses. They seemed interested but had already proceeded with a bond issue without the clauses, saying they were not familiar with our collective action clause reform. As with the Costa Ricans, we would frequently find out that the country was just about to issue new bonds and it was too late to change the clauses in the bonds. We realized that we had to get a detailed schedule of future issues to make this diplomatic effort work.

To demonstrate to emerging market countries that the G7 practiced what it preached, the G7 members endorsed the idea that they themselves would use collective action clauses when they borrowed in foreign jurisdictions. This was very unlikely ever to be the case for the United States because our markets are so large and liquid. But it did affect Italy, and I think this gesture helped make the case that the clauses were not only for emerging market countries.

All the key players in the emerging market bond world were scheduled to attend the meeting of the Emerging Markets Traders Association (EMTA) in New York in December 2002. They invited me to speak, and I readily agreed. It would be an excellent venue to make the case again. In the eight months since my original speech in Washington, there had been plenty of heated debate; it was time to respond. The speech was another exercise in persuasion, addressing the concerns that had been raised with our proposal during the previous eight months of discussion. There was a terrible snowstorm that evening in New York and it was impossible to catch a cab, so we trudged along the streets of lower Manhattan through deep and still-falling snow. I spoke on a cell phone that evening with Paul Wolfo-witz about a completely different subject—the need for a financial package for the Turks in case there was a war in Iraq—and I remember wondering whether I was going to get booed off the stage at the EMTA meeting. I had decided to be aggressive. I would call for 2003 to be the "Year of the Clauses," recognizing that there were still many skeptics. In the end, I was not booed off the stage, but there was no enthusiastic applause either when I made my rallying call. People listened politely, perhaps thinking how improbable my hope was, and clapped courteously at the end.

It took a long time to get back to Washington that night. The airports were closed, so we took the train, which moved very slowly through the ice and snow, frequently coming to a full stop miles from any station: plenty of time for reflection. I had come into government with lots of ideas and hell-bent for reform. IMF reform was perhaps my highest priority. Yet after months of hard work, I seemed as stuck as the train sitting on the tracks in the snow in the middle of New Jersey. I recalled how in recent years people didn't stay very long in my job. The previous four under secretaries served an average of two years. By that measure, my time would be up before 2003 was over. Unless my improbable call for clauses in 2003 came true, I might be gone before accomplishing any reform. Not a pleasant thought. I was sure I would feel better about all this in the morning. After all, tomorrow we were having a retreat for Treasury senior staff to review plans and priorities for 2003 and everyone would be upbeat and optimistic.

The retreat the next day was to take place outside Washington, but because of the snowstorm it was held at the Treasury. When I arrived, the Assistant Secretary for Management told us that the Secretary of the Treasury had a few words to say. Then Paul O'Neill got up, announced that he was resigning, and immediately left the room.

I was stunned. For a few minutes people acted like we would still have the retreat, but that was ridiculous, and we soon filed out of the room. I immediately thought about the implications for all the projects we were working on—not only the IMF reform, but the contingency planning for Iraq, my dealings with the Turks, the war against terrorist financing, the free trade agreements with Singapore and

Chile, and on and on. The one thing I knew was that I had a job to do—to carry out the President's mission. And part of that job would be briefing a new Treasury Secretary, who the President would soon announce to be John W. Snow, the CEO of the railroad company CSX.

A Breakthrough and a Celebration

By January 2003, it looked like some of our hard work was going to pay off. Despite their earlier misgivings, the Mexicans were sending signals that they wanted to issue bonds with collective action clauses. Agustin Carstens visited me on January 21 and again on January 30 with Paco Gil-Diaz, the finance minister, each time going over in more detail how they wanted to issue. They shared in confidence and asked for our feedback on the talking points they would use with investors to explain the collective action clauses. The talking points included wording like "The United States of Mexico will soon issue a new SEC-registered global bond for $1 billion. This bond—and all future bonds issued under New York Law—will include collective action clauses (CACs) . . . as you know, we were worried that the introduction of them could result in increased costs for our debt. After talking with our underwriters and some investors, we think CACs, if designed properly, taking into account investor's worries, don't necessary imply higher funding costs."

As for the U.S. Treasury, the Mexicans wanted to be sure that we would not criticize them if the clauses did not have all the details mentioned by the G10 draft clauses. I assured them that we would be supportive. They asked whether I could get the entire G7 to congratulate Mexico if they put the clauses in their bonds. I said I could do it. They asked if I could be more public and definitive about my opposition to the SDRM. On this issue, I was pleased that I could do even better than this request. I could ask the Secretary of the Treasury to make things clear. I had already had several conversations about this with John Snow, who was sworn in on February 7. He was very happy to drop any U.S. support for the SDRM and put all our effort behind the collective action clauses. Of course, it was essential that we keep all of this very quiet until Mexico actually issued the new bonds.

On February 24, Gil-Diaz and Carstens met with Secretary Snow to discuss their plans. John Snow hit it off immediately with Gil-Diaz and said he would be happy to say that the collective action clauses had won the day, that Mexico would be showing great leadership in putting the new clauses in their bonds, and that we did not need to do any more work on the SDRM. The issue would come two days later, on February 26.

We were all a little worried, perhaps the Mexicans more than me, that for some unanticipated reason the interest rate would be high or that subscriptions of the new issue by investors would be low, though our best guess was that it would be fine. Carstens called me that afternoon and left a message saying that he would send a fax with the news, but then he got me on the phone anyway. "John. I am very happy to say that it was a real success. We were over subscribed. The spread was 312.5 basis points. That means there was no additional premium due to the clauses. It was better than we expected. We really proved the naysayers wrong." I was really happy myself. I congratulated Carstens for his courage, and I said his country had just contributed an enormous amount to the international community. "You are a real hero," I said. That evening, my wife and I invited Agustin and his wife to our Washington apartment. We all celebrated together and I thanked him for Mexico's key role in the reform process.

Mohamed El-Erian, the successful Pimco investor who would later head up Harvard's entire portfolio, called to offer his take and to congratulate me. Curiously, he did not buy any of the bonds, which surprised me because he had been a supporter of the clauses. He wanted to assure me it was not because he did not think it was a success, but because it was *too* successful. He said they did not buy because the price was really too good for Mexico; in his view, the clauses generated a discount rather than a premium. Months earlier, El-Erian had claimed that the clauses would make emerging market debt more attractive to a wider class of investors because those investors could now understand what would happen in a near-default situation.

I immediately called John Snow to give him the good news, and I congratulated Randy Quarles and the staff who had worked so hard on this. Then I called the French, who had taken over the chair of the G7 from the Canadians, and sent them a draft statement to release to the press. After the usual clearance process in our government and the other G7 governments, the statement went out, dated February 26, 2003:

> *The G-7 Finance Ministers and Central Bank Governors welcome Mexico's decision to include collective action clauses in its international bond issue. Collective action clauses are an essential component of the G7 2002 Action Plan for reinforcing crisis prevention and resolution. This step, coupled with Mexico's sound economic performance, reinforces Mexico's leadership role as an emerging market country that is positively contributing to strengthening the international financial system. G-7 Finance Ministers and Central Bank Governors welcome this positive step toward enhancing cooperation between sovereign debtors and their private creditors. They urge other countries to follow Mexico's lead.*

Other countries did follow Mexico's lead and 2003 did indeed become the "Year of the Clauses." *The Economist* was one of the first financial publications to note the change, paying the Treasury a compliment for our work in its May 10 issue, though in a left-handed way: "On the international scene, Team Bush pales in comparison with Robert Rubin and Larry Summers. . . . Yet the Bush Administration may have more influence on one of the most pressing questions in international economic policy than the Clinton crew ever did: how the debts of developing countries can be restructured." Two days later, the *Washington Times* published a crystal-clear editorial entitled "Treasury's Rx for Global Crises," writing that a concept that had been "long embraced . . . by John Taylor . . . is now favored by developing countries. . . . By including Mr. Taylor's recommendations, which have been dubbed collective action clauses, governments can more easily negotiate new terms with bondholders, who would be forced to take a hit on their investment, reducing the likelihood of a full-blown economic crisis and an IMF bailout."

In February 2004, around the time of the one-year anniversary of the Mexican issue, I issued a statement reporting on the amazing progress during the year. By then, bonds with the new clauses had become the template for the investment banking and legal communities. Chile, Panama, Colombia, Costa Rica, Belize, Guatemala, Korea, Italy, Peru, Poland, South Africa, Uruguay, and Venezuela had each completed successful bond issues with collective action clauses for the first time, while Brazil, Turkey, and Mexico's recent issues again included collective action clauses.

The Rules Are Put in Place

With the progress on the collective action clauses, we could now go ahead and implement the "limits" part of the IMF reform, which came to be called the "exceptional access framework." In February 2003, the IMF Executive Board approved this new rules-based framework. To get exceptionally large IMF loans, countries would have to satisfy specific criteria, including sustainability of their debt and a high likelihood of future access to the private capital markets. If the IMF made an exceptionally large loan to a country, the IMF staff would have to write a special "exceptional access report." I was a strong promoter of the exceptional access report as a way to provide accountability. The idea was based on an analogy with monetary policy, where central banks were required to publish inflation or monetary policy reports several times a year to show that they were diligent in following policy principles consistent with controlling inflation.

The two key elements of our reform plan—the clauses and the limits—were implemented. To make these policy changes work well in practice, it was also essential that the IMF mend its past ways in three other areas. First, focus on its core mission of monetary, fiscal, and exchange rate policy rather than spreading itself too thin by getting into areas beyond its competence like labor markets or regulation of industry. Second, reduce the number of conditions in its programs to a manageable level. And third, engage with countries—especially poor countries—without forcing them to borrow, through the use of a new "non-borrowing program." How we implemented this non-borrowing program, which came to be called the Policy Support Instrument, is another financial diplomacy success story. To make the long story short, the reform was officially adopted by the IMF Executive Board in October 2005.

The combination of all these changes represented one of the biggest reforms of the IMF in many years. The reforms were accompanied by supporting actions, some of which I described in chapter 3 on the Argentine crisis: the decision not to continue IMF lending to support poor policies in Argentina in late 2001; the strategy to contain contagion following the Argentine default; and the decision that the IMF should not get in the middle of the debt negotiations between a country and its creditors. By pushing through these reforms—especially the collective action clauses and the limits—the Bush administration fundamentally changed the bailout process at the IMF; or as *The Wall Street Journal* editorial writers put it on June 21, 2005: "the Bush Administration ended the bailout habits of the IMF."

After these reforms were implemented, the situation in emerging markets changed dramatically. Starting in 2003, the number of emerging market crises went down, capital flows to emerging markets went up, and interest rate spreads went down. Throughout all of 2003, 2004, and 2005, there were no significant emerging market crises anywhere in the world. Of course, there are still risks in the emerging market economies, and no sensible analyst would predict that financial market crises are a thing of the past, but it is a remarkable improvement compared to the situation we confronted in 2001.

I was sometimes asked when I served at Treasury whether the reforms helped bring about this economic improvement. I believe that the answer is yes, they helped. The emerging market debt class is more mainstream than exotic. The clauses are providing some clarity about what would happen in a payments crisis. The IMF's new exceptional access framework has held, and the large-scale lending to Brazil and Turkey (made before that framework was put in place) has not continued, as both countries have reduced their outstanding loans from the IMF, the Brazilians all the way to zero.

The policy reforms in the emerging market countries themselves have been the biggest factor in the improvement in their economies. But these changes were probably encouraged by the better incentives—the reduction in moral hazard, if you like—that the IMF reforms and the other buttressing actions accomplished. I was in the Oval Office when President-elect Luiz Inacio Lula da Silva first met with President Bush in December 2002. Lula outlined his commitment to a sound fiscal and monetary policy while pursuing his anti-poverty goals. President Bush enthusiastically approved, joking that it sounded like "good Republican policy." President Lula followed through with his commitments; it is no coincidence that U.S.-Brazil relations shifted away from IMF bailouts toward longer-term pro-growth issues, and that the two presidents initiated a new bilateral dialogue called the "Group for Growth" to address these issues.

The IMF was not the only international financial institution on the reform radar screen in the post-9/11 era. We also pursued a reform agenda at its Bretton Woods sister, the World Bank, a story I tell in the next chapter.

Inside a C-130 cargo compartment traveling to the front lines, reading the *Financial Times*. When Air Force General Mike Dunn, whom I coordinated closely with at the NSC, saw this photo, he joked, "Nice to see that the Air Force can provide such comfort to our traveling global financial warriors." *Courtesy of Sonja Renander.*

A meeting to formulate monetary policy in the boardroom of the Central Bank of Iraq in Baghdad in February 2004. Governor Shabibi and his deputies are on the left. I am on the right with our Treasury advisers. During the next year, we would have many more such meetings, except that I would attend via satellite link from the U.S. Treasury. *Courtesy of Tom Simpson.*

The Iraqi central bank in
Baghdad after looting.
Courtesy of David Nummy.

Saddam's handwritten order to the Iraqi
central bank. The translation is:

Top Secret
  In the name of Allah the most merciful the
most beneficent
  To the Chairman of the Iraqi Central
Bank
  I hereby authorize Mr. Qusay Saddam
Hussein and Hekmat Mezban Ibrahim to
receive the following amounts:
    1- Nine hundred and twenty million
      U.S. dollars.
    2- Ninety million Euros
for the purposes of protecting them from
U.S. aggression.
  Please carry out the request.

Al Hassan Saddam Hussein
President of the Republic
3/19/2003

This cartoon appeared in *The Wall Street Journal* on March 24, 2003, four days after the start of Operation Iraqi Freedom. While the cartoon nicely depicts my thinking about removing Saddam's image from the currency, our actual postwar currency plan envisaged that new Iraqi authorities would choose the new design. *Illustration by Scott Pollack.*

When the Iraqi people went to the currency exchanges from October 2003 to January 2004, they turned in their old Saddam dinars (top) for new Iraqi dinars (bottom). The new Iraqi dinars replaced Saddam's face with historic symbols and figures as illustrated here for the 10,000-dinar note: the eminent physicist Abu Ali al-Hasan Ibn al-Haitham, who was born in Basra in 965, appears with some of his diagrams illustrating his discoveries in optics.

David Nummy (left) shakes hands with Director Atisha of the Pensions Division of the Iraqi Finance Ministry as U.S. dollars are transferred to the Iraqis to pay pensioners in May 2003. *Courtesy of David Nummy.*

Pallets of new Iraqi dinars stored at Baghdad Airport after offloading from a Boeing 747. They are guarded by Saddam in case Qusay comes back for more. *Courtesy of Hugh Tant.*

Global Financial Warrior (and my senior adviser) Sonja Renander with our security detail waiting to board a Blackhawk helicopter for our trip to the Green Zone from Baghdad International Airport in February 2005. *Photo by Richard Arsenault.*

Our Reach Back Team (Task Force on Iraq Financial Reconstruction) during a visit with Jerry Bremer to the U.S. Treasury. From left to right: Roger Bezdek, David Joy, Elizabeth Weiss, Alpita Shah, Anthony Torrice, Teresa Rutledge, Jerry Bremer, Chris Walker, Ann Wallwork, Karen Mathiasen, the author, Tom Simpson, Jim Fall, John Murphy, and Don Hammond. *Treasury Photo by Chris Taylor.*

With Turkish Finance Minister Babacan and American Ambassador to Turkey Pearson before our press conference in Ankara (December 2002). Photos of the press conference were front-page news in Turkey, with captions such as "Top US Treasury and State Department officials' talks come at a time reports mount that Turkey seeks assurances that its losses from war in Iraq will be compensated." *Turkish Daily News, Selahattin Sonmez.*

My view of Turkish Finance Minister Babacan, Foreign Minister Yakis, and President Bush during the February 13, 2003, meeting in the Oval Office to discuss the U.S. financial assistance program for Turkey. *AP Photo / J. Scott Applewhite.*

Our welcome at Herat Airport guarded by U.S. soldiers with M-16s and Afghan mujahideen with AK-47s (September 2002). *Courtesy of Larry Seale.*

My view from the "negotiating room" in the back of Ismail Khan's SUV.
Courtesy of Larry Seale.

Drinking juice and talking finance with Ismail Khan at his palace before heading out to the customs house, accompanied by American Ambassador Robert Finn. *Courtesy of Larry Seale.*

Walking out of the Herat customs house, with Iraq Finance Minister Ghani and Ambassador Finn, after the town hall meeting. Security detail stands close by as we observe hundreds of people who had wanted to come to the meeting but were turned away for lack of space. Impounded cars can be seen in the distance. *Courtesy of Larry Seale.*

Our Afghanistan desk officer (and Global Financial Warrior) Anna Corfield, who accompanied me on the September 2002 trip to Kabul, with security. *Courtesy of Anna Jewell.*

Inspecting handwritten pay records in Kabul with Finance Minister Ashraf Ghani and his payroll chief. *Courtesy of Larry Seale.*

With school children in Côte d'Ivoire on a trip to Africa just after I was sworn in, June 2001.

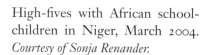

High-fives with African school-children in Niger, March 2004. *Courtesy of Sonja Renander.*

What was measured got done: reading a new text-book with schoolchildren in Nairobi, Kenya, March 2004. *Courtesy of Sonja Renander.*

Soliciting support for our 100 percent debt cancellation (The Bold Proposal) over breakfast in Washington with Bobby Pittman and the finance ministers Osafo-Maafo of Ghana, Diop of Senegal, and Kaberuka of Rwanda. The photograph of a blackboard on the wall is from the school in Nairobi discussed in Chapter 5. *Treasury Photo by Chris Taylor.*

Visiting with Argentine President de la Rua in his office in the Casa Rosada in Buenos Aires in August 2001 to address the ongoing financial crisis in the country, two months after my swearing in. La Nación, *Argentina / Carlos Barria.*

Discussing Argentina's debt negotiation with Finance Minister Lavagna in Buenos Aires airport lounge in April 2004. *AP Photo / Ministerio de Economia.*

A cartoon from *The Economist* illustrating the new collective clauses that, despite naysayers' predictions, became the market standard in 2003. The cleaning agent in the dispenser labeled "New Bond, Now with Collective Action Clause" is used to erase the old financial terms on a bond and make it easier for a country to agree to new terms and thereby restructure its debt. *Illustration by Satoshi Kambayashi.*

Mr. Dollar, or Zembei Mizoguchi, my counterpart in Japan, oversaw the "Great Japanese Intervention," where the Bank of Japan purchased an unprecedented $320 billion in U.S. Treasury securities. *Courtesy of Michelle Mosman.*

Talking strategy in the Oval Office with President Bush just before a meeting with President Duarte of Paraguay. Terrorist financing had been a concern in the tri-border area of Paraguay, Argentina, and Brazil, and President Duarte's cooperation was essential. Also shown in the photo are U.S. Ambassador to Paraguay John Francis Keane (on my left), Roger Noriega of State (on my right), and Thomas Shannon of the NSC (September 26, 2003). *White House Photo by Tina Hager.*

President Bush meets with President Batlle of Uruguay in the Oval Office. It was at this meeting that President Batlle dramatically thanked President Bush and his financial team for the role of the United States in resolving the financial crisis in Uruguay in 2002. On the couch to President Bush's left are Colin Powell, Condi Rice, and me. On the couch to President Batlle's right are Uruguayan Ambassador Fernandez Feingold and Bob Zoellick (April 23, 2003). *White House Photo by Eric Draper.*

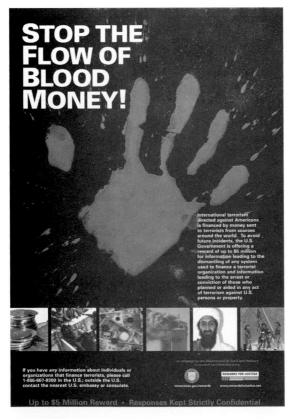

An anti-terrorist financing poster issued in Washington by Treasury and State just after 9/11.

At a G7 meeting at Blair House across the street from the White House on September 27, 2002, where the G7 agreed to apply their policy on collective action clauses to themselves. *Courtesy of International Monetary Fund.*

At a G7 meeting in Constitution Hall, Washington, April 15, 2005, with Alan Greenspan and John Snow. *Treasury Photo by Chris Taylor.*

The negotiating table in my office in the United States Treasury.
Treasury Photo by Chris Taylor.

This Civil Servant They *Really* Liked

Washington retirement parties can really be a bummer. One minute you're a big shot meeting with the president, the next some no-name boss gives you a blunt sendoff over Oreos and punch. Not so for departing Treasury Under Secretary **John Taylor,** who played a big role in Iraq and other international issues. Elbowing their way to the podium to brag on him were Treasury Secretary **John Snow,** Secretary of State **Condi Rice,** White House national security adviser **Stephen Hadley,** and Fed Chair **Alan Greenspan.** Treasury Under Secretary **Stuart Levey**—who?—brought up the rear and joked, "I'm going to send my mom a copy of the program knowing she'll make 1,000 copies for everyone in Akron."

U.S.NEWS & WORLD REPORT

MAY 30, 2005

Farewell to good friends in the Treasury Cash Room and the *U.S. News & World Report* story about it. *Treasury Photo by Chris Taylor. Story copyright 2005 U.S. News & World Report, L.P. Reprinted with permission.*

CHAPTER FIVE

Accountability at the World Bank and Beyond

◆

In World War II we fought to make the world safer, then worked to rebuild it. As we wage war today to keep the world safe from terror, we must also work to make the world a better place for all its citizens. . . . Poverty doesn't cause terrorism. Being poor doesn't make you a murderer. Most of the plotters of September 11th were raised in comfort. Yet persistent poverty and oppression can lead to hopelessness and despair. And when governments fail to meet the most basic needs of their people, these failed states can become havens for terror.
—GEORGE W. BUSH, *March 14, 2002*

The World Bank was created in 1944 at the same Bretton Woods Conference that created the International Monetary Fund. The initial objective of the World Bank was to provide loans to finance post–World War II reconstruction in the war-shattered countries of Europe. Over time, the Bank's objectives shifted to providing development assistance to poor countries throughout the world. Today, the World Bank is made up of two development institutions: the International Development Association (IDA) and the International Bank for Reconstruction and Development (IBRD). IDA and IBRD operate very differently.

IDA focuses on the very poorest countries, with incomes per capita of less than $950 per year. Eighty-one countries with a total of 2.5 billion people are poor enough to qualify for IDA's financial assistance. IDA gets money to provide this assistance from the United

States and other developed countries that donate funds to it each year. The United States is the largest donor, contributing 23 percent of the total since IDA was created. The contributions vary from year to year. In 2004, the United States contributed $1.8 billion to IDA.

IBRD focuses on middle-income countries like Brazil, China, the Philippines, and Ukraine, rather than the poorest countries. IBRD does not receive donations from the developed countries each year. It gets money by borrowing it in the private markets—selling IBRD bonds to investors—and using these funds, it makes loans to the middle-income countries.

In the mid-1990s, around the fiftieth anniversary of the World Bank, many outside development experts began to question the effectiveness of the IBRD and IDA in achieving the goal of reducing poverty. They called for reform. Advocacy groups like "Fifty Years Is Enough" formed and created Web sites to spread the word. A skeptical U.S. Congress cut funding to IDA, and so did other countries.

In the months and years following 9/11, the U.S. government led a major initiative to reform the World Bank. The reform purposely focused on IDA, and thereby on poverty reduction in the poorest countries. Many of the ideas behind the reform had already been proposed during the 1990s, and the simple idea of improving accountability was at the core. The real accomplishment was implementing the ideas. Despite strong initial resistance by many in the international community, the reform came, though it took years of tough negotiations, with many ups and downs. In the end, the international community agreed to create, for the first time ever, a measurable results system at IDA; to cancel 100 percent of the enormous debt poor countries owed IDA; and to open a new window for giving grants rather than loans to these countries. As a result of these reforms, the U.S. Congress began to increase funding for IDA after a decade of cuts. This is the story of how it happened.

A PLETHORA OF CRITIQUES AND REFORM IDEAS

When the Bush administration came into office in 2001, there was no shortage of criticism of the World Bank. Specific recommendations for reform differed greatly, but there was a general sense that the Bank could do a much better job of helping countries reduce poverty, especially given the growing opportunities that better technology and improved communication could bring to the poorest areas of the world. One of the most widely cited critiques of the World Bank was a March 2000 report from the Meltzer Commission, which Congress set up in 1998. Chaired by Carnegie Mellon monetary economist Allan Meltzer—a good friend, whom I had known for thirty years—it included distinguished experts in economic policy from across the political spectrum.

As soon as President Bush nominated me for the international job at Treasury, people in the international finance community began to call, write, and e-mail, urging me to take on the task of reform. Within the government, responsibility for oversight and for U.S. financial contributions to the World Bank falls to the Treasury. As the person in charge of international affairs, I had direct responsibility for the money the United States spent on IDA. If there was to be any real reform, I would be responsible for developing and implementing the reform strategy. As always I would be working in a chain of command, reporting to the Treasury Secretary, who in turn reported to the President. For the big issues, the President would have to approve.

An example of the kind of advice I received is a May 11, 2001, letter from the distinguished and outspoken development economist at Yale University, T. N. Srinivasan. T.N. wrote: "I am convinced that the World Bank has lost its focus and is trying to do too many things for which it has neither a mandate nor competence," and that by taking on this reform task, "you will be doing a great service to the poor of the world." Many others—Meltzer, George Shultz, Jeffrey Sachs, then at Harvard, and Anne Krueger, who served as chief economist at the World Bank—agreed with T.N. The World Bank, distracted by secondary goals, had lost its focus on its key mission of poverty reduction, and needed a more businesslike focus on results.

Many reformers also recommended that the middle-income countries, like Brazil and China, "graduate" from the World Bank and stop borrowing from it so the staff could concentrate on the very poor countries. Such middle-income countries were quite capable of borrowing funds for infrastructure development in the private market, critics argued, and did not need World Bank loans. The middle-income countries, of course, resisted this view, as did the Bank staff, some of whom preferred to work on the middle-income countries rather than the poor countries. In that same May 11 letter, T.N. wrote that "Reports from the Bank rationalizing lending to middle income countries and to China . . . are just self serving."

Others criticized the World Bank for adding to the debt burden of poor countries by encouraging them to borrow too much. Even though IDA loans offered extremely low interest rates and long maturities, the poor countries would eventually find that they were not generating the resources needed to pay the loans back. In many cases, the loans were given to provide funds to deal with pressing social problems, such as HIV/AIDS prevention and treatment. Such projects should not have been expected to generate future revenues to pay back the loans. It seemed to everyone that the money needed to pay back IDA for interest and principal could go to other better uses. Economic development experts and many religious and other non-governmental organizations devoted to economic development shared this criticism. It led to the debt relief movement, which called on the World Bank and others to cancel their debt to the poorest countries. The cause was taken up by popular charismatic celebrities such as Bono of the rock group U2.

In the 1990s, the G7 launched the Heavily Indebted Poor Country (HIPC) initiative to reduce some of the debt that had been built up over the years. The HIPC initiative was a continuation of earlier debt relief initiatives that began as far back as the 1970s and 1980s. While the HIPC initiative and its predecessors succeeded in reducing some of the IDA debt, the World Bank continued to lend to the poor countries, which meant that the debt would grow again soon after it was reduced. With the debt again growing there would be more calls for forgiveness—a vicious "lend and forgive" cycle where neither the borrowers nor the lenders were pleased. In some cases, new loans would raise the debt so rapidly that more debt relief was called for in only three years. The cycle created a disincentive for the governments of the poor countries to develop sound fiscal policies and contributed to the high interest rates in these countries.

To deal with this problem, development experts had proposed a number of reforms. One reform, endorsed by experts across the political spectrum, argued for IDA to simply give grants to the very poor countries rather than loans. The grants would not have to be paid back, which meant that the debt would not rise, and the lend and forgive cycle would be broken. Grants were much more appropriate for dealing with problems like HIV/AIDS treatment. Using grants rather than loans was one of the major recommendations of the Meltzer Commission.

A Charge to Keep

I always welcomed and appreciated the advice I received on economic development issues, and I was committed to reform. I had studied the economic research on poverty reduction and read the recommendations of the development economists. I wrote chapters in my economic textbooks about the great potential for poor countries to reduce poverty through economic growth. As the person now in charge of this area in the U.S. government, I had a once-in-a-lifetime opportunity. I was fired up. Yes, some would probably criticize me, but the only way to avoid criticism was *not* to try to change things, to quietly maintain the status quo. To me, the main reason to take this job was to try to improve the way government worked, and that included the international institutions like the World Bank. Otherwise, why join the government? John Cassidy, who interviewed me for an article in *The New Yorker* a year after I joined the government, asked me why I would take on such a reform when I knew I would be attacked as someone unsympathetic to the World Bank, and even to its mission of fighting poverty. His article accurately reflected my views:

> *"When you demand more of people or institutions, it doesn't mean that you don't like them," Taylor replied. "It means you love them, you want them to do better, so you demand more of the things you*

are responsible for. These calls for better performance are not calls to
do less. They are calls to do more and do it better. I sincerely believe
*that."**

I think you could say I was morally committed to this task. I
decided that my first trip out of the United States as Under Secretary
of Treasury would be to an IDA country. This would demonstrate to
the Treasury staff and others that we would be taking economic
development issues very seriously, and that it was sometimes important to see what was happening on the ground with development
projects and to talk to the people affected. The first trip I took after
I was confirmed was to Côte d'Ivoire, on the west coast of Africa. I
visited several development projects. One was an elementary school
building in the capital city of Abijan. Though not an old school, it
was already dilapidated and had terrible sanitation conditions.
Despite the physical state of the school building, the children
seemed alert and enthusiastic. But when I asked the students if they
had anything to say, one girl of about seven said in French, "I can't
really concentrate because the smell is so bad with no toilets
around." Embarrassed, the teachers even hesitated to translate what
the young girl said, but she said it all. It was the kind of lasting message you frequently get when you talk to people who are on the other
end of our development assistance. Soon after my visit, a civil war
broke out in Côte d'Ivoire, another illustration of some of the difficulties of economic development.

Over the four years I worked in Treasury, I would take many
more such trips to Africa, and to poor countries in Asia and Latin
America. I always made sure I scheduled visits to elementary schools
for me and my staff. When you watch young children in poor countries trying their best to learn basic skills, you have to be optimistic
about the future. Seeing them provided all the moral support we
needed to pursue our reform agenda. When I got back from that first

*John Cassidy, "Helping Hands: How Foreign Aid Could Benefit Every-
body," *The New Yorker*, March 18, 2002, p. 66.

trip, I put a picture on my Treasury desk showing me doing high-fives with a group of those Ivorian schoolchildren.

The greatest motivation for our reform effort came from my knowing that the President of the United States was interested in it and would support it. On April 19, 2001, while I was still awaiting to be confirmed by the Senate, President Bush invited Jim Wolfensohn, the president of the World Bank, to the Oval Office to discuss the World Bank and other development issues. Before the meeting, as is customary for such Oval Office visits, a small group, myself included, briefed the President on some of the key issues facing the Bank. These pre-meeting Oval Office briefings usually took place on the side of the office closest to the Rose Garden. The actual meeting would then take place in an area in front of the fireplace. I was there not only to help brief President Bush on the technical finance issues before the meeting but also as a means of maintaining a consistent policy within the administration. Things President Bush said to Jim Wolfensohn would have bearing on how Treasury performed its oversight role at the World Bank.

The meeting was small—about half a dozen White House staff were there and I was the only person from a cabinet agency. Jim Wolfensohn sat on one of the couches, I sat on the opposite couch, and President Bush sat in his usual chair between the two couches. The President was supportive and encouraging of Jim, saying that he was very interested in the World Bank and its mission. He wanted the Bank to function in a businesslike manner. Gesturing to me, the President gave me a special charge, which I wrote down after the meeting: "I'm going to ask John to watch what you're doing over there," he said, "keeping the World Bank in line with measurable results." While this was just what my job called for anyway, because it came from the President of the United States in the presence of Jim Wolfensohn, it made a special impression on me and others in the meeting. Afterwards, Gary Edson, the international economics deputy at the National Security Council, who also attended, remarked to me how unusual the President's "charge" was. I knew it would be useful to me in carrying out my job in the months ahead.

During Oval Office meetings I attended, it was not unusual for President Bush to refer to *A Charge to Keep*, a painting on the wall next to his desk. The artist is W. H. D. Koerner, and it depicts horsemen charging hard on a special mission. I do not recall if President Bush mentioned the painting at the meeting with Jim Wolfensohn, but he may have. He did mention it at other meetings, including one with me, my wife, son, daughter, and son-in-law. Much of the conversation at that meeting was personal, especially with my son, who had just been commissioned as a Marine officer and was wearing his uniform. But President Bush did take the time to talk about that painting, and how important "keeping the charge" was to him, a message that was not lost on me as I went about my job.

DEVELOPING A REFORM AGENDA

As I began the task of developing a reform package that the United States could pursue at the World Bank, I had several practical considerations in mind. I wanted a long-lasting reform that would be robust enough to survive the inevitable criticism from disparate groups in the international community, many of whom had their own ideas. I also knew that the reform should be aimed at the institution rather than the people at the institution. I knew and respected many World Bank employees. I knew that, as employees of the institution, they would tend to resist reform. But as is so often true in cases of government failure, I felt that the effectiveness problems at the World Bank stemmed from institutional design rather than personnel.

Jim Wolfensohn is a larger-than-life figure, with many admirers. My wife and I appreciated being invited to his beautiful house in Jackson Hole, Wyoming, during the annual monetary conference held in the Grand Tetons. A native of Australia and a self-made success in investment banking, Jim had a reputation for knowing how to get his own way. To be sure, he had many critics, many of whom did not hesitate to express their views to me. I would listen, but I never did feel that antagonizing Jim or others at the World Bank would help our cause. Jim had just been appointed to a second five-year term in 2000 by President Clinton. He had effectively addressed concerns about corruption at the World Bank by setting up an integrity unit to investigate evidence of corruption. He spent a large amount of time dealing with the protestors of the late 1990s and bringing greater visibility to the problems of the poor. When his term was over in 2005 and he retired, he was widely praised. Nick Stern was the World Bank's chief economist when we started the reform effort, and as fellow economists we could mix it up on the technical issues, but Nick was a good economist and I respected him. I made it a point that there was nothing personal about the calls for reform.

That the problems were institutional had another implication for the reform: it was the job of the shareholders who set up the institution to address them. The lack of focus on the Bank's original mission, for example, was largely the fault of the shareholders, including the United States, who kept asking the management and staff to do so many things that they lost the original focus. If the shareholders asked for more focus—more specific results—then the institution would begin to respond.

The reform package I came up with focused on IDA. It had three central elements. First, shift support for the poorest countries from loans to *grants*. IDA financed its loans with grants from donor countries like the United States, so this proposal was really asking IDA to pass on the grants to the poorest countries instead of converting them into loans.

Second, develop a *results measurement system*, with incentives, to be applied throughout the operations of IDA. The new grants (as well as IDA loans) would be tied to measurable results with clear metrics such as kilometers of roads built or number of textbooks delivered. At the country level we would also monitor progress on such measures as the average time to start a business, completion rates in elementary schools, and immunization rates for measles.

Third, to make this reform work we would also call for an *increase in funding* from the United States for IDA. The reform agenda would be controversial, so pledging increased U.S. funding if the reform was implemented would help get international support. By the same token, the U.S. Congress would view the reform positively, which was essential for securing support for the increased funding.

The plan was quite ambitious and seemed like the most far-reaching reform that we could negotiate internationally at the time. In deciding on the package, I worked closely with the Treasury staff, whose experience with World Bank oversight was essential. They made sure that the plan was feasible under IDA's complex accounting procedures and legal framework, and they assessed the likelihood of support and objections from the G7 and other countries. The reform could never have been launched without their expertise.

We decided to leave several popular reform ideas off the agenda. We tabled the proposal to graduate countries like Brazil and China from borrowing from the World Bank. While proposals for middle-income countries had much merit, I considered this issue as a show-stopper. It would cause a confrontation with all the middle-income countries, many of whom would find allies in the developed countries who could prevent us from forming the needed international coalition to adopt the plan. I knew that T. N. Srinivasan, Meltzer, Sachs, and others calling for more ambitious reforms would be disappointed, but I was dealing with the art of the possible.

We also left off the table a proposal to forgive more of the debt owed to IDA by the poorest countries. I personally found this proposal attractive, but it would have encountered strong opposition at that time from Japan, Germany, and France, as well as many in our own government, who thought that the HIPC initiative had gone far enough.

I reviewed the final version of the plan with Paul O'Neill during a plane ride from Washington to Toronto on the afternoon of April 3, 2001. I had written the key ideas on a small piece of paper and went over each one as we sat together in the front row of the plane. I explained that the reforms did not call for radical structural changes such as a new institution, but rather for changing the incentives within the existing institution. I thought it would be tough to get agreement in the international community, but it was doable. He was quite comfortable with the package and quickly agreed. He also agreed to ask Congress for more funds for IDA in the next budget, but the exact amount would require many more rounds of inter-agency discussion, negotiation, and eventual approval by the Office of Management and Budget on behalf of the President.

A Rollout by the President of the United States

To implement the reform, we needed a rollout plan, including a financial diplomacy strategy. Not all shareholder governments assigned World Bank oversight responsibilities to the same agencies. For instance, in the United Kingdom it was the foreign aid agency (the Department for International Development) rather than the Treasury as in the United States and Japan. Thus, we would need different government-to-government communications strategies. Political factors in each country were also important to take into account because each government looked on foreign aid issues through its own political lens. Judging popular support in each country was essential. Getting influential people like Bono to support the plan would help. In the United States, we would have to get support from both the Democrats and Republicans, especially if we were going to get more appropriations from Congress.

I was very pleased when President Bush decided that he himself would announce the key elements of the plan—the grants proposal and results measurement—in a speech before the World Bank. This would raise visibility for the reforms greatly, help garner support in the United States, and demonstrate to the international finance community that the United States took the World Bank reform effort very seriously. The speech was scheduled for July 17, 2001, right before the President would go to his first G8 Summit in Genoa, Italy. I will never forget when Gary Edson called me to tell me that the President would announce the grants proposal. Gary was the Sherpa, the chief U.S. staff person, for the Genoa Summit, and one of his jobs was to put together a package of proposals. The grants idea would be one of those proposals, and by announcing it before the trip there would be more press coverage and a greater chance to discuss the idea at the summit. This was all good news for the rollout strategy.

President Bush met with us in the Cabinet Room the day before the World Bank speech to review the speech's theme, the grants proposal, and the agenda for the entire Genoa Summit meeting. Paul O'Neill, Larry Lindsey, Glenn Hubbard, Gary Edson, and I were there. President Bush was upbeat about the speech and the trip. Near the end of the meeting, he asked who was going with him to Italy. When I did not raise my hand, he asked, "Why aren't you coming, John?" I answered that "The financial crisis in the southern cone needs watching." I was referring, of course, to the ongoing crisis in Argentina, which was causing worries in Uruguay and Brazil. Indeed, in just two weeks I would be in Buenos Aires. But I was disappointed not to go to Genoa. I sent Mark Sobel, who was in charge of Treasury's planning for the G8 meetings. He was honored to go and did a great job.

In his speech to the World Bank, the President said this about the grants proposal: "I also propose the World Bank and other development banks dramatically increase the share of their funding provided as grants rather than loans to the poorest countries. Specifically, I propose that up to 50 percent of the funds provided by the development banks to the poorest countries be provided as grants for education, health, nutrition, water supply, sanitation, and other human needs, which will be a major step forward. Debt relief is really a short-term fix. The proposal today doesn't merely drop the debt, it helps stop the debt."

Why 50 percent? As the speech was being written, we debated whether a specific number would be useful. I thought a high number would be useful as we went into negotiations with our fellow shareholders, and the speechwriters thought it would make for a better speech. But we would have to rationalize the number in some way. The Treasury staff made some calculations which showed that if IDA provided grants to poor countries for all the purposes listed by the

President in the speech, the total would be 50 percent of the World Bank's assistance to those countries. That seemed to be a good rationale and we used the 50 percent number.

SETBACK AND RECOVERY

The initial reaction to the President's grants proposal in the United States was favorable, with more support coming from the more conservative editorial pages in the press. We had discussed the proposal in advance with several environmental, religious, and other non-government organizations. Many of them, including Friends of the Earth and the U.S. Conference of Catholic Bishops, endorsed the proposal. Bono also supported it.

However, the reaction from Europe was very negative, a signal that the international negotiations were going to be a tough battle. Alan Beattie of the *Financial Times* explained the negative reaction in an article published on July 20, the day the summit began: "Mr. Bush's call this week for half the loans made to some poor countries by the World Bank to be converted into grants has alarmed several European countries that are shareholders of the Washington-based institution. Coming soon after the abrupt US decision to abandon the Kyoto protocol on global warming, it has renewed fears about US unilateralism." Already the battle lines were being drawn.

The main complaint with the proposal concerned the "reflow problem," which would come up repeatedly in our reform efforts. As the *Financial Times* went on to say, "one worry . . . about the US proposal is that if the sums disbursed by IDA were not repaid, it would gradually erode the organization's finances."* Reflow is what the poor countries have to pay to the World Bank each year. A decline in payments from the poor countries themselves would not erode the organization's finances because the purpose of the organization was to give more funds to the poorest countries, not get more funds from the poorest countries. Sebastian Mallaby, of *The Washington Post*,

---

*Alan Beattie, "Give and Take," *Financial Times*, July 20, 2001, p. 14.

made the same criticism, saying: "the Treasury's suggestion [is] that the bank should shift from unrepayable loans to grants. This is an excellent idea, but it depends on the World Bank's rich member government's providing the money to make such grants possible."[*] Other criticisms were put forward as well, including the strange idea that poor countries would benefit from the experience of paying back IDA loans; but of course the problem was that they were having a great deal of difficulty paying them back at all.

The World Bank staff and management were also negative about the grants proposal and tended to support the European position. Perhaps they were concerned that the reduction in the reflows would force them to depend more heavily on the appropriations each year from the shareholders. This would be a diminution in the power of the Bank bureaucracy, and any elementary theory of government would therefore predict their opposition.

We were all surprised by the very negative reaction from the European shareholders. Because I was deep into the subject technically, I knew the economics and the accounting were on our side and that the criticism was largely unfounded. Perhaps this knowledge made it easier for me to withstand the harsh criticism from the very people we would have to convince to accept the reform. I remained confident that we would be able to negotiate a good amount of what President Bush had proposed. I tried to be upbeat with my staff and with others in the administration, but they were obviously discouraged by the reaction in Europe.

I was also confident because I knew we had a solid negotiation strategy and we were willing to wait the others out if need be. We had planned to push the reform package at the upcoming IDA replenishment negotiations, using the U.S. financial contribution as leverage. Every three years, donor countries replenished IDA with more funds. The year 2001 was one of those replenishment negotiations. As the largest contributor, the United States did have some

*Sebastian Mallaby, "In a Sticky Spot at Treasury," *The Washington Post*, July 2, 2001, p. A17.

leverage to get the others to accept reforms, assuming that it had enough support on the merits. If we could not finish by the end of 2001 we could continue the negotiations into 2002, and that is what we did.

The Europeans maintained their position through the summer of 2001, but began to show some flexibility in the fall after the 9/11 attacks. The Europeans and the Americans had been cooperating well in other areas, such as combating terrorist financing, and fund-raising for Afghanistan, and I believe a spirit of cooperation spread to other areas. In February 2002, around the time of a G7 meeting in Ottawa, the Europeans formally indicated that they could live with a 10 percent grants proportion. It seemed like a very small move to us, and we decided not to budge; we held firm to the 50 percent number in President Bush's speech. The most acrimonious public reaction to the proposed 10 percent (quoted on February 20 by Agence France-Presse) came from Paul O'Neill: "I say the hell with it. . . . Somebody tell me one good reason for 10 percent."

That the World Bank staff and management lacked enthusiasm for our proposal made things more difficult for us. They had the data to do the number crunching on the controversial and confusing reflow issue, and they always seemed to find that the problem was more severe than our calculations showed. Fortunately, the General Accounting Office challenged their calculations in a study put out in April 2002. The study found that "if donor contributions to the World Bank were to increase by 1.6 percent per year, which is less than the expected rate of inflation over the next 40 years, the World Bank could fully finance the 50-percent grants proposal." So we seemed to finally be winning the battle of the arithmetic; nevertheless, some people still claimed that the proposal would drain the finances of IDA.

We kept holding out. In May, I joined Bono and the Secretary of the Treasury on a highly publicized trip to Africa, which took us from Accra to Johannesburg to Kampala and to Addis. I made many calls to my G7 counterparts during that trip trying to strike a deal; each of us was in touch with our IDA negotiators who would meet in

June—hopefully for the final time—in London. One point that seemed to bring real progress concerned giving loans to countries to fund HIV/AIDS projects, where there was obviously no way to generate revenue to make debt payments. All agreed that this made no sense and it struck some as simply cruel. Traveling through Africa where we saw so many HIV/AIDS treatment centers helped me make that point. It helped enormously that Bono was supporting the grants proposal. I would keep him updated on how my calls to my G7 counterparts were going. At every one of our stops in Africa he would mention the grants initiative, and I would relay the news back to my G7 colleagues on the next call.

I got to know Bono well on that trip, and I always found him to understand the technical issues and try to be helpful. The first time I met him in my first few months at Treasury, I gave him a copy of my economics textbook. I suggested that he put music to some of the words. When Bono later boarded the plane on the trip to Africa, he stopped at my seat to say hello, and the first thing he said was that he had read the book and that he liked it. And after spending some time with him, I knew he did read it. He later returned the favor with a book of poems, *Electric Light*, by the Irish poet, Seamus Heaney. Inside, Bono wrote: "God is in the details . . . Your student with the annoying questions . . . thanks again John for putting the last first. Bono."

VICTORY

After the Africa trip, we reached a final agreement on the grants proposal. Criticism of using loans to finance health projects, such as HIV/AIDS, seemed to move the Europeans in the end. I announced that an agreement was at hand at the G7 meeting in Halifax on June 14. I gave a press conference right before the meeting and the resulting press stories were very good; many commented on how the Europeans and Americans had finally come together after a year of debating and negotiating. It was nearly one year since President Bush had announced the proposal.

The agreement was of course a compromise. It stated that the total percentage of IDA funds going to grants could be as large as 21 percent. Although less than our initial negotiating position of 50 percent, for the first time ever a substantial proportion of IDA funding would go to grants rather than loans. The agreement did not require the same percentage of grants for each country, and for many of the very poorest countries the percentage was much closer to our goal of 50 percent. Some projects, such as those for HIV/AIDS treatment, would get all grant funding. Thus, countries with more projects in those areas would get a larger share of grants in their disbursements. Many of the very poor African countries qualified for a substantial grant share: for example, up to 47 percent in Ethiopia, 46 percent in Mali, 41 percent in Mozambique, 50 percent in Niger, 38 percent in Uganda.

The second part of our reform agenda—a good results measurement system—also made it into the IDA agreement. We employed a novel incentive scheme to create the measurement system quickly and then monitor the results. The incentive was to provide extra funding for IDA from the United States if the reforms were carried out expeditiously. We promised an extra $100 million to IDA in the second year and $200 million in the third year of the three-year replenishment period. During the year-long IDA negotiations, the World Bank staff had started moving toward a better results measurement system so it would be ready to go.

There was a huge sense of victory in the Bush administration, especially after the long-drawn-out negotiations. The NGO committee was particularly vocal in its congratulations. The president of Oxfam, Raymond Offenheiser, testified in Congress on July 19, 2002, that "it is clear to Oxfam that initiating IDA grants is a very, very positive step that we fully endorse." The position the Europeans had taken was criticized; as Reverend David Beckman of Bread for the World put it in that same hearing: "I think it is nutty, the European position has just been nutty."

Given the victory, I now felt we could make a strong case for the increase in IDA funding that we had requested from Congress. On

July 25, I appeared before the subcommittee of the House Committee on Financial Services, which is in charge of the authorizations. I reported that our reform "has been one of the highest priorities of the Bush Administration's international economic agenda. . . . Steady progress has been made on all these fronts, and this progress provides the grounds for today's request for authorization. . . ." The specific request was for an 18 percent increase in the U.S. contribution to IDA, the first increase of that magnitude in many years, and Congress eventually authorized that amount.

In the end, I think that our negotiation strategy made the difference, but it was helped by our fellow shareholders gradually coming to understand our proposal better and by the desire to move beyond such disagreements after 9/11.

THE GRANTS MISSION TO AFRICA

Given the Bush administration's emphasis on results, I felt it was imperative to get a firsthand view of how IDA was implementing the President's grants initiative on the ground. I waited a year after we reached the grants agreement, figuring that this would afford plenty of time to get the program started; then, in the summer of 2003, I told my staff that I wanted to take a "grants tour" to Africa to find out what was happening. When I proposed this idea, some Treasury staff and other people told me that it would be a bit strange for the Under Secretary of the Treasury to traipse around the world looking "under the hood" at World Bank projects. But I thought it was a great way to show how much the United States cared about achieving results on the ground, and my personally assessing a few projects made good sense. I also felt that such a trip could help move things along. I suspected things could be going faster, and it turns out I was right.

I originally scheduled the trip for late November. I asked my staff for a list of the countries that were receiving grants under the new World Bank agreement. They went over to the World Bank offices, a few blocks from Treasury, and came back with a list of about twenty-five projects in Africa. They sent me a memo asking me to indicate which of the twenty-five I wanted to visit. I replied: "Before I decide, please ask the World Bank to indicate which of the projects are operational." They went back to the World Bank, and when they returned the list was reduced to five. "Okay; that decides it," I said. "Let's go to those five." Soon after they started making detailed logistics plans with the U.S. embassies and World Bank personnel in each of the countries, they realized that in truth only one of the projects, a textbook project in Kenya, was up and running. It was really hard to believe. There was only one project where you could actually *see* something. I was disgusted and said, "There's no sense going on the trip." After all the planning with the embassies abroad, my staff was a bit shocked and disappointed with my reaction; but I then added, "By the end of the winter I want there to be at least five grant projects up and running that I can visit." And I scheduled a trip for March 15, 2004.

By the time March rolled around, we did have five live IDA grant projects to visit in Africa. They were located in three countries: Rwanda, Kenya, and Niger. I requested the detailed action plans for each of the projects from the World Bank's operational people— some who worked in Washington, some in Africa—with dates and specific actions to be accomplished. I had the idea that I would get to Africa, go to each of the projects, and check on the progress in each. But what I got back from the World Bank were not detailed action plans with timelines. There were no timelines to speak of, except for the textbook project in Kenya, which, I would find out when I got there, happened to have a very good local project manager, a Brit, who knew the importance of measuring results and a good reporting system. The rest were vague.

It was a great disappointment to me. Jim Adams, the vice president of the World Bank in charge of operations, called me to explain. He admitted that their measurement standards were less rigorous than we were expecting, but at least I was beginning to make it clear to people what we wanted in terms of measurable results. Jim Adams was concerned enough that he decided to come on the trip with me.

WHAT GETS MEASURED GETS DONE

In Africa, I met with high-level government officials—President Paul Kagame of Rwanda and President Mamadou Tandja of Niger; the finance ministers of all three countries, Donald Kaberuka of Rwanda, Ali Zene of Niger, and David Mwiraria of Kenya; and with other health and education ministers. I found that they liked the new grants initiative. In fact, it was very popular and enormously well received in these countries. They were specific in their praise, evidence that they were not just telling me what they thought I wanted to hear. They explained how the grants dealt with the debt problem, but they also pointed to other advantages of grants, including fewer bureaucratic hurdles and a greater commitment by the donors. In Rwanda—where the grants were for HIV/AIDs projects—the health minister was particularly appreciative of what he called the "Bush grants." In Niger, Minister Zeni kept saying, "Long Live the Doctrine of Grants."

These high-level meetings were important, but there is really no substitute for, in General Patton's words, "assuring by personal supervision on the ground proper and vigorous execution" of your plans. My visit to the World Bank projects illustrates how that principle applies to the financial world just as well as it does to the military world. One of the best examples of a good project with measurable results was the school textbook project in Nairobi, Kenya. We visited a school there that was in the poorest slum I have ever seen anywhere in the world. Getting to this school required driving into the middle of the slum, which consisted mainly of dilapidated cardboard structures and unpaved streets turned to mud after rains the day before. When he heard we were coming, the mayor asked that broken pieces of concrete, obtained from some demolition project elsewhere, be thrown down onto the road that we would take through the slum. Apparently he thought that would constitute some form of pavement, but broken chunks of concrete simply became obstacles for our SUV to get around. We went about five miles per hour down very narrow streets crowded with people.

When we got to the school, hundreds of grade school children had come out of their makeshift classrooms and lined up in rows to greet us. I met the principal and he asked me to sit with him and some of the teachers in front of the crowd of children. The kids were lined up all clean and proud. One group came to the front and danced; another group sang for us. They were really good at both. I gave a little talk, saying how pleased I was to see them and that the American people were pleased to be helping them out. They clapped happily at anything I said, so it was pretty gratifying. They asked me to plant a tree in the schoolyard, and they put a sign on the tree with the date and my name. Afterwards, we went to the classrooms and I read books with the children. These were the books that they had received through the new World Bank grants program.

I could see that in this particular school, something was working—they had the texts. But the real highlight was the measurable results system that the parents and teachers had installed at the request of the overall project manager. They put it all on a blackboard, which they proudly showed me. The school was given an allocation of funds to buy textbooks, and the parents and teachers then got together to decide what books to buy. There was some competition among the textbook sellers so they could bargain and negotiate to get the best price and thereby have more to spend on workbooks, or even more books to reduce the "sharing ratio." There were not enough textbooks for each kid to have one, but if they could get the ratio down from four children per book to three, it would be worthwhile. The accounting on the blackboard showed the discount they negotiated. On the bottom line you could see that all but 1 of the 300,000 Kenyan shillings that were allocated had been spent.

Their system had timelines, too. The kids needed to get the textbooks by the start of the school year, and even though the demand for books was high because of the recent shift toward universal education that caused big increases in enrollment in Kenya, they met the deadline. You could see that the measurable results were really making a difference to people. It was a good story. I congratulated Jim Adams and all the other World Bank people who were part of this operation. I asked that a picture of the blackboard be taken, because I knew what a powerful message it could send as an example of parents being interested in their children and how they used measurable results in a development project. I put a life-size copy of the picture on my office wall in Washington and would refer to it often. This example was particularly useful for me because I myself am a teacher and a textbook writer.

Another project I visited was not such a good story. It was a community development project in Niger, one of the poorest countries on earth. Niger is largely dry desert country just south of the Sahara, with terrain much like the state of Nevada. Outside the capital city of Niamey, which sits on the banks of the Niger River, most people live in small tribal villages that have very primitive thatched housing, often with dirt floors. To observe the World Bank projects, I traveled to several of these villages. There are very few roads in Niger, and when we went from one village to another we essentially went overland, as if we were driving off-road in the desert in Nevada. We traveled in this way in a long motorcade of about a dozen SUVs—an amazing sight in this remote desert. The finance minister, Ali Zene, accompanied me, along with his assistants and his security people, and many people from the World Bank and the U.S. embassy— hence the long motorcade. I was pleased to have Minister Zene along as he was a great supporter of the U.S. grants initiative at the World Bank, and he had not been to many of these villages before.

When we arrived at a village, everyone came out of their homes and lined up along the main street, often just a strip of sand. They were in colorful clothing and they welcomed us with songs, clapping, and dancing. I would walk along the line, shaking everybody's hand, and then I would meet with the chief and explain that I was there to assess the new World Bank grants program and ask a lot of questions.

One of the villages I visited had used its World Bank money to build a new "health care facility." It turned out that the facility was a small one-room building of concrete blocks, with no windows to close and no door to open. Inside sat a young nurse with a table, chair, and a cabinet. He covered many villages and happened to be there that day. When I asked him what was in the cabinet, he said it was made to hold medicine, but they had no medicine. The finance minister then opened the door and was amazed to find virtually nothing. The nurse added that the village needed a kerosene-powered refrigerator for some of the medicine but that had not been delivered yet, either. When I asked why, he took me outside for a presentation by a big crowd of villagers.

Their story was long and involved, and it took an even longer time to tell because it had to be translated form one African language, Fulfulde, to another African language, Zarma, and then to French and finally to English. And all my questions had to be translated in the other direction. This was especially difficult when we discussed financial matters such as their village budget. They told me that they had been waiting nearly a year for the refrigerator; along with the medicine, it was to be part of the health care facility project. The people explained in amazing detail how much of their own money they had saved to help pay for the refrigerator, but the World Bank contractors had still not delivered it.

Not surprisingly, this was a case where the Bank had no system in place for measuring results, and there were no timelines. What was not being measured was not getting done. The lesson is pretty obvious when you say it, but it is pretty painful when you see it. Jim Adams and the Bank people could see the problem right away. I didn't even raise my concerns. They apologized and promised to get the refrigerator to the village as soon as possible. "How long?" I asked. "You better be talking about days, not months." But it was not just the refrigerator. The whole World Bank engagement with Niger had similar delivery problems. To be sure, Niger is a difficult country for foreign aid workers. When a famine hit in 2005 after a locust infestation, the United States and the United Nations flew plane-loads of food into the country. But President Tandja, who I met during my trip, claimed that the food crisis was propaganda of the opposition party. Nevertheless, the World Bank completely overhauled its operations in Niger after our visit.

When I returned from this trip, I wrote a short letter to Jim

Wolfensohn. I told him about the enthusiasm expressed for the new IDA grants and the excellent IDA textbook project in Kenya, but I was candid, too:

> *A problem we found on the trip, however, is that the grants could be used much more expeditiously. Recall that the World Bank approved the grant initiative in 2002, after President Bush's proposal in 2001. Yet, in preparing for this trip, these countries were the only ones where we could find any grant program being implemented, and even in Rwanda and Niger the disbursements had only just begun. I must say that this is very frustrating to see in person: very poor people pointed out their own needs for medicine, for textbooks, for small water projects, while we knew that the money was available to fill many of these needs. To be sure, there are complex project management and political problems, but there is a lot of room for improvement. In my view the disbursement delays are more of a problem for loans than for grants.*
>
> *In every country we asked for specific timelines for reaching certain measurable results (primarily outputs) and for ultimate completion of projects. However, few timelines were given and I am concerned that this is a common problem with the implementation of the measurable results initiative. Despite very good intentions, therefore, I must report that much more needs to be done in the field.*

THE "BOLD PROPOSAL"

After finding so much enthusiasm for the grants initiative on that African trip, I felt that we had an opportunity to press for larger grant percentages, effectively completing the President's 2001 proposal. It was three years since I had proposed the grants initiative. The idea was less controversial now, and another IDA negotiation was coming up in the summer and fall. I was glad to be able to attract the enthusiastic and brilliant Bobby Pittman from the NSC to work on these reform issues. I appointed him our IDA negotiator and, in the end, he would negotiate an IDA agreement with World Bank shareholder governments that substantially increased the grant share. Over forty poor countries would get 100 percent of their IDA assistance in the form of grants, and the overall grant percentage for the eligible IDA countries moved up substantially. Starting at zero percent in 2001, it was raised to 25 percent in 2002, and would go to 45 percent in the 2004 negotiations. The ambitious target President Bush laid out in the first year of his administration had effectively been achieved.

I also felt that our success with the grant percentages indicated we should try something bolder. Even though we were able to move closer to our ultimate goal of removing loans as a form of IDA assistance, there was still all that old IDA debt out there, which meant the poorest countries would have to pay service costs to IDA each year.

To test the possibility of a bolder initiative, on April 2, 2004, I called the debt experts, the Africa experts, the World Bank experts, and the IMF experts on my staff into my office for a brainstorming session. I was hoping for a free-flowing, non-bureaucratic discussion, and I got it. The immediate issue concerned what I would say at an upcoming debt relief event on April 22. The Center for Global Development, a new Washington think tank, was sponsoring this event. Toward the end of the brainstorming session, I asked what people thought about a proposal to completely cancel the debt that the heavily indebted poor countries owe to IDA; that is, 100 percent cancellation, well beyond what had been proposed before. If IDA gave grants equal to the difference between (1) the amount of new loans that the country had been getting from IDA and (2) the payment that the country was making on the old IDA loans, there would be no net change in resource flows, so it should be financially feasible. "Think of it this way," I said. "Rather than making a new loan of $100 and collecting payments on old loans of $20, we would cancel the old debt and make a grant of $80." There was a good discussion, with a lot questions back and forth, but everyone who spoke was skeptical of the idea. I asked them to go back and think about it, get some data from the World Bank, do some computer simulations, and then we would meet again for another session.

A couple of weeks later, the staff indicated that they were ready for another brainstorming session. We assembled in my office again, this time with numerical calculations that had been run in the last two weeks. The meeting started off with one of our talented young debt experts saying something along the lines of "John, we have thought about your idea and we have concluded that you are right. Your idea will work. We haven't got all the data yet, and there are more calculations to do, but it's pretty clear, and we all agree. Let's work through the tables to see how."

I was delighted and very proud of the staff. Not only did it look like the proposal would work, but their professional approach in the two brainstorming sessions was essential because their initial reaction would match other people's initial reactions. It was a very different type of proposal that, when you first heard it, didn't make any sense. But once you look at it more closely, it starts to look obvious.

This initiative became the most dramatic part of our World Bank reform effort, and when combined with the grants initiative and the measurable results system, it would completely overhaul IDA. People came to call the 100 percent debt cancellation proposal the "Bold Proposal." I did not choose the name; people just started using it, and it stuck. The idea had been on my mind since we developed the original reform three years before in 2001, but, as I mentioned, it would have been too radical at the time. In retrospect, if we had tried it then, we would never have gotten anything. In policy reform you sometimes have to wait for the time to be ripe.

I talked to John Snow, who picked up on the idea right away and was enthusiastic about it: 100 percent cancellation made sense to him, and it would enable us to demonstrate that we were for large debt reduction in poor countries if people criticized us on those grounds for favoring large debt relief for Iraq—a parallel development I will come back to in chapter 9.

Bobby Pittman and I debated how to proceed. We consulted with Tony Fratto, Treasury's press spokesman for international issues. Tony had accompanied me on many of my trips to Africa, and was passionate about economic development. He also knew how to handle the public relations aspect of this idea, which would be very tricky. We knew the proposal would be controversial, partly because it was so difficult to understand. Moreover, a proposal like this needed full vetting in the U.S. interagency process and approval from the very top. It was the kind of proposal that should be announced publicly either by the President or the Secretary of the Treasury. We needed a rollout strategy, a diplomatic strategy, and a negotiating strategy.

As for the remarks I planned to give at the April 22 Center for Global Development conference, which would be heavily attended by debt relief advocates, I decided to simply signal that the United States could support additional debt relief as part of a general set of principles, but no details that would attract attention. I jotted down the principles in my own cryptic shorthand on a small piece of paper while sitting on the dais waiting to give my speech. Afterward, I handed the piece of paper to Bobby, who fleshed it out and saved it for the record. Over the next few months, we used these principles to discuss the plan. The five principles were: first, debt sustainability for poor countries is essential; second, IDA lending when you know the loan will be forgiven is unacceptable; third, providing grant support is essential; fourth, providing more debt relief will be necessary; and fifth, net resources transfers to poor countries should not go down as a result of the reform.

We were right that the fourth principle would get the most attention. Zanny Minton Beddoes, the economics correspondent for *The Economist* who was moderating the conference, asked me right away: "I think your fourth principle was that we need additional debt relief. What does that mean for the here and now?" I answered, on "the specifics. I think that is something we need to be talking a lot about and figuring out how it will work, developing coalitions. . . ." So, without committing in any way, the discussion had begun.

THE BATTLE FOR IDEAS

There was some faint hope of moving ahead with the debt relief plan in time for the June 2004 G8 Summit, which President Bush would chair at Sea Island, Georgia. I had prepared a memo on debt relief for a conference call with my G7 counterparts leading up to the summit. Without taking a position, the memo included options on debt relief that the leaders might endorse, including "the five principles" and the "Bold Proposal." I wanted to see if there was any interest in either proposal, but there wasn't. The five principles were still too controversial for the G7 at that time. When I said the bold proposal deserved serious consideration, I got dead silence, and perhaps could hear at least one of my counterparts dropping the phone. None of them could believe that the U.S. Treasury was even considering 100 percent debt relief.

The next opportunities to move ahead with the proposal would be at the September 2004 IMF/World Bank meetings in Washington or the UN General Assembly meetings in New York. For either of these, we felt we should indicate to the G7 members quietly, but in advance and specifically, that the United States wanted to support the bold proposal and also delve into the details. I thought that the annual retreat I would host at Stanford, California, on July 19, 2004, would be the perfect place. It would also be timely because at the retreat I would be proposing enormous debt relief for Iraq. I asked Faryar Shirzad, who had replaced Gary Edson as the international person on the NSC, for formal consideration of this quiet diplomatic initiative by other cabinet agencies. The NSC held a meeting and State and the Office of Management and Budget gave us the okay to float a trial balloon to my counterparts. As planned, I described the proposal and the U.S. support for it in California. All my G7 colleagues rejected it. Not only was the proposal hard to understand, but I believe I was experiencing a period of less cooperation in the G7. With the U.S. presidential election coming up in November, my counterparts had to be thinking about the possibility of a change in government in the United States.

Despite the reaction in the G7, I still hoped that the President would announce the proposal during a speech at the United Nations meetings in New York, but in the end that rollout idea did not win approval in the White House. A new, complicated initiative right before the U.S. election did not seem wise, and I had to agree with that reasoning. Instead, Secretary Snow would briefly mention the proposal at the IMF/World Bank meetings in Washington. And in a speech to a group called the Bretton Woods Committee, he announced the possibility of up to 100 percent cancellation of IDA loans.

The Secretary's now public proposal was still rejected by the G7, but the cat was out of the bag. There was broad popular support for debt relief, and with the United States moving ahead on the bold proposal, the other governments felt forced to offer their own proposals. First, there was a proposal from Gordon Brown, the British Chancellor of the Exchequer. Then, the French and the Japanese made proposals. Their alternatives were far less aggressive than the American proposal. Although none called for 100 percent cancellation of IDA debt to the heavily indebted countries, a battle of the plans had begun.

During the winter of 2004–05, the dissension among the G7 over debt relief proposals was widely covered in the press. Nevertheless, I thought we were making good progress. Most important, there was now a universal desire to have a big debt relief package ready in time for the next summit in Gleneagles, Scotland, in July 2005. Instead of fighting about whether there would be debt relief at all, it became a quarrel about what type of debt relief to have. The idea we had floated in the spring and summer of 2004 was no doubt responsible for this change.

In the battle for ideas, I knew it would be important to get influential African ministers on board with our proposals, which would require additional meetings and travel. For example, I invited a group of African finance ministers to my office for breakfast that summer, and was happy to get the support of Rwanda, Ghana, and Senegal. Perhaps the most influential African finance minister is Trevor Manual of South Africa, whom I had come to know well. At Bobby Pittman's suggestion, I decided to travel to South Africa to meet with him personally; it was actually part of one of my multitasking trips, with many issues and many stops: first down to Chile, Bolivia, and Peru; then over the South Atlantic to South Africa; then up the west coast of Africa to Liberia; and then on to Paris and London and back to Washington.

I met with Trevor Manual in Cape Town over a long dinner which also included Tony Fratto, our press spokesman, and Jendayi Frazer, who had just been appointed U.S. Ambassador to South Africa. Jendayi was very supportive of our bold proposal, and partly because she was a good friend of Bobby Pittman, she understood exactly how it all worked. Trevor Manual said he was sympathetic, but now that there were other proposals on the table from other countries, he declined to actively promote our proposal, despite my long trip and the efforts of Jendayi, Tony, and me to convince him. But at least he would not object to it. The trip to South Africa was not for naught, however. I always tried to visit small businesses on my trips to developing countries—usually textile factories or farms— but this time the American Consulate in Cape Town chose the beautiful Fairview Winery in the California-like countryside outside of town. Drinking their "Goats do Roam" wine over a long lunch was the best R&R Tony and I could have hoped for before we headed up the coast to Liberia. We also went to a party that Jendayi hosted for Congolese-born NBA star Dikembe Mutombo at the ambassador's residence in Pretoria, where he told me about the work his foundation was doing, including building hospitals in Africa.

Getting Bono's support for our plan was going to be important. Tony and Bobby had been explaining the plan to Bono's staff in Washington for months and they already had good things to say about John Snow's speech mentioning the bold proposal in September. Tony set up a meeting between me and Bono in Davos, Switzerland, on January 29, 2005. While most people thought Bono was trying to convince me to support 100 percent debt cancellation, the reality was that I was trying to convince *him* of our bold proposal to cancel debt by 100 percent.

After talking about our plan for half an hour, Bono agreed to be very supportive. Tony, who is much more hip than I am, then changed the subject. He started asking Bono questions about his latest iPod and CD. I clearly did not know what they were talking about, so Bono asked his assistant to get a copy of the CD. Bono then started writing something on it, taking a while as if he was thinking what to say. Then, on one side, he wrote: "Dear John, You don't have to listen to this." And on the other side: "You listen to me too much anyway. Bono."

I also wanted to be sure that we had support from the U.S. Congress, and we reached out in a number of ways. We put on a conference for congressional staff, NGOs, embassy officials, and press at the Treasury aimed at explaining the difference between the U.S. proposal and the U.K. proposal. One of the slides at that seminar, which made the U.K. proposal look pretty bad, leaked out. It was soon picked up by Gordon Brown, who called John Snow directly to complain bitterly. The debate over the different debt relief plans was like war itself.

On February 3 and 4, 2005, an important G7 meeting took place in London. On the way to Dulles Airport I got a call informing me that John Snow's chest cold had taken a turn for the worse and he would not be able attend the meeting. So I went in his place—a particularly challenging assignment given that we were going to argue for our debt relief program over Gordon Brown's. Even more difficult was that I also had to publicly register our opposition to another Brown proposal called the International Finance Facility, a scheme in which pledges of future government spending would be used as collateral to borrow funds to assist poor countries now. The scheme could not work legally or technically in the United States so we could not support it.

In London I promoted the U.S. debt relief proposal over the British proposal, but I also made it very clear that we could not support the International Finance Facility. Of course, I was right on message—not only the Treasury's but the entire Bush administration's message. Right before I arrived, Gordon Brown met with Condi Rice—who now as Secretary of State was on her first trip to London—and asked about her support for the facility. Thanks to excellent interagency coordination between State and Treasury, I immediately got a report about that meeting and knew that the U.S. position had not changed. Brown also invited Nelson Mandela to meet with the G7 ministers that weekend, and Mandela asked me directly to support the facility as a way to help Africa. I explained why the United States could not support that particular initiative, but emphasized that aid from the United States to Africa was increasing and had already tripled since the Bush administration came into office.

I received both criticism and praise in the British press for crossing Gordon Brown's proposals, but I got all good marks back in the Treasury and the White House. The chancellor is a charming man, but he was particularly forceful at that G7 meeting. At one time, right before breakfast was to be served at an early morning session at Number 11 Downing, he and I went out on the balcony, closed the glass doors, and then argued the issue while the other ministers watched curiously and waited for us to come back in and have breakfast. I am sure it was a pure coincidence, but I was not served any food until everyone else had finished, and then only after I had asked if there was a mistake.

Despite the heated debates, there was some progress toward our debt relief proposal at that G7 meeting in the form of an agreement to *consider* debt relief up to 100 percent. All of the proposals were still on the table. There was no agreement to support the specific U.S. proposal, however. After the meeting I joined Mervyn King, the head of the Bank of England, and Alan Greenspan to play a quick tennis match at Wimbledon, and then flew off to Iraq on a whole different mission.

Soon after I returned to Washington, on February 13, the *New York Times* published a blistering editorial about our debt relief plan and about my role: "John Taylor, a Treasury under secretary, delivered a personal blow to the British chancellor of the exchequer, Gordon Brown, last week by putting the kibosh on Mr. Brown's ambitious proposal for cutting third world debt." The editorial went on to criticize the U.S. proposal, which it called the "Taylor plan," charging that it was an "accounting gimmick." On February 19, the *Times* got personal, saying that Taylor was "globally unpopular for his eccentric policy views and poor leadership skills." In the world of ideas, eccentricity is not a vice, and I knew that the unpopularity charge was completely bogus. I offered to visit the *New York Times* editorial board to explain our proposal in detail and went in on

March 3; to my knowledge they did not criticize it after that. Deep into the substance of our plan, I felt confident that the U.S. proposal would win the day at the Gleneagles Summit. It was the only proposal that all could sign on to that was significant enough to effect real change and that would work from a budgetary point of view. I remained upbeat with the staff, with John Snow, and with others in the administration.

VICTORY AGAIN

In a White House meeting in June 2005, President Bush and Prime Minister Blair agreed to 100 percent cancellation of the debt of the heavily indebted poor countries, leaving it to their finance ministers to work out the details with the rest of the G7 and Russia in time for the Gleneagles Summit. The prime minister received a lot of good press back home for the White House agreement. John Snow then met with Gordon Brown and they both agreed to the U.S. proposal because it was the only one that could fulfill the Bush-Blair 100 percent agreement. Together, they brought it to the G7 finance ministers plus Russia for approval in London. With the Americans and British now in lockstep, the others did not have much choice but to go along. One week later, the deal was made official in Gleneagles. They had agreed to the "Bold Proposal" lock, stock, and barrel.

On June 30, 2005, in Washington, DC, President Bush announced: "In 2001, I challenged the World Bank to give 50 percent of its aid to poor countries in grants instead of loans. And the bank has moved steadily closer to that goal. With the leadership of Great Britain and the United States, the G8 countries are urging cancellation of $40 billion in debt owed by 18 of the world's poorest nations, including 14 nations in Africa. Twenty more countries can qualify for this debt forgiveness in the future with good government and sound economic policies. We're determined not only to relieve debt, but to erase it, so nations in need can face the future with a clean slate."

It was a spectacular and highly gratifying success.

CHAPTER SIX

Financial Diplomacy and the Turkish Option

◆

I was in the kitchen when I got the call. The State Department Operations Center had tracked me down at my home in Stanford and put Marc Grossman, State's Under Secretary for Political Affairs, on the line. "John, I hate to interrupt you out there in California on Christmas Eve, but the Turks may be nearing a decision on the issue we have been discussing. It looks like you will have to get to Turkey right away to nail down the financial deal. If you can get to Andrews by tomorrow night, the NSC has arranged for a milair flight to take you non-stop the rest of the way to Ankara. I'll try to join you."

I sensed that this mission to Turkey was going to be tricky. I knew that the stakes were high. Turkey had gone through a wrenching financial crisis in 2000–01, and was still reeling from the impact of the 9/11 attacks on tourism and trade. Now, as the year 2002 drew to a close, the Turkish economy was still not out of the woods. Politically, things were not any better. A new, inexperienced government had just been elected in November, and during the election the previous government had gone on a spending spree, raising the budget deficit and leaving the new government to make the tough adjustments. When the new government at first appeared reluctant to make the necessary changes, the financial markets tanked. The Istanbul Stock Exchange had fallen by 25 percent in the last three weeks. On the military front, there was huge uncertainty. A war in Iraq on Turkey's southern border was increasingly likely, and Turkey's military cooperation remained an unknown in the U.S. military strategy. The Turks' imminent "decision on the issue we have been discussing," as Marc cryptically put it on the phone in case the line was tapped, was about whether they would agree to cooperate if there was a war in Iraq. To be exact, the Turks were about to decide whether they would allow us to have a "northern option"—the ability to send thousands of soldiers from the Coalition Forces through Turkey and into northern Iraq. My mission would focus on the financial aspects of this decision.

THE 2000–01 FINANCIAL CRISIS AND THE IMPACT OF 9/11

As I flew across the United States on my way to Andrews Air Force Base that Christmas Day, I recalled how Turkey had been on my radar screen for nearly two years, quite literally from the day I started my job at the Treasury. On my very first day on the job, the top two people at the IMF—Horst Kohler and Stanley Fischer, managing director and first deputy managing director, respectively—came over to Treasury to talk with Paul O'Neill and me about the financial crisis in Turkey. I knew Stan Fischer very well; we had been colleagues in academia and we worked in the same field, monetary economics. On Sundays during my previous stint in Washington, we would run together on the C&O canal with our wives. Stan was a highly respected economist and he had held the number two post at the IMF for the last six years. Tradition dictated that the number two job go to an American, and Stan had been selected for the job by the Clinton administration. Horst Kohler, who would later become the president of Germany, was only one year into his appointment at the IMF, but he was familiar with the issues, having previously held the job that was the counterpart to mine in Germany.

Fischer and Kohler described the financial crisis in Turkey as they saw it. Poor monetary and fiscal policies throughout the 1990s had caused high inflation, high debt, high deficits, and low economic growth. To deal with the problems, the Turks, working with the IMF, developed a series of fiscal and monetary reforms aimed at bringing down the inflation rate and restoring fiscal responsibility. In December 1999, the IMF and the Turks agreed to a program of specific reforms, and the IMF lent Turkey about $4 billion to support the reform program.

Although the Turks made a pretty good start on the reforms, inflation did not come down as rapidly as they had hoped, and by November 2000, less than one year into the reform program, a serious crisis developed. The high inflation rate produced selling pressure on the Turkish currency—the Lira—and interest rates rose sharply. The high interest rates made it more difficult for the government to finance its large deficit, which fueled fears of a default. The Turkish banks held a significant portion of Turkish government debt, and fears of a government default were increasing the probability of a run on the banks. To deal with this crisis, the IMF and the Turks revised the original program. The Turks would reduce the budget deficit further and start to close or reconstitute the weak banks, and the IMF would provide more loans. The revised agreement, approved by the IMF on December 21, 2000, would increase IMF loans from $4 billion to $10 billion. But one aspect of the reforms was still wanting: the Turks kept their exchange rate peg rather than move to a flexible exchange rate. With Turkey's exchange rate peg, there was always a possibility that currency traders would suddenly try to get out of the currency and the central bank would lose all its foreign reserves trying to prop up its value. As a result, the financial pressures continued despite the renewal of the program. The next crisis was just waiting to happen.

On February 19, 2001, just before I joined the Treasury, the next crisis did happen, big time. Press reports of a bizarre emotional outburst between Prime Minister Bulent Ecevit and President Ahmet Sezer at a meeting of the Turkish National Security Council in Ankara appeared to set it off. The meeting was called to discuss Turkey joining the European Union. The fight began at the start of the meeting, when Sezer accused Ecevit of obstructing investigations of corruption in the banking sector. The president then threw a copy of the Turkish constitution at the prime minister, who, according to the *Financial Times*, "reacted with fury, saying he was personally insulted," and abruptly left the meeting, as one of the other ministers threw the constitution back at the president.

That public display of dysfunctional government shocked the markets. It led to heavy selling pressure on the Turkish Lira and sky-rocketing interest rates. Out of options, the central bank now had to abandon the exchange rate peg. When it did so on February 21, the Lira immediately fell by 28 percent against the dollar. The sharp depreciation of the Lira worsened the government's debt problem, because much of its debt was in dollars. Interest rates rose to 7,500 percent and the stock market fell by 18 percent. Not surprisingly, the finance minister was fired and a new finance minister, Kemal Dervis, was appointed.

This was the situation when Kohler and Fischer showed up at Treasury. Despite the mixed results of their program with Turkey, the IMF was encouraged that the country now had a flexible exchange rate and a new finance minister. And despite economic mismanagement by the Turks and the apparent failure of the IMF program thus far, the IMF management felt there was no choice but to move ahead with a new program. In light of the crisis, they felt that more money was needed to support the government during another round of reforms. However, the IMF already had lent Turkey close to $10 billion, and the management was reluctant to put up much more money themselves. They had come to ask the U.S. government to put up the money, as much as $10 billion from the Exchange Stabilization Fund.

I had never heard anyone ask for a $10 billion loan before, but I was surprised at how aggressive the IMF, and Kohler in particular, sounded. This wasn't a soft-touch ask, like, "Would you please consider making a ten-billion loan to help us get back on track with Turkey?" but rather more like, "You and I both know that Turkey is of strategic interest to the United States and Europe. The IMF has already lent too much. You simply must put up ten billion." Later, Stan Fischer admitted even he was surprised at how demanding Kohler was that day. In any case, O'Neill and I listened and said we would have to think about it.

Two days later, the new Turkish finance minister came to Treasury to present the new IMF program and demonstrate his commitment to it. Although Kemal Dervis was new to the Turkish government, he already possessed a great deal of political savvy. He was a good economist, trained at the London School of Economics and Princeton, and had gained practical policy experience working until recently at the World Bank. He made an impressive presentation, speaking with sincerity and confidence: "With a flexible exchange rate Turkey is now better able to bring inflation down, and, as finance minister, I am committed to significantly reducing the budget deficit and to bank reform." I knew that he would try to carry out these good policies; but their success would hinge on how well he could maneuver with the likes of Ecevit and Sezer, and whether they and the other top political leaders in his government had the political will to make difficult and perhaps unpopular choices.

Formulating the United States' position on the IMF request—the first major decision about an IMF crisis operation in the Bush administration—was difficult, but the decision came quickly. Regarding the explicit request for loans from the Exchange Stabilization Fund, we would say no. I recommended this decision, and after the NSC agreed, it became the U.S. position. We would agree to support an IMF program similar to the one that Dervis worked out with the IMF, but only if the Turks agreed to implement some policy decisions before they received the loans. We wanted to be sure that the top political leadership in Turkey, not just the finance minister, was committed to the reforms. These "prior actions" seemed essential to us given the lack of action—not to mention the outburst between the prime minister and the president—during the most recent IMF agreement. We agreed to the size of the loans as originally put forth by the IMF management and Dervis, a decision that would bring the total size of the program to $19 billion, nearly twice the size of the program agreed to in December 2001, and five times the size of the amount from two years earlier. This was a good lesson that once the IMF becomes a partner in the reform of a major country, it also becomes a partner in any shortcomings in the reform effort, and finds it difficult not to double and redouble its lending if the going gets tough. And, of course, if the country's leaders realized this type of response, they might be less concerned about keeping the reforms on track.

There were a number of reasons we decided not to put U.S. funds directly into this operation. First, the use of the Exchange Stabilization Fund had become extremely controversial since the Clinton administration used it in Mexico in 1994. Using it now would create a firestorm in Congress and elsewhere that would likely delay any response to Turkey at all. Second, keeping the responsibility for providing the funds on the shoulders of the IMF would indicate that such support is limited (because the IMF has an overall budget constraint). Third, as a matter of incentives, the IMF management and staff should not expect the United States and other governments to come to the rescue when a program went sour and provide additional funds.

It was essential to get full U.S. interagency support for these positions and we did so, arguing that the proposed approach would place accountability for IMF programs more clearly with the IMF and that it would emphasize the IMF's budget constraint. I was pleased at the strong show of internal support from our government—State, Defense, CIA, NSC—because this unity would help me make our case with other G7 governments. Convincing the other governments and the IMF (that is, Kohler) would establish a good trusting relationship between Treasury and the other foreign policy agencies in the NSC.

I worked toward an international consensus primarily through my counterparts in the G7 finance ministries. Caio Koch-Weser of Germany at first disagreed, arguing that the United States and others should provide bilateral support for Turkey; but eventually he and the other G7 members came around to our position, probably because the United States was firm in its decision not to provide bilateral support. After the G7 agreed, the IMF management came around, too. In the NSC meeting where I informed my colleagues that the G7 and Kohler had agreed to the U.S. position, Marc Grossman and Steve Hadley generously portrayed this as a victory for me personally. Though many people were involved and compared to sundry other things it was not that big a deal, they still warmly congratulated me in that meeting. I think this relatively small success helped in many later dealings Treasury would have with the other departments. I could not have foreseen then that Marc and I would travel to Turkey on a completely different mission in December 2002.

The U.S. decision attracted a lot of press scrutiny because it was the first indication of whether the Bush administration would differ from the Clinton administration in its policy toward the IMF and financial crises. The main criticism was that we were not as tough as we said we would be. As Michael Phillips wrote in a front-page *Wall Street Journal* story on May 14, "the view is different from the playing field than from the bleachers." Morris Goldstein, a senior fellow at the Institute for International Economics in Washington, was quoted in that same article as saying, "When the big decision came on the bailout, they blinked."*

Some noted our new "presumption of no topping up" principle—that is, that the IMF would provide support in these situations without additional funds by the United States or other governments. But they said it was just a minor departure from the Clinton administration. For the most part we were criticized not because people thought we made the wrong decision, but rather because we were

*Michael Phillips, "Bush Policy is Familiar to Developing Nations," *Wall Street Journal*, May 14, 2001, p. A1.

not as radical as they perceived us to be. Perhaps some people actually thought that we were immediately going to stop supporting any IMF programs, but that was at best a caricature. It is true that we did want to make substantial changes in the way that the IMF had dealt with economic crises; but I thought it would be irresponsible to change the policy too abruptly, convinced that a more gradual approach would be better for the financial markets and that it was more likely to succeed than a radical approach.

I kept in close contact with the Turks through the rest of the summer of 2001, supporting Dervis in his battle for reform. Fortunately, the Turks stuck to this IMF program, unlike the previous two. The new central bank governor, Sureyya Serdengecti, who was appointed in March, lowered inflation and established credibility at the central bank. Serdengecti personified no nonsense and seriousness about reducing inflation, and was clear about that objective in every meeting I had with him, whether alone or with Dervis. He was the ideal central banker.

During August and early September, interest rates were coming down and the chances for recovery seemed to improve. Then, 9/11 hit. Soon warnings were issued about the dangers of travel in Turkey and the tourist trade started to drop off. With debt levels still high, any negative economic news could easily trigger a serious crisis in Turkey at a very dangerous time.

To deal with the impact of 9/11 on the Turkish economy, the Turks requested additional IMF funding, again with strong backing from the IMF management. By this time, Anne Krueger had taken over the number two position from Stan Fischer. There was a lot of skepticism in the G7 about the need for additional IMF funding. Lorenzo Bini-Smaghi of Italy was perhaps the most skeptical. Over the course of four G7 conference calls in October 2001, at the request of the G7, and especially Bini-Smaghi, Anne Krueger provided more and more detailed information on how serious the threats to Turkey were. As Krueger put it in a report prepared for a G7 conference call on October 23, Turkey "has been thrown off course by an exogenous shock." By exogenous shock, she meant the

9/11 attacks, which, because of the resulting travel warnings and drop in tourist trade, raised the trade deficit and the budget deficit, requiring an additional $4 to $5 billion. Given the excellent track record of Dervis and Serdengecti and the vulnerability of Turkey's economy to the new terrorist threats following 9/11, we decided to support the additional IMF lending. In the end all the other key shareholders did so too, and I was pleased that no one even asked me about bilateral topping up this time. On November 15, 2001, Horst Kohler announced additional funding, which would add another $5 billion in loans to Turkey, bringing the total package to $24 billion. This announcement had a welcome soothing effect on financial markets.

Dervis and his team continued to pursue the reform program and we continued to support them. I made a three-day visit to Ankara and Istanbul in January 2002 with the express purpose of showing U.S. support for Dervis and the need to continue the reforms. We had some success with press coverage; for example, the *Turkish Daily News* noted: "Commenting on the Turkish economy to journalists, Taylor said on Wednesday there were signs of growth in the Turkish economy but added that it was essential for the government to effectively implement a reform program to ensure future prosperity." But, as frequently happens when making economic policy, the results that matter most to people in the country—more jobs, lower unemployment, faster economic growth—were slow in coming. When elections were held on November 3, 2002, a new government came to power. The Justice and Development (AK) Party, under Recep Tayyip Erdogan's leadership, scored an impressive election victory and gained control of the government. I would have to get to know a new finance minister and deal with a host of new issues.

THE BEGINNING OF CONTINGENCY PLANNING

My interaction with the Turks relating to the war in Iraq—as distinct from the financial crises I just described—began in earnest on October 25, 2002, just before the Turkish elections. I was asked to attend a meeting in Condi Rice's White House office with Turkish Ambassador Fasuli Logoglu and my national security colleagues Paul Wolfowitz, Deputy Secretary of Defense; Steve Hadley, Deputy National Security Adviser; Pete Pace, Vice Chairman of the Joint Chiefs; and Marc Grossman. The others had already been talking with the Turks about the possibility of a military intervention in Iraq. The Turkish Foreign Ministry Under Secretary, Ugar Ziyal (Marc Grossman's counterpart), had visited Washington in the summer to be briefed on possible military options in the event Saddam did not comply with the UN resolutions. On a visit to Ankara in September, Tommy Franks had made the case for Turkish cooperation to General Hilmi Ozkok, commander of the Turkish Armed Forces, but the general said he would not even broach the subject with his government until after the upcoming elections.

We met with Logoglu to inform him that Turkey would soon have to decide on military cooperation, and that the United States would be willing to provide financial assistance to cushion the impact on the Turkish economy of a possible war in Iraq. I was there to indictate, still in very general terms, that we would be ready to discuss an economic package to help Turkey deal with the economic impact should there be a war. To demonstrate our commitment, I reminded him how I had been working closely with Kemal Dervis, the IMF, and the G7 for a long time on Turkey's financial crisis. Of course, we recognized that no decision would be made until after the Turkish election.

After the new government was elected, Paul Wolfowitz and Marc Grossman went to Ankara to discuss political and security issues with officials in the newly elected government. On their visit, the new government and the Turkish press asked for details about the economic impact of a war and possible U.S. economic assistance. At a press briefing after the meetings, Wolfowitz was asked, "Did you talk about the economic situation and aid to Turkey?" and he answered, "One thing that we did talk about is the deep concern in Turkey about the condition of the Turkish economy. We've been working closely with the Turkish Government in the IMF and bilaterally ever since the economic crisis broke. . . . We are determined to support Turkey whatever comes to make sure that the Turkish economy continues to recover. If there is a crisis in this region, we know that Turkey is going to be one of the countries most affected. We want to make sure we deal with that."

When Wolfowitz returned to the United States, we reviewed the economic issues that the Turks had raised. On December 5, the same day I was in New York City to give a talk to the Emerging Markets Traders Association on collective action clauses, we had a long telephone conversation about his trip to Turkey. In his view, the Turks seemed to want some kind of a contingency facility, or credit line, that could be drawn on in case the war had a large economic impact. But he also said these finance issues were not his bailiwick and urged me to follow up with the new finance minister, Ali Babacan, as soon as possible.

Erdogan visited the White House to meet with President Bush on Tuesday, December 10. The meeting took place in the Roosevelt Room. Colin Powell, Condi Rice, Paul Wolfowitz, and others attended. I was there because the next day I would meet with the Turkish finance minister to discuss in more detail any economic issues that came up at the meeting. I was impressed with how smoothly this first meeting between the two leaders went. I was even more impressed because earlier that morning President Bush had also met with President-elect Lula of Brazil for the first time. Though the personalities, the foreign policy issues, and the cultures of Turkey and Brazil were completely different, the President's meeting with Lula also went smoothly.

Viewed from my financial perspective, Brazil and Turkey had many things in common at that time. Two of the most important emerging market countries in the world, they were both struggling to avoid another financial crisis, while their economic policymaking was about to be taken over by unproven political parties with little governing experience and worrisome populist tendencies. It would have been way too much to expect, in the years ahead, that both economies would flourish and the financial relations between them and the United States would blossom despite political strains. President Bush's ability to set a good tone for these relationships from the start and to emphasize the importance of the economics was a good part of the reason why it did.

Erdogan, as leader of the victorious AK Party, was effectively head of the government, but he was not legally able to be prime minister because he had been convicted of violating a sedition law when he read an Islamic poem at a political rally in 1997. Not until after he was formally elected to Parliament in a by-election on March 9, 2003, could he become prime minister. At the meeting with Erdogan in the White House, the President spoke admiringly of Erdogan's leadership and his party's strong victory, thanking him for his commitment to democracy and freedom. He spoke movingly about the importance of religion for both men, Christianity and Islam, respectively. He committed to support Turkey's membership in the European Union. And he emphasized the need for Saddam Hussein to abide by the UN resolutions or pay the consequences.

A GAP TOO WIDE?

The economic talks with Turkey relating to a possible war with Iraq began the next morning, December 11, at ten-thirty when the newly appointed Turkish finance minister Ali Babacan and I met in my Treasury office. I prepared in great detail for the meeting because of the complexity of the financial issues and the potential gravity of the military issues. Coordination and clearance within our government about what I would say was essential, so I made sure that NSC cleared everything, and I had no qualms about representatives from State and Defense joining me in that meeting. My keeping exactly on message was extremely important for our overall effort. This meeting would not be a negotiation but it would set the stage for future negotiations.

Babacan and his staff arrived exhausted; their train from New York had been delayed for hours the night before by a heavy snowstorm that coated the tracks with ice. Despite the rough trip, they were eager to proceed as planned. Babacan had a serious, business-like attitude about him. He looked very young, and at the age of thirty-two he was indeed quite young to be a finance minister. After getting an MBA from the Northwestern Business School, he worked for a financial consulting firm in Chicago for a few years, and then went on to run his family's textile trading company in Turkey before joining the new government. I perceived a lack of experience in our first few meetings, but he soon grew rapidly into the job, and deserves ample credit for the eventual recovery of the Turkish economy.

We reviewed what the United States was prepared to do, war or no war, including projects like modernizing the Turkish military bases. We also discussed the possibility of additional financial assistance in the event of a war. In light of the recent Wolfowitz meeting in Ankara, I probed to see what kind of financial package the Turks would prefer.

I indicated that we could provide assistance in the form of grants or loans, but that Babacan had to recognize certain important budget rules in the United States. "There is a trade-off between loans and grants," I said. "A $1 billion grant, for example, would be the budgetary equivalent in our system of about an $8 billion loan, depending on the interest rate and the maturity of the loan." The trade-off between loans and grants is one of the more confusing parts of our budget law. Only a handful of experts on the Treasury staff and in OMB know the details, so I had anticipated that this part would be tough to explain. Regardless, I wanted to get it on the table to see if he had interest in having the flexibility to switch between a loan and grant assistance. A loan would be for a larger amount, perhaps useful for a large, but temporary economic shock; it would have to be paid back. A grant would be for a smaller amount and would not have to be paid back. Babacan and his staff did seem interested and they asked for more examples of the trade-off, which we agreed to supply.

Babacan and his staff then made their presentation. They had prepared well, too, and they handed out several tables. They had completed a series of simulations with an economic model, which indicated that the cost to the Turkish economy of a war in Iraq would be huge. They showed me a table with two model simulations; one simulation (they labeled it "Optimistic Scenario") estimated the impact to be a loss of GDP of $92.2 billion over the years 2003–07; the other (labeled "Pessimistic Scenario") showed a loss of $138.1 billion.

	Optimistic Scenario	Pessimistic Scenario
Short Term (2003)	21.6	29.7
Medium Term (2004–2007)	70.6	108.4
Total (2003–2007)	92.2	138.1

These calculations were germane to our discussion because the Turks used them to determine how much the United States would have to pay to compensate the Turks for losses resulting from a war in Iraq. The calculations demonstrated, Babacan argued, that the United States would have to hand over at least $92 billion! As a result, the economic problem of estimating the impact of a war on the Turkish economy was placed at the center of the discussion. I know a good deal about economic modeling, so I asked a number of detailed questions about their model that only economists care about, and the Turks agreed to get back to me with more information. But no matter what they said, I simply could not take their calculations seriously. I felt the numbers were worthless, although I did not put it quite that way at the time. I was much more diplomatic; it was our first meeting, after all, and I wanted the initial discussion to be civilized and professional. I simply pointed out that they had inappropriately extrapolated from the first Gulf War, a time when the Turkish economy performed poorly. That episode of poor performance stemmed from bad economic policies in Turkey and a sluggish world economy. It had little if anything to do with the first Gulf War.

Despite my objections, the Turks held on to their estimates. This, of course, was part of their negotiating strategy. I reminded myself that Babacan was an experienced textile trader, and thus probably knew a thing or two about bargaining. But if $92 billion was going to be their "ask," then there was about to be a huge "bid-ask" gap to deal with. Our very best "bid," which I then knew, but did not of course tell the Turks, was between $4 billion and $6 billion, and I knew how hard it was to get that, requiring approval all the way to the top of our government. This was not going to be an easy negotiation.

At the end of my meeting with Babacan, we designated "point persons" on each side to go over the technical budget and econometric issues. We agreed to meet soon again, which would turn out to be my Christmas meeting in Ankara.

Another factor that complicated the negotiations was a rumor circulating that I was fired or was about to be fired from my job. It was certainly not the best thing for building up a negotiator's credibility or authority to speak and deal for the administration. "Don't worry about what Taylor thinks of our calculations," you could imagine the Turks saying in private, "he's on his way out anyway." Paul O'Neill had announced his resignation as Treasury Secretary on December 6, right in the middle of the complex planning that surrounded the financial issues relating to a possible war. On December 19, *The Wall Street Journal* reported as fact that I was fired too, writing in "Washington Wire": "Following Secretary O'Neill out the door are his deputy, Ken Dam, and Under Secretary of Treasury for International Affairs John Taylor, who the White House sees as indecisive." Ken Dam did leave the Treasury early the following year, but I was never asked to leave, and in fact I was working closely with people in the White House, making countless decisions relating to Iraq, Afghanistan, and the broader global war on terror. In reality, I was probably being *more* decisive than they would like; so the story was completely wrong. But many people had read the *Journal* story and taken it for the absolute truth. In fact, people, including my foreign counterparts, sent condolence letters or called to express their sympathy. Sometimes I would call a foreign economic leader, or a counterpart in our government, and the conversation would begin like this:

"I thought you left the Treasury."

"No. I'm still here. What gave you that impression?"

"I thought I read it somewhere. Well, glad you're still around."
Milton Friedman even sent me a nice condolence note:

Dear John,
    I write to express my sympathy and regret at what I read in the papers that you will be leaving your position at the Treasury. Perhaps it was inevitable with the change of Secretary, but it is a dirty shame anyway and I cannot believe it is justified by performance.

I called Milton right away to tell him it wasn't so.

Years later I asked Alan Murray, who had been Washington bureau chief for *The Wall Street Journal* for ten years before leaving in February 2002 to join CNBC, about that story, and I explained, using my example of negotiating with the Turks, the damage that false stories can cause. He did not remember the story, of course, but said "Washington Wire" stories "aren't subject to the same level of reporting and editing scrutiny" as news stories, and he hoped that people understood that. In retrospect, I wish they could have put a warning label on that column.

KEY ATTRIBUTES OF THE FINANCIAL PACKAGE

Based on my preliminary discussions with Babacan and his team, I decided that the financial package should have two major attributes, both of which in my view would best help the broader foreign policy strategy.

Flexibility—whether it would be a grant or a loan or freely convertible from one to another—would make the package more attractive to the Turks and hopefully offset some of the "bid-ask" gap. To achieve this flexibility required some "out-of-the-box" thinking on our parts and the possible creation of a financial instrument that had never been conceived of or used before. Our Treasury debt experts and OMB budget experts would have to use their imagination.

The second attribute, borrowed from a doctor's creed, was to "do no harm." There was a danger that giving the Turks a large grant or loan would allow them to deviate from the wise, but sometimes tough, fiscal and monetary policy that happened to be part of the IMF program. One way to ensure that the package stayed true to this attribute would be to insist that in order to get the grant or the loan, the Turks would have to continue the same economic policies that were in their current IMF program. I decided to go to Ankara with the goal of developing and negotiating a financial package with these hallmarks.

FINANCIAL COVER

I arrived at Andrews Air Force Base at 4:00 a.m. on Thursday, December 26, 2002, for a five o'clock flight. When I walked into the passenger terminal, Marc Grossman was already there; he was talking on his cell phone, rather impatiently and with a worried look. Bob Pearson, our Ambassador to Turkey who had arranged the trip with the Turks, was on the other end of the call. Marc had also served as U.S. Ambassador to Turkey so he could size up the situation there quickly. Marc explained that the Turks wanted to cancel the trip. A high-level U.S. delegation would attract a lot of press attention about the war in Iraq at a delicate time for the new government. Having officials from State (Marc Grossman) and Defense (Bill Luti, a deputy assistant secretary) fly to Turkey now would make it appear like the United States was pressuring the Turks to make a decision about whether coalition troops could deploy into Iraq through Turkey. The Turkish NSC also had planned a meeting while we were there, which could add fuel to such speculation.

To deal with the appearance problem, Marc suggested and I agreed that we should stress that the mission was primarily about financial issues, which had the great advantage that it was the truth. I was going to Turkey to follow up on my Washington meeting with Babacan, even though political and security issues were obviously tied in to our discussions. To highlight this mission, I would very visibly head up the delegation, appear publicly in that position in press briefings, and chair all meetings with Turkish officials, whether on finance, foreign affairs, or defense issues. Bob Pearson also agreed to this plan, and he worked out the arrangement with the Turks while we waited at Andrews.

Although this solution meant the trip could proceed as scheduled, it certainly increased the pressure on me. I knew that most of the press questions would focus on political and military issues and that I would be far afield of my expertise. This would be less of a problem in the internal meetings, where I could lead off and then defer to Marc or Bill on the details. To deal with this in the press briefings, I would stay as close to a previously agreed message as I possibly could, especially on the non-economic issues. Nevertheless, I was apprehensive, imagining what I would say at a press conference in Ankara when a reporter asked me, as head of the delegation, questions about the Kurdish leaders in northern Iraq, or how the Turkish bases were going to be refurbished, or one of a million other questions I knew almost nothing about.

We took off on schedule at 5:00 a.m. Washington time on a sleek Gulfstream V corporate jet. When we arrived in Ankara at about 11:30 p.m. that night, we were greeted, as expected, by a large number of reporters and TV cameras. Just in case, I had worked on some simple talking points with Marc on the plane, and I kept to those points as the press surrounded me at the airport. Happily, I stayed on message; and the reporting was accurate. As reported by the Associated Press on December 27, 2002: "'We will continue to discuss the economic reforms in Turkey and the good progress that has been made in those reforms, the state of the Turkish economy and the possible impacts on Turkey of a possible conflict in Iraq.' Taylor said on his arrival in Ankara late Thursday. 'The purpose of course is to avoid such a conflict.'"

AGREEMENT ON A FLEXIBLE FRAMEWORK

We first met with Minister Babacan and his economic team in the finance ministry, followed by an informal lunch with him at a local restaurant. We would have over four hours to discuss the financial issues in depth.

I began the meeting by reviewing the total amount of support we could offer. "We can provide $4 billion," I said, "consisting of $2 billion for Economic Support Funds [ESF] and $2 billion in Foreign Military Assistance in the event of a war with Iraq in which Turkey cooperated fully." The Turks could use the ESF funds, a U.S. budget term, for a variety of non-military purposes; the rest would be restricted for military purposes. I knew that it would be possible, at the right time, to increase that amount and that we could ultimately offer up to $6 billion in assistance. But I could not offer that amount on this trip unless the political and security issues were fully agreed to, which seemed unlikely. I did, however, make it clear that we could go above $4 billion, but not by much; "nowhere near double digit amounts" was the way I put it.

I also made it very clear that we could be flexible in providing loans rather than grants. I told them we had worked out the details in Washington and brought some sample calculations. I had experts back in Washington ready to do more calculations if needed. David Loevinger, the Treasury Deputy Assistant Secretary in charge of Turkey, accompanied me to Ankara, and he was in close communication with Treasury and OMB staff back in Washington. As in all my other endeavors, it was important to put together a good team of people and motivate them, and I was very pleased that our "Team Turkey," under David's direct command, was another highly motivated group of global financial warriors. Whenever we asked them, no matter what time of day it was in the United States, they would do mathematical calculations for different maturities of the loans, different interest rates on the loans. For example, one of their calculations showed that a $1 billion grant could be converted into a $10 billion loan.

"So, if you take $1 billion of the $2 billion in ESF funds and convert it into a $10 billion loan," I said, "you could have a package that would amount to about $13 billion rather than $4 billion. Also if you add in the nearly $500 million in procurement by the U.S. military and another $500 million for base renovation, and maybe throw in another $1 billion for oil guarantees which some of our allies in the

Gulf might consider, the 'headline' financial support package would be $15 billion." This example apparently leaked, because the press began reporting that the U.S. package ranged from $4 billion to $15 billion.

In my view we had already come a long way toward achieving my first objective, making the package as attractive as possible within the overall budget constraint. The loans would make the package sound larger and, even more important, could be more useful to the Turks in the event of a large short-term impact from the war. As for the second objective, I made a point that we would insist that any support package have economic conditions comparable to those in the IMF program on the fiscal and monetary side.

When it came time for his part of the presentation, Babacan reiterated that the war would cost Turkey between $92 and $138 billion. I again replied, somewhat less diplomatically than in our previous meeting, that their numbers made no sense. The estimates were naive, essentially made up. The Turkish economy would recover from any war shock much faster than in the Turks' simulations, there would be economic benefits for Turkish firms to participate in the inevitable reconstruction, and a free Iraq would benefit Turkey's trade. I also reiterated that the Turkish economic policy had improved significantly in recent years.

Babacan then went on to say that Turkey was very reluctant to tie the U.S. economic support to conditions in the IMF program. He added that while they were committed to the fiscal policy and the reforms, they were making a point of developing their own views, independent of the IMF. He argued that by tying the U.S. support to the IMF, we would thwart that healthy process. Babacan's remarks worried me because implicit in them was an apparent willingness to depart from the sound fiscal and monetary policy that had just started to serve Turkey well. Yes, the previous government had spent too much before the election, but Babacan had to get them back on track. They seemed to be slipping despite our pleas and warnings.

I explained that it was essential to relate U.S. support to good economic policies because we did not want our package to under-

mine the IMF and hurt Turkish policy, which was beginning to show
positive results. For example, it would be tragic if the U.S. support
was wasted defending an unrealistic exchange rate. It was important
for Marc Grossman and Bill Luti, as representatives of non-economic
agencies, to support me on this in front of Babacan, and they did so
strongly. They understood well that I wanted to make sure that the
program did not put the Turkish economy at even greater risk.

As for the flexibility of the financial support package that I proposed, Babacan liked the concept. He agreed to our idea of leverag-
ing to a larger loan amount in part because it would take the
headlines announcement well above the $4 billion mark. We agreed
on this financial framework in general terms and it was now time for
our legal experts to begin drafting a formal agreement. Babacan asked
if we might consider adding even more "flexibility and adaptability,"
as he put it. He wanted to know if we could build some contingency
into the financial agreement under which Turkey could decide, after
seeing how hard the Turkish economy was hit by the war, whether it
would take the support as a loan or a grant. In other words, could
Turkey switch from grants to loans after the legislation passed the
U.S. Congress as a fail-safe against another financial crisis? This
flexibility was very attractive to the financial types in the Turkish government. I said I would see whether our budget laws would permit
this additional flexibility.

Although we agreed to this framework we did not, of course,
agree to the total size of the package. In fact, to my surprise, Babacan
did not reduce the size of his demand at all, and still expressed reservations about the link to economic policy. They were clearly tough
negotiators.

After having lunch with Babacan, where we discussed a much
broader set of economic issues, we went to the foreign affairs ministry and met with Ugar Ziyal, Marc Grossman's counterpart, and a
number of generals from the Turkish General Staff. This meeting
occurred just after the Turkish NSC meeting had adjourned. Ziyal
informed us that the NSC had made no decision on military concerns relating to a possible conflict with Iraq. He indicated, however,
that the Turkish government did want to provide a northern option

for coalition troops, saying, "We will not deny you a northern option," but added they were not ready to announce it at that time. There were a number of important details to be worked out, including how many coalition troops there would be and the role of Turkish troops in northern Iraq, a very sensitive issue for both the Turks and the Kurds. In any case, to proceed with any plan, they would have to pass legislation in the Parliament.

I reviewed with the Turkish political and military leaders the progress I had made with Babacan on a flexible financial framework, though not the dollar amount. I reminded Ziyal that we would insist on the Turks complying with the terms of the IMF agreement—especially the budget—because we did not want the money wasted, nor did we want the Turks to shake up the markets and renew the previous crisis.

After the meeting with Ziyal, I gave a press briefing in front of the foreign ministry building. Not surprisingly, there was huge press interest in our meetings, and what they meant for a possible war and its economic impact. Although we could say nothing about an agreement on the military side, I decided to emphasize that we had made headway on the financial side. I reported that we had agreed on a framework for the economic package. On December 28 the AP quoted me as saying, "We've established an agreement on the overall structure of the assistance" in an article entitled "Top U.S. Officials Offer Aid to Buffer Turkey's Economy from a Possible War in Iraq."

I tried one more meeting with Babacan on the morning of December 28 to see if we could move closer on the numbers. He remained firm, saying, "Your figure is not quite acceptable," even if the loan amounts brought the total above $15 billion, to $25 billion. Though we had made progress, I knew that the United States could not provide anything close to what Babacan was asking, so we had work to do. On our plane ride back to Washington that Saturday, Marc and I wrote up a report on the trip with follow-up tasks. For Treasury, the main task was to flesh out the financial agreement and see if it was possible to build in the increased flexibility Babacan had suggested.

KEEPING THE INTERNATIONAL COMMUNITY INFORMED

The press reports about my mission to Turkey generated a lot of complaints from the IMF and the G7, as everyone wanted to know what I was doing there. They were naturally concerned that a U.S. support package could adversely affect the incentives for Turkey to follow good policies and thereby undermine the IMF program. In fact, there were worries—and I shared those worries, based on my visit—that the new government in Turkey was already getting off track.

When I got back to Washington, I asked my staff to set up a G7 meeting as soon possible. Most of my G7 colleagues were going to Milan to attend a conference with academic finance experts. With all that was going on, I could not attend this meeting. However, the others agreed to have a special meeting with me on video from Washington on January 11 during a break in their meetings in Milan. I wanted to review the situation and reassure my G7 colleagues and the IMF. Anne Krueger joined the meeting and led off by expressing her concerns that the Turks were not staying on track on their fiscal and banking reforms. I conveyed my own concerns—which were quite consistent with Anne's—based on my recent trip.

My colleagues—especially from Germany, Italy, and Japan—pressed me for more details about the size of a U.S. financial assistance package and whether it was conditional on military actions. They expressed concern that the possibility of a package had contributed to the Turkish government's recent backtracking on reform. I replied that we had been warning Turkey not to backtrack and that a package would not go forward if Turkey were off track on its economic policies. In light of this, it made no sense to blame a possible assistance package for policy procrastination in Turkey. I could not, of course, give out any numbers because we were still talking with the Turks, but I reiterated that any financial support we gave to Turkey would not undermine the reform effort there. I explained that preventing policy slippage remained one of our major objectives. We would insist on economic conditions consistent with the IMF program's conditions. I emphasized that my entire government—not just the Treasury—was insistent on this.

This discussion seemed to alleviate concerns about the U.S. assistance package, and by the end, all my G7 colleagues had agreed to contact the Turks and urge them to get back on track with monetary and fiscal policy immediately. The messages would travel either directly to Babacan through finance ministry channels or through regular diplomatic channels.

TOWARD FULL FINANCIAL AGREEMENT

In the meantime, the lawyers had nearly completed the full legal details of the financial agreement, and on February 9, I returned to Turkey to finish it off. I met for many hours with the Turks, dealing with each of their concerns and trying to convince them to accept our total amount. I recall meeting with Babacan in his office at one or two in the morning, going over his numbers again and again, and explaining that they would simply not work. At this point, we had reached agreement on everything except the total amount, and I had made it clear that the United States could go no higher than $6 billion, a 50 percent increase in the offer from my previous trip, and that the Turks could leverage this into a much larger loan amount if they wished. Nevertheless, the Turks were still insisting on their original extraordinarily large numbers. We decided to leave a space in the legal agreement where the final dollar amount would be filled in. Babacan then made plans to travel to Washington with the Turkish foreign minister, Yasar Yakis. They wanted to make their case for a larger amount at the highest levels of our government.

They arrived in Washington on February 13, and Babacan spent a good amount of time at the State Department going over military and political issues related to a war in Iraq, which would begin in just over a month. They then went over to the White House, first meeting with Condi Rice in her office. Regarding the financial agreement, she made it very clear that the United States could offer support of $6 billion, but under no circumstances could it go higher, and that the flexibility that Treasury had offered them would deal with all their concerns in the case of a serious economic impact. She said that it would be useless to ask the President for more. We all then walked across the West Wing from Rice's office to the Oval Office to meet with the President.

President Bush started the good, cordial meeting by complimenting them for being such astute negotiators, "good horse traders," and for their success in getting such a large and flexible package out of the United States. Then, despite Rice's strong hints not to push, Babacan and Yakis went ahead and asked for more, but to no avail. After the Turks left the Oval Office, I mentioned to the President that the package was an amazingly good deal for the Turks; and even if it were a better deal, they would have asked him for more. He agreed, saying, "Maybe it's too good a deal."

Remarkably, even after meeting with President Bush, Babacan and Yakis wanted to continue debating the size of the package. They wanted to speak with Secretary Powell, so he offered to have them come over to his house late that night. Powell was the last to arrive, having just returned from a meeting of the UN Security Council in New York where he had spent much of the day debating with the French and the Russians about Iraq's non-compliance with UN Security Council resolutions. Al Larson of State also joined us. Powell, Grossman, Larson, Yakis, Babacan, and I went into the dining room and sat around the Powells' table. The Turks kept asking us for more. I explained how the package was large, well designed, flexible, and certainly appropriate in size for the circumstances. Colin Powell explained that their request exceeded the State Department's entire foreign aid budget! We were all exhausted. Nevertheless, they kept insisting, left that night without a final agreement, and returned to Ankara the next day.

I was greatly disheartened, as I am sure everyone else was. It was about that time that I recollected asking General Pete Pace in an NSC meeting about the costs of not getting the northern option. As usual, he wore his olive-brown Marine uniform with four stars and all his ribbons. He was then the second highest ranking officer in the U.S. military and soon would be promoted to number one. He answered in his usual soft-spoken manner. With all the other uncertainties of war he could not say definitively, but his best guess at that time was that it would raise the number of casualties. By how much he could not say. Pace's soft-spokenness later became the subject of a good laugh in a Situation Room meeting the following October 8. Zal Khalilzad was on the phone from Kabul. After about five minutes into a presentation by Pete Pace on a crucial military issue in Afghanistan, Steve Hadley, who was chairing the meeting and had noticed a puzzled look on Zal's face, asked: "Did you hear Pete, Zal?" Zal candidly admitted, no, he hadn't, and everyone in the room laughed. Steve asked Pete to repeat the presentation, this time in a louder voice. Then Steve added: "Before you start again, Pete, I have two observations about this. First, Zal we love you. Second, there is nothing in this world like a soft-spoken four-star Marine general."

In a last-ditch effort to get the Turks to accept, I offered the possibility, if needed, of a short-term loan from the Exchange Stabilization Fund. I had learned during Babacan's February 13 visit to Washington that he was worried about a lag between the start of a war in Iraq and Congress passing legislation for their financial agreement. He felt that Turkey would be vulnerable during such a period. To alleviate this concern, I suggested a very short term "bridge loan" and asked our lawyers to see if we could use the Exchange Stabilization Fund to make it. After a flurry of legal work, they said we could do it. The scenario the Turks had imagined seemed like a very low probability, but Babacan seemed comforted once he knew how the loan from the Exchange Stabilization Fund would work. I do not know the exact reason for the final decision, but soon after Yakis and Babacan returned from Washington, having heard from the very highest levels of our government that they were not going to get any more, the Turks agreed to accept the financial package. They signed the agreement, including the $6 billion budgetary impact and the flexibility between grants and loans, on February 27, 2003. I was elated, as was Dave Loevinger and the entire Team Turkey that had worked so hard and so long on this agreement. It was high-fives all around.

THE VOTE

With the financial agreement in place, all the experts on Turkish politics—both inside and outside Turkey—predicted that it would be only a short time before the Turkish government would bring the necessary legislation to their Parliament and it would be approved. But the experts were wrong. On March 1, to our great surprise, the Turkish Parliament denied permission for U.S. troops to enter Iraq through Turkish territory. More specifically, they failed to pass a law authorizing 62,000 U.S. troops, 255 warplanes, and 65 helicopters to use Turkey as a base for invading Iraq. There would be no northern option. The Fourth Infantry Division, which was already sitting on ships in the Mediterranean off the coast of Turkey, would not be given permission to enter Iraq through Turkey.

Though passage by a large majority was expected, the measure lost by 4 votes. The government, expecting a large majority, had not required voting along party lines. When members of Parliament thought the measure would win anyway, many decided to vote against it—which would be popular, given Turkish public opinion at the time.

The Erdogan government was as surprised as everyone. They thought that they had plenty of votes and could afford a little leakage. With the loss, they became concerned that they had also lost their financial support package from the United States to cushion the economic impact; they were very worried about an adverse affect on the markets. The Turkish ministers met for many long hours that day deliberating about what to do, but bringing the legislation back to the Parliament was not a possibility. Tommy Franks would begin the war in Iraq on March 20 without bringing the Fourth Infantry Division down from the north.

THE MILITARY AFTERMATH: ALL FOR NAUGHT?

Looking back on that March 1 vote, I can say that I was very disappointed at the time. It was not just that all our hard work and the tough negotiations seemed to go for naught, but the loss of the northern option for the war in Iraq. But what exactly was the military impact of losing that option? There are many possibilities to consider.

If the Turks had allowed the coalition a northern entry point, we would have had to allow several thousand Turkish troops into northern Iraq with us. This would have likely generated suspicion among many Iraqis of our motives and made unification with the Kurds more difficult. Even today, the Turks worry about the formation of an independent Kurdish state that would carve out parts of Turkey and Iraq.

On the other side, if the Fourth Infantry Division had entered from the north, rather than from the south, it would probably have crushed some of the forces that eventually became part of the insurgency. Much of this is speculation. Historians will be theorizing and debating the what-ifs for a long time.

But one of the most intriguing theories suggests that all our work with the Turks was not in vain after all. In a meeting of the National Security Council on March 25 in the Situation Room, President Bush raised the subject of Turkey. According to Tommy Franks's memoir, *American Soldier*, the President said, "It looks like we've reached the end of the string with Turkey. Nothing we can do will persuade them to let our troops transit their territory." Franks then said, "Mr. President, I'd like to keep the Fourth ID up there another twenty-four hours. Our deception is holding. We've got eleven Iraqi divisions fixed in the north. I want to keep them there until Buzz Moseley's airmen can reduce their effectiveness."*

What was the deception that Franks referred to? It was a highly

---

*Tommy Franks, *American Soldier* (New York: Regan Books, 2004), p. 500.

classified and compartmentalized effort to provide false information to Saddam Hussein and the Iraqi military. A U.S. military officer with the code name "April Fool" had been approached by an Iraqi intelligence operative to provide information about U.S. war plans. But April Fool was operating as a double agent, and he immediately contacted his superiors in the U.S. military about the request. For several weeks in late 2002 and early 2003, April Fool met and sold the Iraqi operative contact detailed, but fake, operational information. In Tommy Franks's words, the fake storyline went as follows: "The Coalition was planning to build up only a portion of its ground force in Kuwait, while preparing a major airborne assault into northern Iraq. . . . C-17 transports would deliver tanks and Bradleys. . . . This small armored force would then be reinforced by the 4th Infantry Division, which the Turkish government would permit—at the last possible minute—to pass through Turkey and steamroll its way south to Baghdad."*

The purpose of the deception was to convince Saddam to keep a major part of his army north of Baghdad to defend against the Fourth Infantry Division, far away from the Coalition Forces attack from Kuwait. It appeared to work. Much of Saddam's Republican Guard and regular army divisions remained in the north, and interviews with Iraqi leaders after the war indicate that Saddam was fooled by the deception. Perhaps unwittingly, the financial package, our trips to Ankara and the Turks' excursions to Washington, the long negotiations, and the press coverage probably played a role in these very successful deceptions. If all this had not occurred, maybe Saddam or his team would have seen little chance of an attack from the northern entry and ordered his divisions to go south.

THE ECONOMIC AND POLITICAL AFTERMATH

The vote also had economic implications. When Dave Loevinger and his Team Turkey first learned of the vote, they immediately

*Ibid., p. 435.

came and told me there would be adverse effects on the Turkish economy. The markets had expected a substantial financial aid package for Turkey, like the one that was agreed to on February 27. They were just as surprised as we were at the vote, and now Turkey would not receive the package. We were getting good reports back in Washington from Ambassador Pearson and his economic team at the American Embassy in Ankara, and we stayed in close communication with them about how to proceed.

In an effort to bolster confidence in their economic policies, right after the no vote the Turks wisely submitted an improved budget and then focused on getting back on track with the IMF program, which they did. In a sense the no vote shocked the Turks into dealing more effectively and more aggressively with their economic reforms. It was another unforeseen benefit of the no vote.

In an April 29 call from President Bush to Prime Minister Erdogan, the President emphasized the importance of staying the course with the good economic program. On May 2, Secretary Snow said in public that Turkey "should stick to the IMF program." Eventually we decided that it would be wise for the United States to offer Turkey a financial package, though much smaller than the one we had been discussing before. It would be $1 billion, rather than $6 billion, in grants, and if they wanted to, they could leverage up the $1 billion to a larger amount of loans. This agreement had some "military conditionality," namely, that the Turks would not move troops into northern Iraq. In the end, the Turks could not accept that condition politically. The speed of the invasion meant that there were none of the economic impacts that the Turks had worried about. Hence, the need for a financial support package diminished greatly and there was no rush to finish this agreement. In the end, the grant/loan agreement was not signed until September 2003.

Fortunately, as we hoped and encouraged, the Turks kept with the good economic policies and the economy responded wonderfully. They never even used the grant funds or the loan, and eventually, in March 2005, the U.S. Congress pulled the money. To make sure that the financial markets did not misinterpret that decision, we made clarifying statements to the press. In an interview in New York the day Congress pulled the money, I said that the Turks have taken steps to have a better monetary policy, better fiscal policy and it's working," a quote which was widely picked up in the Turkish press.*

Turkish economic performance continued to improve. Inflation came down, interest rates came down, and economic growth got stronger. In a meeting I had with Babacan in Davos in the winter of 2005, he spoke proudly about the benefits of "crowding in": as he tightened the budget and growth based on government spending slowed down, private capital spending crowded in, and the economy grew even more rapidly. Capitalism was alive and well in Turkey.

The close vote on the northern entry, conducted freely, without any obvious interference by the Turkish military or any other power group, also demonstrated that democracy was alive and well in Turkey. Though democracy has unequivocal strategic benefits for the global war on terror, as President Bush emphasized in his second inaugural address, one cannot expect it to deliver the right tactical decision in every instance. The long-run economic and political benefits of that no vote could very well outweigh the short-run costs, whatever they were.

*"U.S. Treasury's Taylor Praises Turkish Economy," *Turkish Press Review*, March 7, 2005.

CHAPTER SEVEN

A Plan for Financial Stability in Iraq

◆

*A*s our team of financial experts and I were brokering a financial agreement with the Turks relating to the northern entry into Iraq, another Treasury team of financial experts was assembling in Kuwait. Should a war in Iraq take place, they were ready to carry out a mission that we had been planning for months in Washington. The team would enter Iraq as soon as possible after Saddam Hussein's government fell and implement a series of steps to secure the country's financial system and prevent a financial collapse. We wrote up specific terms of reference for what each person on the team would do, though we all knew that we'd have to call "audibles" once they were on the ground in Iraq. Although we did not know it then, at about that same time, Saddam was instructing the governor of the central bank in Baghdad to remove one *billion* dollars, largely in U.S. currency, from its vaults, and hand it over to his son Qusay, an action which itself could threaten financial stability in Iraq.

Recruiting and choosing the right people for this difficult mission was not easy. One otherwise qualified Treasury staffer told me he was too worried about Saddam using chemical and biological weapons to go, saying that he did not want to have to wear a gas mask. In the end I chose three highly capable and willing people to lead the team, all of whom had practical financial experience and had served previously in difficult environments around the world. Van Jorstad, who would be the overall leader of the three, had served in Russia as a banking adviser and had been CEO of a bank in Colorado. George Mullinax, who would make the initial contacts with the Iraqi state banks and the central bank, had also run a bank in the United States. David Nummy, who would make initial contacts with the finance ministry, had served in Afghanistan, in Kosovo, and in Russia just after the fall of the Soviet Union. He also knew about finance ministry operations, having served as Assistant Secretary of the Treasury for Management in the first Bush administration.

We started our work on a plan to deal with the financial aspects of a possible military intervention in Iraq in the late summer of 2002, about one year after 9/11. Much of this work was highly classified at the time, and we developed it on a contingency basis because we did not know whether there would be a military intervention. But just as General Tommy Franks had to develop a war plan at CENTCOM, we had to develop a financial reconstruction plan at Treasury and be prepared to execute it.

These financial operations constituted some of the most complex parts of reconstruction, whether you assess it from an economic, political, security, or logistical viewpoint. Their planning and execution occurred on many levels—from broad policies set by the President to financial calculations done by Treasury economists, and security provided by the Fourth Infantry Division. On each of these levels, many different agencies of our government and of other governments participated. As the principal person responsible for managing this effort, I relied on the same management principles that served me well in other operations I have written about in this book. For a successfully executed plan, you first have to gather the available facts, then analyze the many options and ideas and come up with a strategy. To move from strategy to tactics, you have to set up a flexible organizational structure with high-caliber people. At each level of the organization you have to require that people follow the maxim: "Tell them what to do, not how to do it." Using an analogy from map reading, as a leader, I could not zoom in too often or too closely, except to spot-check or make adjustments when needed.

GATHERING FINANCIAL INTELLIGENCE

The first task was to get the facts, which meant an assessment of the financial situation in Iraq—the state of the currency, the central bank, and the banking sector. Our first intelligence report was completed by a highly skilled and methodical young analyst we brought over from the Central Intelligence Agency. She combined existing intelligence resources with the latest information she could gather on the current prices for basic goods and services and on the condition of the banking system. Her report was very good (so good that the CIA realized, with a possible war in Iraq looming, what they were missing and insisted that she return very fast). But I was dismayed that our information about the economy was so sketchy. I am an avid consumer of economic data and enjoy using it to spot trends or regular patterns, so I was probably more disappointed than others.

One reason for the lack of data was that Iraq was essentially cut off from legitimate commerce with the rest of the world. In addition, the Iraqi statistical agencies had atrophied under Saddam. In more conventional cases when I needed data from emerging markets or poor developing countries, I could request assistance from the IMF, which collects data and analyzes economies around the world. The last Article IV consultation (the technical term for an economic analysis of a country) for the IMF in Iraq was twenty years ago. I asked for a copy of that old report from the IMF, dated August 5, 1983. Although obviously extremely out of date, I found it useful to read about the damage done to Iraq's economy going back to the time of the Iran-Iraq War, including the closing of oil pipelines running through the south. Iraq lost access to the deep water terminals near Basra near the Persian Gulf as a result of that war, so the oil had to travel in more limited volume through Syria and Lebanon to the Mediterranean Sea.

In any case, we had very little to go on. I had written my PhD thesis on economic policymaking under uncertainty, but this was more uncertainty than anything I, or maybe anyone else, had ever seen. Even with the poor data, there was no doubt that a quarter century of repression and economic mismanagement under Saddam Hussein had reduced the size of the economy to a small fraction of what it was before his regime took over. In 1979, GDP in Iraq was $128 billion; by 2001, it had declined to as little as $25 billion. Income per capita had plummeted also, impoverishing the Iraqi people. While the world economy prospered, the Iraqi economy degenerated and the Iraqi people fell way behind. The United Nations has a Human Development Index that measures quality of life and can be used to measure how far Iraq had fallen under Saddam. The country went from a rank of 76 in 1990 to a rank of 127 in 2001.

The banking system was in shambles. Electronic transfer of funds, widely available to people in developed countries, was virtually nonexistent, making Iraq's payment system the equivalent of a Model-T Ford. The central bank existed almost solely as a vehicle for Saddam to make loans to supporters of his regime. Inflation had eroded the salaries of most government workers, who subsequently had to depend on the food delivered by the UN-administered Oil for Food Program.

There were two Iraqi currencies in circulation. The Saddam dinar was used primarily in the south and the Swiss dinar was used primarily in the northern provinces of Kurdistan. People had different views about the origin of the term "Swiss" dinar. Some say it arose because the currency was as sound as the Swiss franc, others because the original plates were produced in Switzerland. The two currencies were very easy to distinguish: one showed Saddam's face on it; the other featured classic symbols and images of Iraq's antiquity. The supply of the Swiss dinar could not increase very much because no new bills had been printed since the first Gulf War. This helped preserve the value of the Swiss dinar over the years, though the physical state of the currency itself was showing signs of age. The constrained supply of these bills meant there was very little inflation in the Kurdish provinces.

In contrast, the supply of the Saddam dinar increased by large amounts as Saddam resorted to the printing press to pay for his spending outlays. This made for very high rates of inflation in Iraq outside Kurdistan, which caused the value of the Saddam dinar to fall sharply. A Saddam dinar was worth less than 1 percent of its value compared to when Saddam first starting printing it. While the supply of money did not grow in the north, keeping inflation low, it grew rapidly in the south, causing rampant inflation. This situation exemplified Milton Friedman's famous phrase that inflation is always and everywhere a monetary phenomenon.

An active currency market operated in the streets of Iraq. The two currencies could be exchanged and, not surprisingly, the Saddam dinar was worth only a fraction of the Swiss dinar. In 2002, the Swiss dinar was trading at about 10 dinars per U.S. dollar and the Saddam dinar was trading at about 2,000 dinars per dollar. This implied a cross exchange rate of 200 Saddam dinars per Swiss dinar. The Swiss dinar appreciated relative to the Saddam dinar in anticipation of the ouster of Saddam.

In addition to its plummeting in value, the Saddam dinar had other problems. It was easily counterfeited, so if you weren't careful you might get caught with a worthless bogus bill. But the dinar had another much stranger problem, which to a monetary economist vividly illustrated how little Saddam paid attention to providing basic services to the people of Iraq. Only two denominations circulated: a 10,000-dinar note, which was worth about $5; and a 250-dinar note, which was worth about 12 cents. Imagine what it would be like to go shopping at the local mall if you and everyone else only had five-dollar bills and dimes to buy and sell with! Yet that was the situation in Baghdad.

Wherever possible, we tried to obtain additional or at least corroborating information from the private sector. The CIA hired a private consulting firm—Oxford Economic Forecasting—to put together an economic model of the Iraqi economy. The model provided a good analytical framework and allowed us to experiment with alternative simulations and consider different contingencies, including the impacts of long and short wars. To estimate the model, the consulting firm pieced together data from old sources, so it required a lot of guesswork. For example, to estimate Iraqi GDP, they simply assumed that the GDP was a fixed multiple of oil revenues, after which they then pieced together data on oil revenues from various international sources.

Iraqi Expats and the Future of Iraq Project

In my financial work on Afghanistan I had learned a great deal from people like Ned Nadiri, my economist friends who happened to be Afghan expats, so I sought out Iraqi expat economists I knew. I asked Salih Nefti, an American Iraqi who came from Kirkuk via Turkey, to meet with me. I also called Imad Moosa, an Australian Iraqi who came from Basra and whose mother still lived there. I had co-authored an Australian version of my economics textbook with Imad and I respected him greatly. He would be one of the people I asked to be part of our team in Iraq. He agreed and served with distinction, even having a chance to visit his mother in the months after Saddam's fall from power. Imad was later tragically caught up in an airport security mistake when he landed at LAX on a flight from Sydney en route to attend an economics conference. Security officers handcuffed him and sent him back to Australia under suspicion, presumably because his Australian passport indicated that he had recently been in and out of Iraq. When he said that this was for work on behalf of the U.S. Treasury in Iraq, the officers apparently believed this was too far-fetched.

Expats participating in the Future of Iraq Project, which was set up under the auspices of the State Department, also provided a great deal of useful information. The idea behind this project was that Iraqi expats with knowledge of certain areas—economics and finance, for example—would write papers about the current state of the Iraqi economy and share their views with each other and with U.S. government officials. I found the work done under this project to be helpful in pulling together information and in making initial contacts with Iraqis, but it was by no means a postwar financial plan for Iraq, and I assume the same was true in other areas.

It was through the Future of Iraq Project that I first met Sinan Al Shabibi, who would become the governor of the central bank. Shabibi was living in Switzerland and had worked for the United Nations Conference on Trade and Development. Before he emigrated from Iraq, he worked at the government's planning ministry. Shabibi and I became close friends over the next three years as we worked on issues involving the currency, monetary policy, the IMF, and the Iraq debt. From the very outset, Shabibi was extremely appreciative of the work we were doing on Iraq. I greatly admired him for his courage and willingness to help his country. In those early planning days in the fall of 2002, Shabibi wrote useful papers about currencies, inflation, monetary policy, and other issues as they pertained to Iraq. Nasreen Sideek, who was living in Erbil, the Kurdish area of Iraq, and was planning minister in the Kurdistan regional government, also participated actively in this project. People like Shabibi and Sideek with expertise in finance and economics formed the Economic and Infrastructure Working Group of the Future of Iraq Project.

These early contacts with Iraqis revealed to me the human face behind the misery suggested by the economic data. One paper, by Sabri Zire Al Saadi, entitled "New Currency, Fiscal and Monetary Policies: Guidelines for the Transitional Government of Iraq," provides an example. With obvious emotion and disgust he wrote: "It was beyond the imagination of the Iraqis that the foreign exchange value of the Iraqi Dinar (ID) in the late seventies . . . [would] one day deteriorate by almost 660,000%. . . . Adding to its low value [is] the dominant ugly picture of the dictator . . . the introduction of a new currency is essential for gathering support for the new regime. . . ." Papers like Saadi's reaffirmed our negative assessment of the situation in Iraq.

A helpful meeting with Shabibi, Sideek, and Saadi took place in my office on January 30, 2003. Everyone sat around my big mahogany table, the Iraqis on one side and my staff and I on the other. I was eager to listen and question, and to hear the Iraqis' views on the currency. They unanimously expressed a strong interest in introducing a new Iraqi currency as quickly as possible after the regime change. As Shabibi put it and later wrote in a paper: "The immediate measure facing the new authorities is to issue a new currency, change the existing currencies with it, adopt an exchange rate regime for it and implement the necessary action to protect and support the currency." He wanted to put an X over the face of Saddam during the interim period, telling us that this is what the Iranians did after the ouster of the Shah. Shabibi wanted the new Iraqi dinar to be in operation, "hopefully not later than 6 months after the regime's change." I asked if the Iraqis who were now in Iraq would feel the same way. Nasreen Sideek, who was living in Iraq at that time, said, "Of course they would," and the others agreed. In truth, this type of thinking closely resembled where Treasury's plans were heading at that time. The Iraqis' indication that this was something that the people of Iraq would want was obviously of enormous value.

GETTING ORGANIZED FOR A NEW RESPONSIBILITY

It became clear to me by January 2003 that if the financial reconstruction plans became operational, Treasury would assume full responsibility and I would need a more focused and operationally oriented organizational structure at Treasury. On January 22, 2003, Steve Hadley called a NSC deputies committee meeting in the White House Situation Room. We were to discuss National Security Presidential Directive 24, which would formally set up the Office of Reconstruction and Humanitarian Assistance (ORHA) under retired Army Lieutenant General Jay Garner's leadership. ORHA would address humanitarian issues that were likely to arise in the period immediately following a war. At the meeting, Jay Garner explained that different agencies would be asked to assign experts to work as part of the group. After preparing in Washington, they would then travel to Kuwait. In the event of a military invasion and the fall of the regime, they would deploy to Iraq and get the government ministries up and running. As civilians, they would not move into Iraq until there was a "permissive environment." This meant the financial planning we were doing would become part of ORHA, along with other areas ranging from the provision of basic government services to running the government-owned oil facilities.

Soon after the NSC meeting, Condi Rice, then still National Security Adviser to President Bush, invited me to a one-on-one lunch in the White House mess. I was still in the midst of a big leadership change at the Treasury. That same day John Snow was preparing for his confirmation hearings with a "murder board," which works like a flight simulator. By fielding tough practice questions from Treasury staff in a simulated hearing, you prepare for the real thing. On my way over to see Condi, President Bush took a few minutes to chat as he and Andy Card were walking outside the Oval Office onto the colonnade and I was walking past the Rose Garden. It was only small talk, but I remember and appreciated its upbeat and friendly tone, given all the changes at Treasury and the rumors swirling. Condi and I covered a range of international finance issues, but Condi emphasized—and this may have been the main reason for that lunch—how crucial Treasury's role would be if there was a military intervention and Saddam's regime fell. Treasury would be operationally responsible for the finance area.

At the NSC meeting, General Garner emphasized that the people we assigned to ORHA would report to him on the ground, thereby defining the chain of command in the field. This reporting relationship made sense to me and I tried to maintain the same chain of command throughout the financial reconstruction in Iraq when the personnel changed. However, to deal adequately with the technical finance issues that Garner would not be expected to know, and deliver on Condi Rice's request, I had to work out the terms of reference, stating what each person in the field would be responsible for in the financial areas. I would then have to provide a "reach-back" service in Treasury through which we could monitor financial developments, give guidance, and provide technical support.

As an example, here is part of David Nummy's terms of reference:

- within the first 48 hours of intervention . . .
  - ensure that assets and records of the Ministry of Finance are secured by the military . . . including cash, bank deposits, securities, gold . . .
  - establish the foundation for an interim administration . . .
- within one week of intervention,
  - initiate an assessment of all Ministry of Finance functions, including the payments system and so on through the first month.

Of course, to execute this plan, David would have to have a team. As soon as David and his two colleagues, Van Jorstad and George Mullinax, were chosen, we all went about attempting to fill out the rest of the team. I tried to stay closely involved in this selection process and insisted on speaking personally with everyone we sent to Iraq. Despite scheduling conflicts, I managed to do so. Jim Fall, a dedicated senior career Treasury employee with over thirty years of service, was in charge of our technical assistance office and was invaluable in this recruiting effort. When Jim retired in 2005; the Treasury lost one of its best, most experienced people.

Later on, the team on the ground would expand. In May, Peter McPherson would go over and serve as financial coordinator, coordinating the work of the central bank, finance ministry, and private banking teams. Peter was then president of Michigan State University and he had served as administrator of USAID, Deputy Treasury Secretary, and vice president of the Bank of America. Peter initially agreed to spend an extended "summer vacation" in Iraq; he stayed there through September 2003.

REACH-BACK: THE TASK FORCE ON FINANCIAL RECONSTRUCTION IN IRAQ

To provide the people on the ground with support back home, I created a special Task Force on Iraq Financial Reconstruction and assigned Larry McDonald, an experienced manager with knowledge of Middle East issues, to run it. I was attracted to the concept of a task force because of the very successful task force I had set up after 9/11 to coordinate the international efforts to freeze terrorist assets. I made sure that the new task force report directly to me. This would serve to raise its profile, ensure good communication, and demonstrate to all staff that their assignment was a very high priority. The task force would provide reach-back service to people deployed in Iraq and form the analytical center for designing our financial reconstruction plans.

I knew the task force would work best if, once we went operational, all the members were in close proximity to each other—perhaps in the style of the terrorist financing "War Room." I decided to house the task force in the old "market room" at Treasury. Earlier in my term, we had streamlined international affairs by closing the market room and decentralizing its functions—tracking developments in currency and securities markets—to individual analysts tracking specific issues. Still pretty much empty, the market room was ideal for setting up this task force.

We recruited excellent people, both from Treasury and other parts of government. I was delighted that we could recruit, with Alan Greenspan's approval, one of the best monetary experts at the Fed, Tom Simpson. Tom would prove to be invaluable. We also recruited an international affairs veteran, Karen Mathiasen, who graciously gave up her more senior office director position to join the task force as a staff member. Karen would focus on fund-raising for reconstruction in Iraq and bird-dog activities related to Iraq at the IMF and the World Bank.

People from all over Treasury, not just international affairs, and some from other agencies staffed the task force. We had experts on the payments system from Treasury's financial management system working under the supervision of Don Hammond, the Fiscal Assistant Secretary. Their work was essential. We also were moving into new legal areas, which would make the work of General Counsel David Aufhauser and his legal team equally essential. Everyone rose to the occasion. I think they realized we were at a turning point in history and that Treasury was going to play a key role. Turf battles were rare and teamwork was pervasive.

I stressed the importance of staying within the chain of command. The people that I would send to Iraq would formally report to Jay Garner and later Jerry Bremer. In concept, my Washington reach-back team would provide analytical advice when necessary and assist when interagency or other work needed to be done in Washington, including higher-level approval and the requests for added resources. The reach-back team would also monitor the situation, making sure that the overall strategy was on track. If the financial strategy had to be adjusted—as undoubtedly it would as conditions changed on the ground—the task force would be responsible for making sure everyone who designed the financial strategy—people like Tom Simpson—would know, and that it went up the chain of command appropriately far. I insisted on good reporting from our people in Baghdad for this purpose, and when necessary either went to Iraq myself or sent assessment teams.

Many of the issues related to the finance side were highly technical and not really relevant for the NSC deputies. But it was appropriate and helpful for technical people in other agencies—State, Defense, USAID, the Council of Economic Advisers—to weigh in and participate. To keep things simple during the early days, I insisted that other agencies that wanted to be involved in the financial part of this operation send people on detail to our task force. I wanted to provide full information, but I did not want to complicate the operations by setting up another interagency coordination team.

Maintaining the distinction between reach-back versus on-the-ground chain of command proved essential as a management principle for dealing with multiple levels and a plethora of participants at each level. There were, of course, interagency groups that focused on other parts of reconstruction, such as fund-raising. A very effective interagency group, first established for Afghanistan reconstruction, was co-chaired by Al Larson of State, Dov Zakheim of Defense, and myself. We focused entirely on fund-raising issues—calling donors and arranging for a donors' conference in Madrid. I have not covered this here because, while very time-consuming and successful, it was similar in concept to the Afghanistan fund-raising efforts described in chapter 2. Steve Hadley chaired an ORHA Issues Group, which coordinated in Washington the tasks that had been assigned to ORHA. Later on in the operation, in the fall of 2003, the interagency coordination process was reorganized into a new Iraq Stabilization Group, with security, political, and economic cells.

A MANAGEMENT TOOL FOR KEEPING TRACK OF THE STATE OF PLAY

Among the first of my assignments for the task force was the creation of a single document that would summarize all our contingency plans and evolve over time as we made progress. This was to be a "living" document. We called it "Contingency Plans for Reconstruction of Iraq's Financial Institutions and Financial Markets." It summarized, as of a particular date, a set of contingency plans for the reconstruction of Iraq's financial institutions and financial markets. The plans emphasized the restoration of sound operations at the finance ministry, the central bank, and the commercial banks. The document would contain the latest thinking on our currency plan, including goals, strategy, and tactics. It also laid out contingency plans for monetary policy, the budget, the external debt, the banking system, and a host of other financial issues.

The overriding objectives that underlay these plans were to:

- assess as quickly as possible the state of the financial institutions and markets;
- avoid financial chaos—hyperinflation, frozen payments systems;
- secure Iraqi assets—inside and outside Iraq—for the benefit of the Iraqi people;
- help the Iraqi people establish property rights, the rule of law, and free markets; and
- develop sound, well-run financial institutions that can be handed over to the Iraqi people as soon as possible.

The contingency plans provided detail on these strategic objectives and laid out operational steps and timelines for achieving them.

The Main Goals

As we began planning, my overriding goal was to prevent a monetary and financial collapse in Iraq when Saddam's regime fell. If the currency collapsed, the ensuing hyperinflation would cause havoc and distress among the Iraqi people. I also wanted to provide a lasting single currency for the country and establish a sound monetary policy, both essential foundations for economic recovery and growth.

To achieve these goals, we would have to reform the defective dual currency system. A difficulty in designing such a currency reform plan, however, was that we did not know which Iraqis would head up financial matters in a transitional government; and whoever was in charge, we did not know what their position would be on matters related to currency. That was one reason why our interaction with the Iraqi expats in the Future of Iraq Project was important. We wanted to make a choice that would be accepted by the Iraqi people.

The Different Options

One of the fascinating things about currency reforms is that everyone seems to have an opinion. Everybody wanted to weigh in. Within the Treasury, many people had views about alternatives for dealing with the two Iraqi currencies. People in the State and Defense Departments also had concerns. Paul Wolfowitz called me to convey how important it would be to quickly dispense with the Saddam dinar. People in other countries had other ideas.

There were four main options for reforming the Iraqi currency. One proposed to make the Swiss dinar the national currency immediately. The Swiss dinar was already in circulation in the Kurdish areas, and it was reasonably stable. Using it would signal to the Iraqis that the stability of their currency was being restored after years of abuse under Saddam. Moreover, we could use the old plates to print the money. I had called Mervyn King, then deputy governor of the Bank of England (he later became governor), to see if he could ask around quietly and determine whether the British printing firm De La Rue, which had produced Swiss dinars in the past, still had the plates. He agreed to look into it, and eventually found the plates. Hence, this seemed like a good option from an economic perspective.

However, regional political experts in the State Department argued that it would be a bad idea. Adopting the Swiss dinar as the national currency would cause tension between the Kurds in the north and the Shiites and the Sunnis in the rest of the country, who might reject the Swiss dinar as a "Kurdish" currency. From an economic point of view, I found this option the most attractive and workable, as did many of my economist colleagues at Treasury. Nevertheless, while seemingly the most simple, this option would still require printing and distributing the notes very quickly if it was going to stave off the chaos we were trying to avoid. In any case, the opposition from political and regional experts was strong, and the rationale behind that opposition was persuasive.

A second option was to introduce a completely new currency. This would serve as a unifying force for the country and avoid the potential conflict between the Kurds and others. This was more complicated than the first option; we would need to design and manufacture new plates, which would take time. So, it would require even more time than using the Swiss dinar. Moreover, designing a new currency would not be advisable until after the Saddam government fell and Iraqis could provide their own input.

A third option was to use military scrip, an idea that the Defense Department wanted to explore. Pete Pace, then Vice Chair of the Joint Chiefs, had asked me to look into it. At the end of World War II, the occupation armies in Germany and Japan used military scrip—a temporary substitute for money. The military would pay the scrip to the soldiers, who would then spend it in the local economy. Various means were used to encourage the shopkeepers to accept the money, including offering to exchange it into the local currency at a set exchange rate. The main advantage of scrip in the case of Iraq was that it would give us time to work with the Iraqis on a new currency and all would understand that it was temporary, as it was in all previous occupations. Eventually, once a new government was in place, a new currency could replace the scrip. However, it was not clear that local Iraqis would accept this military scrip on a massive scale even on a temporary basis. Although scrip had been used by the military during past occupations, our research could not find examples where a local population used it extensively.

A fourth option proposed to use dollars and effectively "dollarize" the economy, as in El Salvador, Panama, or Ecuador, where the dollar is the official currency. This plan would allow us to skip over the design phase and start distribution of the currency immediately. It would also provide the financial stability we were looking for because the dollar is a widely accepted stable currency. The disadvantage was that it would give the appearance that the United States was trying to take over Iraq on a long-term basis. In light of this, the State Department political experts were even more strongly against dollarization than they were against using the Swiss dinar.

Whatever option we chose, we needed to achieve both interagency consensus within the U.S. government and international consensus with our coalition partners, especially the United Kingdom, Australia, and Spain. We held many interagency meetings, especially in the period from December 2002 to February 2003, and there was a lot of lively debate. The discussions were for the most part civil and people refrained from end runs or other Machiavellian techniques. They were genuinely trying to find a way forward, but a basic difference of opinion between State and Treasury held us back. The State Department, especially the Middle East regional bureau, argued against using the Swiss dinar in the whole country for the political stability reasons outlined earlier. At Treasury, we were worried about financial stability, and were therefore willing to go with option one. If option one was not acceptable, however, then none of the other options was, either. We seemed to be at an impasse.

The Two-Stage Plan

In my view the only solution to this problem, and it was pretty obvious once you thought about it, was to design a two-part plan, and this is what we eventually settled on by February 2003. Stage One would be put into operation immediately with the commencement of the military operation in Iraq. Stage Two would launch later and depend on developments on the ground, including the speed of the military operation and the preferences of the new interim or transitional government.

In principle, Stage Two might be one of several options, and it was not necessary to decide which one before the military operation began in earnest. Stage One would last long enough to allow us to consult with the Iraqis in the transitional or interim government on the second stage of the plan; we could therefore get their buy-in. We would also have time to work on logistical issues like distribution, which would depend on the conditions on the ground. I felt the Iraqis would end up accepting a currency that had all the features of the Swiss dinar, but under the two-stage plan, they could decide for themselves.

Stage One: Paying Iraqis in U.S. Dollars

In the first stage, which was to last for only a few months, we would pay the Iraqi people—government employees, workers at state-owned enterprises, pensioners—in *U.S. dollars*. Paying Iraqis in dollars had a number of rationales. First, the U.S. dollar was used and traded in Iraq and, as in most countries, the Iraqi people were familiar with it. Second, the dollar was a stable currency and itself would provide stability. Third, it would allow us to avoid printing the Saddam dinars in any significant quantity, thereby preventing inflation, or a drop in the value of the dinar. Of course, paying in dollars had to be a short-term or interim part of the plan, because we did not want to give any impression that the United States was going to dollarize

Iraq. No one in the interagency objected to the two-stage plan, and it also appealed to our international coalition. Coincidentally, the U.K. Treasury was thinking along the same lines and readily approved of the idea.

Making the first stage of the plan operational presented a series of challenges. A serious problem was that we had no appropriations from Congress to make payments in dollars. How would we get the dollars to pay the Iraqis? After some brainstorming, we came up with an ingenious idea: As we prepared to put together a plan to freeze the assets currently controlled by Saddam after his regime fell, I found out that the United States had frozen regime assets during the first Gulf War. We estimated that about $1.7 billion remained frozen in banks in the United States, funds that were just sitting there for all these years unusable by Saddam.

Could we use Saddam's frozen assets to pay Iraqis after his government fell? After researching the legal implications, our Treasury lawyers determined that it was in fact legal for the President to require U.S. banks to "vest" the frozen funds, or assign rights to them, to the U.S. Treasury. To do so, the President would use emergency powers, as updated by the USA Patriot Act. This meant we could implement Stage One of the plan without getting funds appropriated—a process we could not count on in the days immediately following a military intervention. The plan dictated that on or near the start of Operation Iraqi Freedom, President Bush would issue an executive order calling on U.S. banks to vest the frozen funds with the U.S. Treasury. The banks would actually send the money to the Federal Reserve Bank of New York, which would serve as Treasury's fiscal agent.

With these funds in the bank, we would then be authorized to send the actual cash to Iraq. Logistically, we would do so by shipping small-denomination dollar bills from the New York Fed's warehouse in East Rutherford, New Jersey. The cash would be loaded onto trucks and driven down the New Jersey Turnpike to Andrews Air Force Base, where it would be loaded onto military aircraft and flown to Iraq.

In order to determine who exactly to pay, we would have to wait until Saddam's regime fell and our people arrived in Baghdad to work with the civil servants in the finance ministry on payroll lists. David Nummy would then be on the ground in Iraq to make this determination. We knew that the payments system was based on cash so that the dollars would have to be shipped around the country.

GETTING THE PRESIDENT'S APPROVAL FOR STAGE ONE

I had discussed these ideas with Secretary Snow many times as we developed a final plan, but we needed President Bush's approval for the go-ahead. On the morning of March 12, 2003, in a meeting of the National Security Council in the Situation Room, I distributed a handout consisting of three PowerPoint slides and entitled "Currency Decision for Post-Saddam Iraq." When it came time for the financial part of the briefing, Secretary Snow led off the presentation.

He started in his typically generous way by saying that "we are lucky to have such a distinguished economist as John Taylor working on this plan." He then described the plan, using slides to outline the interim dollar concept. With the first slide, he explained that "As soon as control over the Iraqi government is established," we plan to "use US dollars to pay civil servants and pensioners." We would "allow other currencies—Swiss dinars, Saddam dinars—to circulate with dollars at flexible exchange rates. . . . Later depending on the situation on the ground we would decide about the new currency or simply use Swiss dinars in place of the Saddam dinar." President Bush asked for more information on how we planned to pay the pensioners and I answered that we would obtain lists from the finance ministry and then get the word out to the pensioners to visit various central locations to pick up the cash.

The second slide, labeled "How we will do it?", focused on operations, indicating, for example, that we could ship $100 million in small denominations to Baghdad with one week's notice, and that we would pay people the "equivalent of what they are paid currently in real terms." President Bush objected to that aspect of the plan, saying that he wanted to pay people "more than what they were getting paid under Saddam." We adjusted the plan accordingly.

The third slide was labeled "Alternatives" and covered the three options that we could pursue after the interim plan was in place. This discussion went quickly because there was no reason then to decide what to do. President Bush approved the plan with the understanding that we would decide among the three options at a time when we knew the situation on the ground. Before the meeting, I had mentioned to Secretary Snow that I had discussed the plan with Alan Greenspan. At the end of the briefing, Snow mentioned that Greenspan approved. Secretary Powell joked: "Hey, do we really need his sign-off on this?"

DEALING WITH LAST-MINUTE GLITCHES

An executive order from the President requires full interagency legal vetting, and while the Treasury lawyers were confident that the order was legal, there was always a risk that lawyers from another agency could find a problem during the vetting process that could derail the plan. I was worried that the plan would be stuck in the interagency vetting process if and when the war started; that I did not know when the war would begin deepened my concern. The vesting order was exactly the type of complex issue that can get the interagency process bogged down—there are many equities and risks. In fact, approval of the executive order did get held up in the interagency process in the last few days. The major concern was that the vesting would result in lawsuits from victims of Saddam Hussein who might want to make claims on the frozen funds. If, for example, they had been harmed by Saddam's regime, perhaps by injury to themselves or their loved ones in the first Gulf War, they may want compensation.

This was a serious matter, of course, but I did not want it to hold back our plan. While the legal debates were cleared up in time, I had to bird-dog the process, emphasizing the need to expedite the vetting process in interagency meetings. The financial rationale for rushing was obvious to financial types like me, but other people thought it was equally important to get the legalities right. I explained the situation to David Aufhauser, Treasury's general counsel. He understood the urgency and worked out a clever compromise in which the executive order would contain an exception for people who had already initiated claims. Moreover, explicitly stating that using the frozen funds for the Iraqi people was in the interest of the United States would reduce the legal basis for future claims. We judged that the exception would be small and the U.S. interest clause would diminish legal problems.

Soon, another bureaucratic roadblock popped up. By way of a complex accounting process, our payments experts—Don Hammond and his team—had to make sure that authorization to disburse the funds shifted from the Secretary of the Treasury to the Secretary of Defense so that the military could take charge when the money was moved onto the military plane at Andrews Air Force Base. The Treasury legal staff and payments experts had to jump over many legal hurdles to make this happen. Of course, it was not an everyday occurrence to ask the interagency legal process to approve the Secretary of the Treasury handing over responsibility for hundreds of millions of dollars in cash to the Secretary of Defense. And even more unusual, these funds were not appropriated by Congress, which put them in a whole different legal category. I could understand that people wanted to check on legal and political issues and make sure it was okay. I just didn't want the process to delay paying people in Baghdad.

Finally, there was one crucial precaution to take care of. We wanted to make sure that in the event of a war, the military entering Iraq would not say or do something inadvertently that would cause the value of the dinar to fall sharply. In order to keep the dinar from depreciating, the military needed to issue a statement assuring the Iraqis that the Saddam dinar would be accepted for payments and that no one in the coalition would do anything to cause it to fall. Pete Pace was particularly concerned about this problem, and we worked closely with Doug Feith's office in the Defense Department to resolve it. Doug drafted language on March 19, which I edited and cleared before it was sent to the appropriate people at CENTCOM for use in the orders to troops in the field. His draft stated among other things that the military should announce that the civilian authorities "will accept those dinars as legal tender for fees, taxes, sales by state entities. . . ."

GOING OPERATIONAL

So, with all the last-minute details attended to, the President issued Executive Order 13290, "Confiscating and Vesting Certain Iraqi Property," on March 20, 2003, exactly as planned. According to Section 1 of the order, "All blocked funds held in the United States in accounts in the name of the Government of Iraq, the Central Bank of Iraq, Rafidain Bank, Rasheed Bank, or the State Organization for Marketing Oil are hereby confiscated and vested in the Department of the Treasury, except for the following. . . ." The exception was that any funds that had already been claimed in a legal suit would not be vested, as Dave Aufhauser had arranged in his compromise. As planned, the executive order also stated that "I [GEORGE W. BUSH, the President of the United States of America] intend that such vested property should be used to assist the Iraqi people and to assist in the reconstruction of Iraq, and determine that such use would be in the interest of and for the benefit of the United States."

Now, with the order issued, we needed to set up an account at the New York Fed. Secretary John Snow sent a letter to New York Fed president Bill McDonough stating: "Pursuant to Section 15 of the Federal Reserve Act, the FRBNY [Federal Reserve Bank of New York] is hereby authorized and directed, as fiscal agent of the United States, to . . . Establish a new account on its books in the name of 'U.S. Treasury Special Purpose Account' . . . until FRBNY receives further instructions from the Department of the Treasury. . . ." Sixteen commercial banks known to hold blocked Iraqi property received letters, including Citigroup, Bank of America, and JP Morgan Chase.

The amount of money sent by the banks to the New York Fed amounted to $1.7 billion, just about equal to our estimates of the frozen money. Thankfully, the exception held back very little money. Now we could move the funds.

As fund requests arrived from Iraq, Don Hammond authorized the New York Fed to withdraw the dollars from the account. As planned, the cash was removed from the Fed's warehouse, placed on armored trucks—including large armored tractor trailer trucks—and shipped by a convoy to Andrews Air Force Base. Once the money arrived at Andrews, the seals on the armored trucks were broken, the money was counted, and it was transferred from the truck pallets to special pallets ready to fit into the military transport plane. Once the cash was loaded on the plane, Treasury personnel were no longer responsible for the cash itself. That responsibility shifted to the Department of Defense. What happened to the money once it left Andrews was Brigadier General Edgar Stanton's assignment. He headed the 336th Finance Command, a group that provided the total financial management support for the military operation in Iraq. The 336th was given responsibility for implementing the cash plan on the ground, receiving the funds by air transport, and then disbursing them appropriately in Iraq. This was an unusual but appropriate part of their operations, that also included military pay and commercial vending services.

Some of our Treasury experts drove down to inspect the first few transfers from the armored trucks to the transport planes at Andrews. When they returned and reported to me that a successful shipment was on its way across the Atlantic, we all felt a deep sense of pride and accomplishment. The trip to Andrews to watch the loading was not unpleasant duty for Don Hammond and the people on his team, who had worked so long on this project.

CHAPTER EIGHT

Iraq Achieves Financial Stability

◆

W hen U.S. troops arrived in Baghdad and began searching through the palace grounds after Saddam's government fell in early April 2003, one of the soldiers
discovered some aluminum boxes filled with money. Each box held
$4 million in hundred-dollar bills, and there were at least one hun-
dred boxes. Some of the money was shrink-wrapped and marked as
having come from U.S. Federal Reserve regional banks, such as the
Federal Reserve Bank of San Francisco. Wisely, the soldiers reported
their discovery immediately and arranged for it to be shipped to
Camp Arifjan in Kuwait. The aluminum boxes were moved to Baghdad Airport and loaded onto C-130 transport planes. Because of the
valuable cargo, the pilots were not told where they were going until
after takeoff. When the money arrived in Kuwait, the soldiers of
the 336th Finance Command carefully counted it and stored it. The
soldiers were required to wear gym clothes—shorts and an Army
T-shirt—as they removed the currency from the boxes and fed them
into the counting machines, so no one would be tempted to stuff a wad
of hundred-dollar bills in their pockets. They counted $700 million.

A few days later, on April 23, our Treasury team—Van Jorstad, David Nummy, George Mullinax—arrived in Baghdad. When they met the central bank employees, one of the first things they were told was that Saddam had removed a billion dollars' worth of currency from the vaults—920 million U.S. dollars and 90 million euros—just before his regime fell. They told our team that Saddam gave written orders for the central bank to hand over the money to his son Qusay.

The central bank employees said they were worried about the loss of the dollars, and when we found out, we worried too. A central bank needs an adequate supply of foreign currency—foreign reserves—to carry out its responsibilities for maintaining financial stability. Especially during periods of enormous uncertainly like this, foreign reserves help provide stability for a country's currency—the Saddam dinar in this case. Like a defensive weapon, they ward off speculative attacks on the currency, which could cause a sharp depreciation or even a collapse. If people began to lose confidence and started selling the dinar, the central bank could use the foreign reserves—dollars or euros—to buy the dinar, supporting its value and restoring confidence. Also like an effective defensive weapon, the central bank had to have a large stockpile of foreign reserves to convince the markets that it could overcome any selling pressure. Saddam had nearly depleted the bank's foreign reserves, and this put the Iraqi currency in a precarious situation. The risks of a currency collapse were higher than I had anticipated, which increased the importance of a successful implementation of our currency plans.

IMPLEMENTATION OF STAGE ONE IN IRAQ

As stated in the terms of reference we worked out back in Washington, the main mission—for which David Nummy had the responsibility—was to assess the situation in the finance ministry, make contact with finance ministry officials, and begin to pay people. In other words, execute Stage One.

David and the rest of the team worked and slept in Saddam's old palace. They provided situation reports to me and the task force in Washington by satellite phone. In one of David's first calls after he arrived, he gave me the lay of the land, starting, at my request, with his personal situation: "Living conditions are bad here; there's no running water, there's broken glass all over the place, and there's a huge amount of dust flying in through the open windows. But at least we have five hundred rooms! Yesterday some people going to the Ag ministry were shot at, so it's not really a permissive environment yet. To get around you need armored personnel carriers." Van Jorstad corroborated: "We're sleeping in an inch thick of dust causing respiratory problems in the mornings and there are no windows in the part of the building that we're housed in. And we're already running low on insect repellent!"

David's description of the situation in the finance ministry was grimmer, and also pointed to a serious obstacle to the execution of Stage One of the plan. "The finance ministry and the central bank are completely looted and damaged by fire," he reported. It looked like all the payroll records were destroyed, making it impossible to determine who should be paid and how much. This was not the report I was hoping to hear.

You can imagine how overwhelming it was to handle these problems in such a difficult environment, with the buildings damaged and no place to work, but dealing with them was David's highest priority. Although their buildings were virtually destroyed, soon the employees of the ministries began to show up and stand outside, trying to figure out what to do next, asking our soldiers what they should do. After getting a tip from the military that a group of Iraqis from the finance ministry wanted to meet with him, David arranged a meeting at the convention center. About twenty people showed up. It was of course hard to determine immediately whether they were supporters of Saddam or serious members of the Baath party, but after describing their responsibilities in the ministry, David was convinced they were professionals, not political hacks. From that meeting on, the Iraqis took a professional approach and tried to work cooperatively with David.

At that first meeting, David explained that he intended to get the government up and running as soon as possible and he wanted to pay people. The Iraqis understood the goals perfectly, and once David got to meet, build trust, and talk in detail to them, they told him that before the looting and destruction of the buildings started, they had removed and saved the employment records. The director of the pension office in the finance ministry had downloaded the records of every pensioner in Iraq—1.8 million people (not including pensioners in the northern Kurdish area) and their families—onto floppy disks and put them on a personal computer, which he then took home. Further, the central bank employees said that they too had moved records and computers to an old central bank headquarters building nearby. Some of the records were copied by hand and some onto old computers that had not been updated in fifteen years. They put the records in safekeeping in anticipation of the war. Despite the damage and the looting, it looked like our team would be able to use the records of pensioners and civil servants and start paying them. A huge obstacle to the plan had been removed, thanks to the foresight and diligence of the Iraqis.

David had to work closely with General Stanton and the 336th Finance Command to actually make the payments. As he reported back to me, "General Stanton assured our team that he was prepared to receive, store, secure, and transport currency to destinations that would serve as points of disbursement. He wisely made it clear that he views revealing details of the movement of large amounts of currency as imprudent."

Within a short time we were paying most civil servants in the country, totaling around 1 million in the center and south and 320,000 in the north. It took a few weeks to figure out how much to pay people because Saddam used a system in which base pay was very small and actual pay depended on one's loyalty to the regime. But even before our team had worked out a pay scale, they began emergency payments to railroad, port, and other key workers in Baghdad—a total of 3,226 workers, according to our initial reports. At the start, each worker received $20 in emergency funds. The military would deliver the dollars to the Iraqis, who would hand out the money to other Iraqis while U.S. government employees watched.

Although people in most parts of the country were happy to receive U.S. dollars, some oil workers in Basra said they wanted to be paid in Saddam dinars. No one seemed to have a good explanation, but the U.K. military, who had responsibility for Basra, supported this idea, and I decided it would be acceptable if limited to a few cases. That the team on the ground checked back with Washington on this adjustment in the plan, and that we responded promptly, indicated that our "reach-back" operation was working well.

All around, things were rolling. The first ten currency shipments from New Jersey arrived in Kuwait and were then delivered to Iraq. Eventually shipments were sent directly to Baghdad. The cash was in small denominations, as requested: $1, $5, $10, and $20 dollar bills. As later documented by Roger Bezdek of Treasury staff, who was integral to the operation, nine cash shipments totaling $1.708 billion of vested assets were made to Iraq. In sum the cash weighed 237.3 tons.* But the most important news was that there was no financial or currency collapse. The dinar did depreciate sharply at the start of the military operation, but the currency soon appreciated back to near its pre-invasion level. Thus one of the major objectives—and my major concern since I had been given this responsibility—had been accomplished.

We endeavored to communicate with the wider world about what we were doing. We thought our successes would help inspire confidence and international support. And there were several stories in the major papers in April about Stage One, with headlines like "Dollars Are Sent to Iraq to Replace Dinars: Stopgap Move Is Intended for Emergency Payments in Effort to Quiet Unrest" (*Wall Street Journal*, April 16) or "3,226 Get $20 as U.S. Begins Work on Iraq's Economy" (*Washington Post*, April 30) or "Iraq to Run On Dollars Till It Gets New Currency" (*New York Times*, April 18). In this

*Roger H. Bezdek, "Using Vested Assets for the Reconstruction of Iraq," *Public Fund Digest*, vol. 5, no. 2, 2005.

last story I explained that "We will pay in dollars initially. It's an interim measure, and we're not going to do it any longer than we have to. But the dollar has value and it's a stable currency." As for the new currency, I mentioned that there were several options, but that "This is something the Iraqis will have to decide on and have a lot of ownership on."

On April 29, I went over to the Pentagon for a meeting that Paul Wolfowitz had set up for deputy department and agency heads who, like me, had personnel assigned to ORHA. He had arranged for a video conference with General Garner from Baghdad. We assembled in the Pentagon's communications center, took our places around a large conference table, and waited for Garner and his team to be beamed in from Saddam's palace. When the connection was secure, Jay Garner reported on the state of play. He reported on the progress in establishing working relationships between the Americans and the Iraqis in the ministries, going over each ministry in detail. When I asked him to elaborate on conditions in the finance ministry and central bank, Garner noted the severe damage to the buildings and praised David, Van, and George by name for their extraordinary work in, as he put it, "standing up" the ministries and getting people paid. Garner reported that the payments had lifted the mood of people in Baghdad during those first few confusing days.

Stage Two: The Iraqi Currency Exchange

Given the success of Stage One, we decided it was clearly time to move on Stage Two of our plan. More and more, conditions on the ground indicated that we could and should move quickly. The image of the Iraqi Central Bank with its foreign exchange reserves depleted was enough to send shivers up the back of a monetary economist like me. We did not know how the security situation would evolve, and despite the success of Stage One, we could not be sure that financial conditions would not sour before the currency reform. Moreover, recalling the pleas of the Iraqi expats, I wanted to help the Iraqis get

Saddam Hussein's face off their currency as soon as possible. When I saw that Stage One was working, I began to push ahead on Stage Two, circulating advocacy papers and frequently raising the issue at NSC meetings on Iraq.

In one paper, Tim Simpson and I laid out the steps so that people could see the need to start now: "to carry out this second phase of the currency plan, the following actions must be taken. . . . It will take several months. . . . so it is essential to begin now: 1. Contact De La Rue to say we are interested in their doing the printing and . . . negotiate a contract. 2. Authorize the use of vested Iraqi assets to pay for the printing of the dinars. . . . 3. Finish the contract with De La Rue. 4. Begin printing," and so on.

At the same time, I tried to expedite things internationally. As early as March 23, I telephoned Jon Cunliffe, my British counterpart, and explained that we would be calling on them to help us move quickly to the next stage. Later on, during an April 1 conference call with Cunliffe and representatives from Australia, Japan, and Spain, I stressed the same urgency. Jon said that there was too little clarity about the structure of the Iraqi government to move quickly on issues like currency.

On April 11, I had a breakfast meeting with these same representatives in a small room off the side of the restaurant in the Watergate Hotel. Although we made progress on other issues, our "coalition of the willing" was not so willing to move ahead quickly on the currency before we were further along in establishing an Iraqi government. At this time, we were still meeting quietly and separately from our German and French colleagues because of the highly charged political tensions due to disagreement about the war. When I saw our G7 counterpart from Germany, Caio Koch-Weser, having breakfast in the main part of the restaurant, I expected the tensions to spill over to the finance area, but he did not notice us.

John Snow raised the currency issue with Chancellor Gordon Brown in several calls. Regarding the currency plan and British support for it, Brown simply said that the "IMF could help us on this. We will try to get more information from De la Rue." Reading between the chancellor's lines you could tell that the British Treasury was not yet ready to move ahead, although Mervyn King of the Bank of England, a recognized monetary expert, was even more convinced than I that we should move now.

We also made an effort to discuss our plans with the Arab world. On May 1, I held a briefing at the Foreign Press Center with Al Larson and Dov Zakheim. When Thomas Gorgussian of *Al-Wafd* in Egypt asked a question about the currency, I used the opportunity to get the message out. He said: "Secretary Taylor, how and when are you going to solve the issue of Swiss dinar and Saddam dinar and American dollars?" I answered: "With respect to what will ultimately be decided about the currency, that is a decision for the people of Iraq to make. And we're going to be very happy to work with the international community. The International Monetary Fund has already begun to work on this, but to give them the assistance that they need to make it a smooth operation—and just one comparison with Afghanistan, if I may—we also gave advice to the Government of Afghanistan, and when they came in, and they had the interim authority, they decided that they were going to do a new currency. We assisted them, and it was a very successful operation. That may be how it works in Iraq, but it's really their decision."

Where appropriate, we also tried to provide information about our rationale for expediting the new currency to the U.S. media. Michael Phillips of *The Wall Street Journal* wrote a story on the various options for a new currency (what I call Stage Two here) on May 19, "U.S. Wants Fresh Supply of Iraqi Currency," which described the policy situation well. I was quoted as saying, "We can be very flexible on the design, but we have a strong emphasis on speed."

The President's Approval for Stage Two

To move ahead—whether now or later—President Bush would have to review the situation and sign off on the next stage of the plan. The President was interested in the currency issue, and at a number of NSC meetings in April and May on other topics, he asked questions about the currency and financial issues more generally. I would always try to address them briefly, and during one of those NSC meeting conversations, Condi Rice interrupted, "John is preparing a full briefing so that we can address all these financial issues systematically." President Bush agreed.

The NSC scheduled me to make the full presentation to President Bush on May 9. Our Iraq Financial Task Force did a superb job preparing the slides in advance. Frank Miller of the NSC suggested that it would be best to circulate the slides to State, Defense, the Joint Chiefs, the CIA, and other agencies before presenting them to the President so that no one would feel out of the loop. I agreed.

I briefly summarized the May 9 meeting in the prologue to this book. It started on security and political issues and then moved on to "Iraq Financial Issues," which was the title of the ten-page Power-Point briefing we had prepared. I began with a quick review of the situation in the Iraqi currency markets. One of my briefing charts showed how the value of the dinar had declined sharply at the start of the war, but then recovered rapidly and had since stabilized. As is typical in charts of currencies, an *upward* movement in the number of dinars per dollar is a *depreciation*, which causes no end of confusion to people who do not study the currency markets every day (which included, of course, everyone in the Sit Room that day except me). "Next time, let's do the briefing charts on the currency so up means appreciation, not depreciation," I told the Treasury staff when I debriefed them about the meeting with the President later that day and thanked them for their work.

As usual there was a lot of back-and-forth with President Bush during the NSC briefing. He asked, "Why did the value of the dinar recover?" I answered, "Well, we worked hard to make this happen by using dollars on an interim basis and by emphasizing that the dinar would still be accepted for payments." I reviewed the currency plan that the President had approved back on March 12, referring to the bullets on a slide labeled "Interim Currency Plan":

- Vest frozen assets and use some of them to finance dollar payments to civil servants and pensioners;
- Make payments to civil servants and pensioners in U.S. dollars;

- State publicly that dinars, dollars, and other currencies will be accepted as a means of payments;
- State publicly that both types of dinar will be redeemed when final decisions of currency regime is made;
- Do not set exchange rates; let market determine.

I then listed measures that showed how each element of the plan was working, using a slide labeled "Interim Currency Plan—On Track":

- Frozen Iraqi assets successfully vested in March ($1.7 billion)
- Dollars shipped to the region
    - $20 million arrived on April 12, 2003
    - $76.1 million arrived on May 6, 2003
- Mechanism established for making "emergency" $20 payments
    - U.S. military transports cash to payment location and delivers to Iraqis
    - Iraqis provide receipt for funds, pay against employee list
    - Signed pay list returned to Coalition observer
- Payment complete to date
    - 74,000 port workers, oil workers, rail workers, and others paid on several locations in the south and Baghdad
    - 338,000 civil servants/pensioners paid in Northern Iraq
- Some deviations from the plan decided on the ground
    - Equivalent of $2.9 million in payments made in dinars by UK military

I explained how, with Stage One continuing successfully, it was necessary to move ahead with Stage Two as soon as possible so that Iraq could have a single high-quality currency without Saddam's face on it. After some further questions concerning market reaction and logistics, the President agreed.

I emphasized that once we introduced the new currency, decisions about what kind of monetary policy to choose would be made by the Iraqi Interim Authority, which we would work with closely. Setting up an independent central bank would be a high priority.

GOING OPERATIONAL WITH STAGE TWO

After obtaining the President's approval, we needed a date to start the operations and we needed to work back from that date, setting timelines to make sure the objectives were completed on time. By this time, the organizational structure and people on the ground in Iraq were changing. On May 6, President Bush announced that Jerry Bremer, a former State Department anti-terrorism official, would be the administrator of the newly created Coalition Provisional Authority (CPA), which would replace ORHA and Jay Garner. Peter McPherson, whom I had already hired, would therefore join the CPA rather than ORHA, and report to Bremer, much as Jorstad, Nummy, and Mullinax had reported to Garner. The CPA would have ground responsibility for Stage Two of the plan.

On June 4, I testified before the Senate Foreign Relations Committee about the currency plan. Dov Zakheim and Al Larson also testified that day. I viewed this as an opportunity to report on how Stage One of our plan was working and to publicly thank our team in Iraq: "These successes are due to the work of experienced and dedicated people and to the contingency plans laid out months in advance of the war." And I went on: "We began selecting people for our financial teams back in January. The first wave was deployed to Kuwait in March. These were some of the first people who went to Baghdad in April. . . ."

Even during this early period, the congressional hearings on Iraq were contentious. Some expressed skepticism about whether there had been enough prewar planning for reconstruction. Perhaps because my financial issues were technical, many of the tough questions were addressed to the others, and in particular to Zakheim. Frustration was clearly evident from, for example, Republican Senator Chuck Hagel of Nebraska: "Dr. Zakheim, could you provide this committee with a number of the American troops in Iraq?"

"Well, I believe the actual number right now is a classified one."

"You're kidding? We have newspaper reporters at the table here, and they may want to tell you, because we read about it almost daily in every major newspaper."

Democratic Senator Joe Biden of Connecticut asked about reopening the ministries. I answered, "In the case of the finance ministry, our people are working with the civil servants in that ministry and have been since the day they arrived. . . . Same with the Central Bank. They are engaged with the people who have been employed for 30 or 40 years in the central bank, very qualified dedicated people. They are thinking about the currency and what monetary policy should look like. . . ." Senator Biden seemed satisfied, responding, "That is all I want to know . . . how each and every one of the ministries is working, relative to the way you just described the Central Bank."*

SETTING A DATE CERTAIN

Several days after testifying to the Senate Foreign Relations Committee about the plan, I went to Baghdad to visit our team and nail down a specific date to start the currency exchange. I was very pleased with how things were going. Our team was housed in Saddam's old palace, and living conditions were improved compared with the first situation reports from Nummy, though still quite spartan.

I was greatly relieved to meet former Navy Admiral David Oliver, the top CPA budget official and the person who would later take charge of the currency distribution in Iraq. I wanted to have a savvy budget person who could work with the Iraqis on their budget planning. In other post-conflict situations, the IMF would provide this assistance, but the IMF was not doing this in Iraq. As soon as I met Dave, I knew he was agile with numbers and could make sensible assumptions, a rare skill. I reviewed his budget estimates and com-

*"Iraq Stabilization and Reconstruction: International Contributions and Resources," Hearing before the Committee on Foreign Relations, United States Senate, June 4, 2003, pp. 26, 71.

pared them with what we were doing in our reach-back operation in Washington. They matched closely. Dave was one of those practical budget people with whom I liked doing business.

My meeting with Jerry Bremer in his Baghdad office also went well. He decided to give the currency plan a high priority, and had discussed the plan with members of the Iraqi Governing Council. Not surprisingly, they wanted to go ahead with the currency exchange. They wanted to use the old prewar design, the Swiss dinar, but to change the denominations by adding more zeros so that it would exchange one for one with the depreciated Saddam dinar. After consultations with our team and with the Iraqis, Bremer decided that the exchange rate for Swiss dinars would be 150 new dinars per 1 Swiss dinar, and 1 new dinar per 1 Saddam dinar. This generated a little resentment among some Kurds because the exchange rate was then well above 150. All this sounded fine to me and I was pleased that Bremer had decided to start the plan and set a date for the exchange. The exchange would begin on October 15 and end on January 15, 2004. My trip to Baghdad had achieved its purpose.

On July 7, 2003, Bremer issued the official order on the currency plan:

> . . . On October 15, new Iraqi dinar banknotes will be available to the Iraqi people. . . . We have not designed a new currency for Iraq. Only a sovereign Iraqi government could take that decision. So we have taken the designs from the former national dinar (the "Swiss" dinar). But the new notes will be impossible to confuse with the "Swiss" dinar, as both the colors and the denominations will be different. . . . The new dinars will be printed in a full range of denominations: in 50s; 250s; 1,000s; 5,000s; 10,000s; and 25,000s. They will be higher quality and last longer. They will be very hard to forge, and thus be notes in which all Iraqis can be confident.
>
> On 15 October, these new notes will be ready. . . . After Oct 15 you will have three months to swap your existing notes for the new ones, so there will be no need to rush. There will be plenty of new notes available.

The currency exchange was now officially launched. It was going to be a tremendous undertaking. We had worked through the strategy in Washington, and now it was time to address tactical issues, such as the physical printing of the currency, distribution, communication, and security. The Treasury task force in Washington provided essential help with these details, including estimates of how much currency would be needed. Tom Simpson first calculated that the swap would require 2,300 tons, or the equivalent of twenty-seven 747 planeloads. Our team also worked with the Secret Service on an anti-counterfeit program.

Tom Simpson and Tom Ferguson, director of the U.S. Bureau of Engraving and Printing, negotiated the printing contract with the British firm De La Rue. This was a highly expedited contract and would require using a number of printing plants around the world simultaneously. To further expedite the process, the CPA paid for the printing, which allowed it to use existing Iraqi procurement rules, with the flexibility to proceed quickly with De La Rue. Applying U.S. rules would have required a lengthy proposal process.

With great diplomatic and logistical skill, Ian Much, the CEO of De La Rue, and James Hussey, the director for currency, put together a consortium of printing specialists. I have never come across a bunch of people in a business firm who were more excited about a project—proud to be able to contribute and doing the job with amazing speed. The Spanish agreed that their Royal Mint would print some of the notes, and, in the end, they produced nearly half of the 250 dinar notes free of charge.

On July 23, 2003, there was an NSC meeting at the White House. The President opened by thanking Don Rumsfeld for the military's accomplishments in rooting out Saddam's sons, Uday and Qusay, from hiding in Mosul. They would no longer be persecuting and torturing people, having been killed in the attack by American forces. The President then called on General Abizaid, who, via video, reviewed the security and political issues, reporting on Uday and Qusay's demise, and other recent events. Jerry Bremer then went over some accomplishments in his area. First was the announcement of the new currency plan; second was the submission of the first Iraqi budget; and third was the new independent central bank law. Understandably, these financial announcements did not bring about the same euphoric reaction as the news about Uday and Qusay—either in the Sit Room or in the media—but I knew they were important and was delighted that Jerry chose to highlight them. But it was way too early for high-fives. In fact, trouble was already brewing.

An Appeal to Replenish the Central Bank's Foreign Reserves

By June 2003 we learned that the hundreds of millions of dollars found on Saddam's palace grounds was the money he stole from the central bank and I requested that it be returned to the bank. I argued that case in an NSC deputies' meeting that Jerry Bremer attended. I explained the problems of running a central bank with little or no reserves, and the worries I still had about a collapse of the currency, at least until the new currency was in circulation. But despite my plea and urging by Tom Simpson and all the financial experts at Treasury, most people in our government, including Jerry Bremer, did not think putting hundreds of millions of dollars back into the central bank was the best use of the money at that time.

In most people's minds, using the funds for reconstruction projects to help the Iraqi people was a better idea. With no congressional appropriation required or complex procurement rules to follow, the found money was ideally suited for this purpose. In fact, the 336th Finance Command set up a new reconstruction system whereby brigade commanders would be given $25,000 for reconstruction purposes. Commanders would then be capable of making an immediate positive impact on the Iraqi people by initiating projects like water systems and sanitation repair. The $25,000 program worked so well that the amounts were quickly increased, creating a $100,000 program. The $100,000-per-commander program was funded largely by the money that had been stolen by Qusay from the central bank.

A MID-COURSE CORRECTION

By mid-August, I became concerned about the operations of the currency exchange. Some things were going fine. For example, the contract with the British printers De La Rue was on track. De La Rue had already arranged to do the printing in seven different locations around the world: Sri Lanka, Malta, Kenya, Spain, Germany, and two in Britain (London and Newcastle). I was also getting reports that the transportation plan for the currency was being successfully contracted.

On August 8, Tom Simpson held a briefing in my office with a number of people who were scheduled to leave for Baghdad that evening to work on the currency exchange. Several people came from the consulting firm Bearing Point who, under contract from USAID, would help out with logistics. A young woman from the Secret Service came by, bringing a new manual she'd prepared on ways to detect counterfeit Iraqi currency during the exchange. Copies of this anti-counterfeiting manual were to be distributed throughout Iraq to the people who would be working on the exchange. However, I was concerned that this work, however professional its execution, was only just underway. My questions revealed that there were no plans in place to train people—for example, in counterfeit detection—in Iraq. I asked that they get back to Tom as soon as they arrived in Baghdad to let us know what was happening with on-the-ground training. When they arrived, they did not seem to be able to learn much about the operation at all, indicating some serious communication and coordination problems on the ground.

But the most convincing evidence that we had a problem on our hands was revealed by our "reach-back" process. Around mid-July, Elaine Grigsby and Tom Simpson developed a detailed checklist and timeline for the CPA staff in Baghdad to follow for the currency exchange process. Elaine drew on her experience working on the Afghanistan currency exchange the previous year. Tom and Elaine set up weekly conference calls with the CPA people who would run the currency exchange, to monitor their progress on the plan and to provide assistance—exactly what a "reach-back" service should do. On the Treasury end of these calls, experts from the Secret Service and the Bureau of Engraving and Printing participated along with Elaine and Tom. But over time, the CPA participants in Baghdad started providing less information and showed less willingness to participate in the process. This raised, in Tom's words, a big red flag, and he and Elaine came to me with their concerns. They were afraid that we were behind in training the Iraqi people how to work at the distribution points, set up the distribution points, and arrange for facilities at the logistic hubs in the north and south, as well as in the public outreach, the anti-counterfeiting plans, and the currency destruction process. These two professionals would not raise an issue like this with me without serious cause, and I said I would address it with Bremer as soon as possible.

Moreover, security looked like it was going to be an increasingly difficult problem. On August 19, a terrorist attack tragically killed the highly skilled United Nations envoy to Iraq, Sergio Vieira de Mello. On August 20, the attack and its implications were taken up at an NSC meeting. The President was on video from his ranch in Crawford, Texas. Condi Rice was in the Situation Room along with myself and several others. Colin Powell was in New York, and Jerry Bremer was in Baghdad. The President opened, and in a forceful but inspiring tone said: "This is an ugly day for freedom. It should strengthen our resolve. We need to remind people of that. We are not going to retreat." He expressed concern that the World Bank and IMF were leaving Iraq. Later in the meeting, I mentioned that another UN Security Council resolution might help get the IMF and the World Bank back, and Colin Powell said he was working on that. Although the resolution was passed, neither institution would return to Iraq for several years. If they met with the Iraqis, it would always be in Amman, or Washington, or some other city. The IMF could have been helpful in advising the central bank on its operations after the currency exchange. Because they left, we had to increase the number of our own monetary experts on our team in Baghdad.

When Jerry Bremer next visited Washington, I shared the concerns that Elaine and Tom raised about the currency operation. Bremer had gone public that the exchange was to begin on October 15 and we did not want to disappoint people or shake their confidence with a delay. Worse, we did not want to start the exchange and find out there were some major flaws. He told me that he too was concerned. We agreed that we needed to do two things: first, have some monetary experts assess the situation; and second, hire an operational person—someone who could bridge military and financial issues—to focus on this full time in Baghdad. I asked Tom Simpson and Elaine Grigsby to go to Baghdad to review the situation and make recommendations. Until we found someone to handle operations, Jerry assigned David Oliver to take full charge of the currency exchange. I had great respect for Dave, and I was greatly relieved by news of his participation, even if it would be temporary.

David Oliver immediately set up a currency exchange "war room" in Saddam's old palace in Baghdad with plans and maps on the walls and with all the key players—the financial people, the PR people, logistical experts, security contractors, the military, and so on. From this war room, he set up a process to run things on a day-to-day basis. He put up a white board and each day he would write down on it the assignments for people. The next day they would return and report that they had accomplished their mission, or else have a very good excuse.

The person Dave found to run things on a permanent basis was Hugh Tant, a retired Army brigadier general who was therefore well connected in the military. Thirty-three of General Tant's associates perished in the 9/11 attacks on the Pentagon, where he was responsible for budget issues before retiring on October 1, 2001. I interviewed Hugh in my office before he left for Baghdad, and he also got a briefing from Tom Simpson. I thought Hugh was just the right guy—experienced, determined, and patriotic. It was clear that during these interviews Hugh began to realize the enormity of the job he was agreeing to do. It was a hot Washington August day and Tom Simpson recalled his briefing. "As I briefed Hugh, the sweat started to come off his brow and he seemed to get hotter and hotter as I told him the details and our concerns. After we were done and Hugh was walking out the door, he told me in a worried voice, 'I've never failed before and I don't want to fail this time.'" That was the kind of attitude that so many people had during this operation that was essential for its success.

After Dave Oliver took charge of the currency exchange in Baghdad, things got back on track. To prevent further glitches, I insisted on daily situation reports ("sitreps") from Iraq to Treasury and other finance ministries in our coalition. Dave Oliver did just that.

Dave's first sitrep was dated September 14. It began: "John Taylor sent a team out here to review our plans for the Iraq Currency Exchange and to remind me that there were people in Canberra, London, and Washington who were very interested in the currency exchange and I might be able to reduce the angst if they saw some regular reports. My apologies. We will begin with daily reports until I feel they are no longer useful." He then started with the first report; and later, after Hugh took over, he would continue to write them until the exchange was completed.

The first sitrep went on: "We have established a 'war room' here with all our reference material, and the plans on the walls so everybody can see both what should be done today, in the next few days, the potential bottlenecks and our worries." He also reported that the first wave of the security force—570 Fijians—was about to arrive.

BACK ON TRACK

In Dave's next sitrep, he wrote: "We have started incorporating the initial recommendations and insights from the U.S. Treasury advisers (Elaine Grigsby and Tom Simpson) into the project, particularly our risk mitigation plan and in the audit process," and he reported that "The new project manager, BG (ret) Hugh Tant, arrived." From that time on things moved efficiently and professionally. Symbolically, the Iraqi Currency Exchange, which quickly became ICE for short, adopted two mottoes: "Teamwork That Works" and "Delivery Under Fire."

On September 17, the first shipment of currency arrived in Baghdad. The project had entered the execution phase. The money was flown from Manston Air Base, in England; the 747s were provided by a British firm, Hanover Aviation Freight. The Iraqi deputy central bank governor, Ahmed Al-Jabouri, went to England so he could fly back with the currency. By this time, the public relations plan had been developed and part of the strategy was to give the exchange this kind of high-level attention and publicity.

On September 25, the third shipment arrived, and importantly the two Russian-made IL-76 aircraft, which could carry up to 40 tons each, also arrived. These planes would make the deliveries in the north and south hubs. As Hugh Tant put it, "The very sight of these magnificent birds felt like 80 tons were lifted from our shoulders!!!"

And on October 15, "Today is a monumental day!!!!!" Hugh Tant wrote. There was some press coverage, but the bad news stories always seemed to get much more coverage than good news stories, a fact that became old news to us real fast. The most important news that first opening day was that the exchange was orderly. Larry Blume, one of our Treasury experts, visited four banks in the Al Mamsour area of Baghdad and spoke to the managers. "Security was good: about 20 Iraqi guards outside each bank, and central bank security people inside the bank. The crowds were light. People seemed to like the new currency. The public messaging that there would be plenty to go around seemed to be working."

Hugh Tant's ability to work with the military, using personal relationships to deal with the problem of coordinating different government agencies, made him very effective. He was working for Bremer and the CPA, but as a recently retired general he personally knew generals serving in Iraq, including Rick Sanchez, the top commander in the field. Tant and Sanchez had lived across the street from each other for a year at the Army War College. The way Hugh Tant put it was, "I'd just say, 'Hey Rick, I need this,' and it would happen." Another friend of Hugh Tant's was Ray Odierno, the commander of the Fourth Infantry Division. In November when the attacks in Samarra intensified, Odierno provided military escorts to back up the ICE security people. Depending on the security environment, the escorts could include infantry fighting vehicles, or even tanks and

Apache attack helicopters. The ICE security people themselves were former soldiers, working for the British firm Global Risk Strategies. Of the seven hundred security people, many hailed from Fiji, but others came from Australia, New Zealand, South Africa, and the United States.

During the month of November, reports indicated that the attacks on the convoys were increasing. On November 9, I asked Hugh Tant whether he needed more help. He answered immediately:

> *At this point we only need more prayers. I know that everything is being done to thwart the terrorist attacks with the force that we have and so we are going to continue our mission as planned. Our deliveries will be complete in the near future. Our efforts then will be to continue to haul old Dinar back to Baghdad for verification and destruction. Our convoy personnel are trained to the task and the military over here gives us excellent over watch support. We are fortunate to have had only a few incidents. Vigilance and persistence will get us through this. Thank you again for your support.*

On November 22, I learned of yet another incident that could threaten the operation. A DHL cargo aircraft (a 747 not involved with the currency swap) was hit by a surface-to-air missile shortly after takeoff from Baghdad International Airport. The flight crew returned to Baghdad and was able to land the aircraft, but the wing had been damaged. After this attack, our contractor, Hanover Aviation, said they did not want to fly 747s into Baghdad any more because the insurance rates became prohibitive. But this roadblock was cleared, too. Hanover would fly their 747 planes to an airfield in the UAE where the currency was loaded off the 747s onto two 707s for the flight to Baghdad.

In spite of the complications, the exchange continued. Remarkably, throughout all these attacks the currency exchange never lost any money. Some people asked me whether we might not want to delay the end of the exchange. I held firm that we could not even entertain that possibility. I also felt we shouldn't even discuss the idea openly. Deadlines are important and rumors of delay would have a negative impact as people would put off coming to the banks to get their new dinars. Also, delaying such a public event would create credibility problems for the United States and the CPA. I recall how, even then, the President insisted that we not delay the upcoming Iraqi election, which would take place about one year later. Perhaps in a small way credibility about meeting deadlines in the currency exchange helped build up credibility in other issues.

I requested that the Iraqis put out the word that the exchange would definitely end on the date planned. On December 20, Ahmed Al-Jabouri, the deputy central bank governor, held a press conference for Arab language media, including Al Jazeera, in which he stated: "Iraqi citizens have until January 15th to exchange their remaining old money. . . . Old dinar will be worthless after that date. There will be no extension to the January 15th deadline."

On December 24, Hugh Tant sent around, in place of his usual sitrep, a poem he called "The Soldier Outside My Door." He didn't give the author's name, but I later learned that it was written by Michael Marks, who titled the poem "A Soldier's Christmas." It is about a young soldier in a foreign land protecting a family's home from an attack by the enemy. The narrator, a member of that family, asks the soldier to come inside and get warm, but he respectfully declines:

> *"My Gramps died at Pearl on a day in December."*
> *Then he sighed. "That's a Christmas Gram always remembers.*
> *My dad stood his watch in the jungles of 'Nam,*
> *and now it is my turn and so, here I am.*
> *I've not seen my own son in more than a while,*
> *but my wife sends me pictures, he sure has her smile."*

> *"It seems all too little for all that you've done,*
> *for being away from your wife and your son."*
> *Then his eye welled a tear that held no regret,*
> *"Just tell us you love us, and never forget."*

It was a patriotic prelude to what would happen in January.

On January 15, 2004, the appointed day, Hugh Tant's sitrep opened with:

> *The Iraqi Central Bank had a big victory today—a great win for the people of Iraq. Today represents the culmination of a tremendous effort by a team of people from all walks of life. These quiet professionals hailed from Australia, Canada, Fiji, Great Britain, New Zealand, South Africa, and the USA. All of one mind: to help the Coalition Provisional Authority achieve success in support of the Central Bank of Iraq and the Iraqi people.*

In only a few months, enough currency to fill twenty-seven 747 planeloads was flown into Iraq from seven different printing plants around the world and then delivered by armed convoys to 240 locations around the country, distributed to a population of 25 million Iraqis in exchange for their old Saddam dinars and Swiss dinars, which were then collected into trucks, shipped to incinerators, and burned, or simply buried.

The new currency proved to be very popular. It was a currency that people wanted to hold, so much so that the new dinar started to appreciate against the dollar. As people bought dinars from the central bank with dollars, the dollar foreign reserves of the central bank began to rise. When they rose above the billion-dollar mark, I breathed a sigh of relief, noting that they now had as much as when Saddam's son Qusay had stolen the money. But the reserves kept rising. In about a year, they reached $5 billion. Financial stability was achieved.

MEANWHILE, BACK AT THE WHITE HOUSE

As the plan was being executed in Iraq, in Washington the White House was following it with great interest and commenting on its progress.

On October 11, 2003—the Saturday just before the exchange would begin—President Bush made it a key part of his radio address, saying, "This coming week, the Iraqi economy will reach an important milestone with the introduction of a new currency. . . . Following World War II, it took three years to institute a new currency in West Germany. In Iraq, it has taken only six months. And the new currency symbolizes Iraq's reviving economy."

At an October 14 NSC meeting in the Sit Room, I presented President Bush with a small wad of the new Iraqi dinars.

"Are these for me?"

"Yes, sir. You see you have all six denominations." And pointing to the one with Hammurabi, king of ancient Babylonia, I said: "Here's Hammurabi." He took them, thanked me, and seemed genuinely appreciative. Tom Simpson, Larry McDonald, and the staff back at Treasury were particularly pleased to hear that the President of the United States now had the currency they had worked so hard on.

On October 28, in a press conference in the Rose Garden, President Bush answered a reporter's question about progress in Iraq: "We put in a new currency in place. For the financial types who are here, you'll understand how difficult that assignment is. And yet it seems to be going well. It's an achievement that is a very important achievement for the future of Iraq. A stable currency, a new currency, a currency without the picture of the dictator or the tyrant or the torturer, however you want to define him, is important for the future."

On November 12, one of the President's opening questions for Bremer at an NSC meeting was: "How is the currency exchange going? Is it going well?"

"Yes. It's going very well. We are 38 percent done and it is occurring all over the country."

At the December 19 meeting on Iraq—the last NSC meeting of 2003—the President made an upbeat year-end statement on U.S. foreign policy, and in a brief discussion of how the dinar was appreciating against the dollar joked, "That's Snow's strong dollar policy at work," causing everyone in the Sit Room to erupt in laughter.

During the week of January 15, 2004, when the currency exchange ended, I gave a final report to the NSC deputies. I concentrated on the importance of getting the message out, one that accurately described the amazing success of the program. It was time for high-fives, though in the decorum of the Sit Room the quiet round of applause was more rewarding.

STANDING UP A MONETARY POLICY

Although January 15, 2004, marked the end of the currency exchange, it was only the beginning of our work with the Iraqis as they conceived and implemented a new monetary policy. Now that there was a national currency, the central bank had to develop a process for regulating its supply and therefore preventing inflation. The Iraqi Governing Council had issued a central bank law, which was modeled after laws in a number of countries with independent central banks, not only the United States. Maintaining price stability was to be a central objective. Sinan Shabibi already had been appointed the governor of the bank, and the law called for the appointment of a policy board. But how exactly should Shabibi and this board conduct monetary policy?

To control the supply of money, Tom Simpson recommended setting up a currency auction at the central bank, and Simon Gray, of the Bank of England, worked with the Iraqis to set up the auction in Baghdad. The auction was essential for the operation of monetary policy because by buying and selling dollars with dinars in the currency auction the central bank could increase or decrease the Iraqi money supply—the supply of dinars in Iraq. Buying and selling dollars would also have an impact on the exchange rate. If there were upward pressure on the exchange rate, the central bank would offset this pressure by selling dinars and buying dollars. The key decision for the central bank was how much to increase the Iraqi money supply, a complex issue for any central bank. Central banks like the Fed or the European Central Bank have hundreds of monetary economists to address this issue; our small team of economists in Baghdad expressed concern about whether this newly constituted central bank could capably address it.

Baghdad, February 2004

In February, I traveled to Baghdad for a second time to go over these issues and to give our support to the team, now under the direction of Olin Wethington. Tom Simpson joined me this time. I met up with him on February 18 in the United Arab Emirates, after I had flown in from Afghanistan on a C-130. We then boarded another C-130 for the flight to Baghdad.

On this trip, I had much better accommodations than on my first visit in 2003, when I slept on the floor at Baghdad International Airport. Tom and I shared a small room in a trailer among a group of trailers behind the palace that served as the headquarters for the CPA. Our security protection was also improved because by that time Treasury had hired Global Risk Strategies to provide security, so that our finance experts could get around Baghdad. The security forces raised the expense of our whole operation by a considerable amount.

We visited the central bank to inspect the currency auction room. We reviewed progress on how they were monitoring inflation. I suggested to Shabibi that we have a mock monetary policy board meeting while I was there, so Tom and I could participate and actually get a feel for the technical discussions. We tried it out and Shabibi liked the format; it turned out to be the first of many monetary policy meetings with the U.S. Treasury and the Central Bank of Iraq. After that first meeting, we used videoconferencing to hold meetings with Tom Simpson and me in Washington and Shabibi and his staff in Baghdad.

On this visit to Baghdad, we explained why the central bank needed to be transparent and state publicly its intentions like other modern central banks, in order to reduce uncertainty in the markets. The central bank had been keeping the exchange rate stable. I told them it was time now to focus on keeping inflation low. The primary goal of any central bank should be to keep inflation low. Having an accurate measure of inflation is essential. If you don't have a measure of inflation, it is impossible to know how you are doing, or make adjustments if you are off track.

PAYING FOR THE INFLATION DATA

Watching inflation in Iraq wasn't easy because the data were so poor. One of our monetary policy experts in Iraq, Bill DeWald, recognized the seriousness of the problem early on, and tried to address it. As a former director of research at the St. Louis Fed, Bill had extensive practical experience advising policymakers and he was a genuine expert in monetary economics. I was pleased and grateful when he said yes when I asked him to go to Iraq to advise the central bank on monetary policy. One of the first problems Bill found was that the statistical office in Iraq was not regularly tabulating or publishing the consumer price index (CPI), which is a basic measure of inflation. The statistical office was months behind and reluctant to move ahead. When Bill mentioned this to me, I complained to the planning minister, who was in charge at the statistical office, when he was on a trip to Washington. He agreed to take care of it and publish the CPI each month, at a regular date.

After some time went by there was still no action. As Bill put it to me later, "The people at the top will say yes to everything you ask, John, but then they can't get the bureaucracy to deliver." To a monetary economist like Bill, not having inflation data was simply unacceptable, and he felt he could not do his job without it. He got so troubled that he finally decided to work directly with the staff at the statistical office and to pay them to do this task with his own money. It was only then that work proceeded. With this catalyst they got started with the tabulations and eventually they regularized the process.

Of course, there were innumerable roadblocks. One time Bill visited the statistical office to see how things were going and he found that no one was working.

"Why aren't you working?" he asked one staff member.

"Because the power is out."

"But I thought you had a generator for times like this."

"Yes, we do, but we do not have any fuel for the generator."

"Why don't you get some fuel?"

"We do not have any money to buy fuel."

Exasperated, Bill offered to give them the money to buy the fuel—again, it was his own money. They took it, bought the fuel, and got back to work.

Eventually, the inflation reports improved and inflation could be more accurately tracked. At the end of 2004, the data showed inflation beginning to pick up as the first election approached in January 2005. Governor Shabibi and his staff attributed the increase in inflation to special factors related to shortages caused by the deteriorating security situation, especially with the upcoming election. As they could only use the currency auctions to control the money supply, they were constrained in how much they could respond to an increase in inflation. We urged them to set up another auction, a Treasury Bills auction, to help control the money supply. Then they could buy or sell Treasury Bills to change the money supply without directly affecting the currency markets or running the risk of depleting their foreign exchange reserves.

BAGHDAD, FEBRUARY 2005

I traveled to Baghdad for the third time in February 2005 to discuss this and other issues with the Iraqis, and to support our team serving there, now under the direction of the resourceful Keven Taecker, our financial attaché. My visit came on the heels of the election, which proved to be very successful, the first of three successful elections in 2005. Security on this trip to Iraq was much tighter than on my first in June 2003, and even more than on my second in February 2004. I was traveling with Sonja Renander, my senior adviser. Surrounded by armed soldiers and security people, we flew from Baghdad International Airport right into the Green Zone, where the U.S. Embassy was located, on a Blackhawk helicopter, cruising fast and low to the ground to avoid being an easy target.

Finance Minister Mahdi invited me to his home for lunch to discuss the monetary policy issues with Governor Shabibi. It was a simple one-story house on a quiet street off a much busier street, probably made even quieter because it was closed off with concrete barriers at either end to prevent terrorist attacks. Getting to his house required me to leave the Green Zone and travel into the neighborhoods of Baghdad. As we drove through the streets, the buying and selling of TVs, kids' toys, and refrigerators seemed as busy and thriving as on my first visit, but now I was in a convoy guarded carefully by U.S. soldiers in Humvees. When we arrived at Mahdi's house, Sonja and I walked from the convoy to the front door donning flak jackets and helmets—now obviously required gear—and after we entered the house, we hung them up on a hook in a small entry hall near the front door. Other people attending the lunch did the same. Soon the entry hall was filled with flak jackets and helmets.

This time the embassy's regional security officer had decided that it was too dangerous for us to travel to the central bank. The narrow streets, close quarters, and heavy traffic in that area would make us easy targets. As a result, we held most of our meetings in the Green Zone, where security was much better. The opportunity to visit with Mahdi and Shabibi together at the minister's house was a welcome change.

The central bank continued to accumulate foreign reserves, now climbing above $5 billion. Amazingly, it was still accumulating these reserves in the form of cash, storing the billions in its basement vaults. With reserves this large—$5 billion and climbing—this was an untenable situation. The Central Bank of Iraq did not have its own account at a foreign central bank where it could earn interest. Aside from the possibility of theft and damage, the bank was not earning interest on these huge sums of cash. That interest could be used for any number of projects, including a fleet of armored cars for moving cash around the country. The central bank was worried about depositing this money outside Iraq for fear it would be attached in a legal suit against Saddam.

To deal with this problem, President Bush issued an executive order that allowed the Iraqi central bank to deposit funds in its own account at the New York Fed and remain immune from attachment. Once the order was issued, the Iraqi central bank opened its own account at the New York Fed. Even at the low 2 percent interest rate on deposits at the time, they were able to earn $100 million a year by depositing $5 billion of their reserves.

I held a press conference while I was in Baghdad to tell everyone who would listen that the Iraqis continued to make progress on the financial front, a year after the currency exchange: ". . . it's now in a very favorable situation where the Central Bank of Iraq is earning income that it would not otherwise have earned, and that income can be used for the betterment of the Iraqi people." Even some Iraqis at the press conference saw some bad news in this good news. They asked questions like, "Why didn't they open an account . . . in Iraq itself?"—which implied that the Iraq government would lose independence or control of the money if it were in an account in New York.

But whether it was reported in the press or not, the Central Bank of Iraq had begun to conduct monetary policy like other effective central banks around the world. The monetary policy video meetings with the Americans continued, with Tom Simpson, now back at the Fed, continuing to volunteer his valuable policy advice.

CHAPTER NINE

Negotiating the
Mother of All Debt Deals

◆

I t was Friday, November 21, 2004, and we were on the verge of closing the biggest international debt deal in history: an agreement to cancel 80 percent, or ultimately $100 billion, of the debt that Saddam Hussein had run up to support his cruel dictatorship. The world's great powers had been at odds over the issue for a year and a half, the division corresponding exactly to the division over whether to intervene militarily in Iraq back in March 2003. France, Germany, and Russia were on one side; the United States, Britain, and Japan on the other. The significance of the deal went well beyond the dollar amounts, however astronomical they would be. If the Iraqis had to pay back more than a small fraction of Saddam's debt, it would jeopardize their ability to prosper economically, and this in turn could derail their quest for democracy and security.

The U.S. strategy for the debt negotiations had been developed in the weeks immediately following Saddam's fall from power, and on the eve of the final negotiations, the strategy was on track and we were ready to close. Our debt experts had sifted through old debt records found in the rubble of the looted and trashed government buildings in Baghdad. Our mathematical finance experts had completed the computer simulations under every conceivable economic scenario. Our representatives in Iraq and at the IMF had worked persistently until they were satisfied with the IMF's calculations about how much debt reduction was necessary for the sustainability of the Iraq economy. A distinguished presidential envoy—James Baker III—had traveled to major capitals in Europe and Asia to make the case. The leaders of the G8 set a deadline that the negotiations had to finish by the end of December 2004, and I had just completed the penultimate round of negotiations with my counterparts in the finance ministries of the G8, setting the stage to reach the final deal.

The final negotiations would not take place at a single table in a single room, but rather at tables in rooms all over the world. President Bush was in Santiago, Chile, negotiating a last piece of the puzzle over lunch with President Vladimir Putin of Russia. Treasury Secretary Snow was in Berlin negotiating with Finance Minister Hans Eichel of Germany. Finance Minister Adil Abdul Al-Mahdi of Iraq was in Paris negotiating with President Jean-Pierre Jouyet of the Paris Club, the international forum for debt deals. And I was bird-dogging the process from Berlin—using my BlackBerry's dual cell-phone and e-mail capability—in touch with the State Department, the White House, and Treasury teams in Washington and Paris.

Before the weekend was over, we achieved the 80 percent debt cancellation we had hoped for. The amount exceeded our predictions and represented a tremendous surprise victory for the Iraqi people and for all those in the U.S. government who had worked so hard with the Iraqis to achieve it. There was a lot to be thankful for that Thanksgiving when we came home from the final negotiations of this, the mother of all debt deals.

WHAT WERE THE U.S. OBJECTIVES?

Our overriding objective was to negotiate the largest possible debt reduction for Iraq within the limits of international law. Achieving this objective would enable the Iraqi economy to grow without the burden of large debt payments. It would also ensure that the substantial financial resources that coalition donors—mainly the United States—were plowing into Iraq would not simply flow back out to creditor governments including, for example, France and Russia. Saddam had stopped making payments on the debt long before the war, and countries like France and Russia would never have seen the money anyway if the coalition had not overthrown Saddam. We knew that the U.S. government was eventually going to cancel all of Iraq's debt to the United States, and the closer we could get other countries to full cancellation the better.

Another objective, at least from the perspective of those of us interested in the smooth workings of the international financial system, was to avoid breaking any principles or precedents that could damage future international negotiations of government debt. Many of these principles and precedents were incorporated in the conventions of the Paris Club, an organization created back in the 1950s when creditor governments got together to decide whether or not to reduce debtor governments' debt, and by how much.

The name may conjure up images of one of those Les Bains-style midnight-to-dawn Parisian nightclubs, but in reality the Paris Club is the most powerful international organization dealing with sovereign debt in the world, though few people outside government understand what it is or how it works. Many of the debt deals that the Paris Club handles involve a combustible mixture of raw international politics and rocket-science financial engineering. This high-stakes negotiating makes for fascinating work for young professionals, so it was not surprising that being the U.S. representative at the Paris Club was a job nearly every young member of my Treasury staff wanted.

Like other international organizations, the Paris Club was in need of reform when the Bush administration took office. The main problem concerned what I liked to call "serial rescheduling" or "recidivism." The original purpose of the Paris Club was to help poor or emerging market countries restructure the debt that they owed other governments, such as the United States or France or Japan, so that the countries could grow and borrow without soon getting into debt trouble again. Asking the Paris Club for debt relief was originally meant to be a one-time, or at least rare, occurrence. Instead, it seemed like every few years the same countries would come back to the Paris Club for more relief. They were not getting back on their feet, which meant that the Paris Club was not working.

THE EVIAN APPROACH: A "TAKE-NO-CREDIT" REFORM INITIATIVE

Early in the Bush administration we decided to pursue a reform of the Paris Club to address the problem, and I added it to my priorities list for the international affairs staff in 2001. Our approach to reform was very low key. A loud proclamation from the U.S. government on the need for reform would certainly kill any chances for success. If we were going to reform the Paris Club, which the French Treasury had run with pride for nearly fifty years, the initiative would have to come from the French themselves. Our window of opportunity would be the year that France chaired the annual G8 Summit. This summit would take place in Evian, France, in June 2003, and preparations for deliverables—new policy initiatives or accomplishments—at that conference would begin in the summer of 2002. If one of the deliverables was Paris Club reform, but presented as the initiative and accomplishment of the French, we would have achieved our goal.

In suggesting ideas for reform, we even shied away from using the word "reform," which would imply of course that there was something deeply wrong with the Paris Club—an unnecessary embarrassment for the French. Rather, we suggested our reform ideas quietly and at opportune times. When one of the foreign affairs ministries in the G8 suggested a poor idea that all the finance ministries hated and wanted to shoot down with an alternative idea, we would suggest the Paris Club reform.

In the end, this strategy worked well and we achieved the kind of reform we were looking for. Known as "the Evian approach," it became a memorable accomplishment from the French-chaired Evian Summit. Under this reform, the Paris Club would determine the amount of debt reduction granted to a country using quantitative financial methods based on how much relief the country needed in order to grow on a sustainable basis without generating another debt problem—a position called "debt sustainability." If a country was granted debt relief on Evian terms, it would have to make a serious commitment that it would not return to the Paris Club. Of course, we all realized that a current government could not commit a future government to anything, but at least the Evian approach provided the country an exit strategy from the Paris Club on a more permanent basis than before the reform. The old Paris Club procedures were more ad hoc, based on simple percentages (like 33 percent or 50 percent) of debt reduction, often appealing to a previous debt reduction agreement with another country.

The Evian approach was an accomplishment in its own right, but an unexpected benefit—certainly unexpected in 2001—was that it proved ideal for achieving U.S. goals for debt reduction in Iraq. The reform would make it possible for us to work within the Paris Club framework. For example, if someone in the Paris Club argued, "Poland's debt was forgiven by 50 percent in 1990; so there is no reason to forgive Iraq's debt by any more than 50 percent," a typical argument before the Evian approach, we would counter that "No, Iraq needs 90 percent debt reduction to be sustainable." To help make the debt-sustainability analysis objective, the IMF would be responsible for running the numbers, rather than any single government.

THE U.S. STRATEGY

Even though it would be possible to work within the Paris Club to reduce Iraqi debt, some argued against such a strategy to achieve our goals. David Mulford was perhaps the most influential advocate for avoiding the Paris Club. David had been Under Secretary for International Affairs during the first Bush administration and was now president of Crédit Suisse First Boston. Later, President Bush would appoint him Ambassador to India. David wrote an op-ed in the *Financial Times* on June 22, 2003, in which he argued that "the Paris Club should not be the forum for negotiations."

There were two reasons people recommended against using the Paris Club. First, the Paris Club's financial principles—even with the Evian reform—would not permit us to use the "odious debt" argument to leverage substantially more debt relief for Iraq. Under this argument, debt run up by an "odious" dictator who harmed his own people should be canceled as soon as that person is removed from office. While no one disagreed that Saddam was odious, there were economic and political reasons not to employ the argument, mainly because it would raise precedent issues. People might argue that some future leader in some other country was odious, when the case was nowhere as clear as Saddam.

Second, French officials ran the Paris Club. The president, for example, was Jean-Pierre Jouyet from the French Treasury. I got to know Jean-Pierre well while he was my counterpart, and we worked together along with John Snow and Francis Mer to keep French-American financial diplomacy working, even when the overall diplomacy effort was faltering because of disagreements about the war in Iraq. Nevertheless, some argued that by serving as secretariat and chair of the meetings, the French could influence the outcome to their advantage, moving the agreement in the direction of their government position, which of course differed greatly from that of the United States.

In March 2003, while the major military operation to overthrow Saddam was still underway, I asked Clay Lowery, an outstanding former representative of the Treasury at the Paris Club, to examine the different strategy options and list the pros and cons of each. There were basically three options. As per tradition, we could negotiate through the Paris Club. Alternatively, we could work with a different group comprised of countries that were sympathetic to a large debt reduction. This group would include the United States, the United Kingdom, Japan, Spain, Italy, Poland, and Saudi Arabia. A third

option was for the United States to forgive the Iraqi debt it held
without any negotiations with other countries; because the United
States held less than 5 percent of Iraq's debt, this would do little good
unless we could get the others to join in.

A lot of interagency discussion and debate about these options
took place. The Treasury and State career staffs did not feel comfortable end-running the Paris Club. I, however, was concerned that a
purely traditional route would not leave us with much flexibility and
leverage, and after discussing my concerns with John Snow in early
April, he agreed. We decided on a strategy that in some sense combined the options but gave us leverage and flexibility, as well as a little time. Our strategy was a contingent one, in which we would allow
for explicit changes as the negotiations proceeded.

First, we would say that we would work within the Paris Club following the principles of the Evian approach. This required getting a
good debt-sustainability analysis done by the IMF, which hopefully
would reveal that Iraq needed a very large debt reduction.

Second, we would be prepared to move outside the Paris Club if
we thought that it was not working, either because the French were
not playing a sufficiently objective role as secretariat or because the
Evian approach was being thwarted.

Third, we would obtain international agreement not to ask for
any debt payments from the Iraqis for at least a year. This "holiday"
on debt service would relieve any short-term pressure on the Iraqis
and give us time to negotiate. With over $100 billion at stake and no
Iraqi government yet in place, we knew it would take at least a year.
The term "moratorium" was too strong a word for this type of defer-
ral, so we generally stated that "we would not expect the Iraqis to
make the payment," but the meaning was the same.

Fourth, after reaching an agreement on a substantial amount of
debt reduction—not 50 percent, but something closer to 80 percent—the United States could move unilaterally with 100 percent
cancellation of U.S.-held Iraqi debt, but would not say anything
publicly about it in advance.

Having the option to circumvent the Paris Club at a later date was essential. First, it would place pressure on the French: if they did not enforce the rules of fair play, we would move to a different playing field. As State's Al Larson nicely put it, "I expect the French are prepared to play ball as long as it is in their playing field." Second, it allowed us to get full support in the administration, both from those who were skeptical about the Paris Club—perhaps because they had heard the critiques from people like David Mulford—and from those who wanted to use the Paris Club. Starting with the Paris Club, but having an options play to either run with or pass by the Paris Club at a later date, meant all could be on board with the strategy.

Clemenceau Tactics: Holding Firm in a "Triple Process of Compromise"

With the U.S. objectives and a strategy in place, we had to consider our negotiating tactics. As in many negotiations, the main issue concerned how extreme a position to take and how long to hold it. The unusual nature of these multigovernment debt negotiations became the key determining factor in my view. Not only were many governments involved, but within each government many agencies were involved. In the U.S. government, responsibility for international debt issues is literally split halfway between State and Treasury. At every level and at every meeting, State and Treasury would have representatives. For instance, a State Department person would head the U.S. delegation to the Paris Club while a Treasury Department person would provide the financial expertise to the delegation. This split responsibility placed an extra high benefit on close cooperation between State and Treasury, and an extra high cost on turf battles. My close personal relationship with Al Larson, the Under Secretary of State with responsibilities for the Paris Club, was essential.

The same type of split between State and Treasury occurs in other governments. Of course, on the big issues, President Bush, perhaps working through the NSC, would resolve interagency disputes and disagreements, but frequently tactical issues were too small for the President's involvement. This meant that tactical disagreements had to be negotiated directly by the agencies. This situation creates a danger for international negotiations in which we, in the U.S. government, would weaken our external position too early in order to negotiate an agreement inside our government, a tendency aptly called "negotiating with ourselves." Our tactics had to prevent us from negotiating with ourselves.

Because this negotiation involved coalitions of countries, it also involved negotiations within coalitions. In the case of the Iraqi debt deal, the G8 was usually split into two coalitions: one consisted of the United States, Britain, Japan, Italy, and eventually Canada; the other consisted of Germany, France, and Russia. Of course, countries within our coalition had different views about strategies and tactics and had their own national interests at stake.

One of the great historical works on international financial negotiations is John Maynard Keynes's best-seller *The Economic Consequences of the Peace*, which he wrote in 1919. In addition to being a world-renowned economist, Keynes was very active in public service, most famously working on international finance issues for the British government in World Wars I and II. Until he quit in disgust, Keynes was present during the negotiations of the Treaty of Versailles after World War I, which he thought was an economic disaster because it placed an immense burden on the German economy. Keynes wrote how the French took advantage of the coalition negotiations to achieve their desired outcome. The Allies—the French, the Americans, the British—first had to decide on a position among themselves and then approach the Germans with that position. Keynes called it "a double process of compromise, first of all to suit the ideas of their allies and associates, and secondly in the course of the Peace Conference proper with the Germans themselves."

Keynes was convinced that French President Georges Clemenceau knew how to exploit this process to get his own way, and this was why the treaty turned out to be exactly what he wanted, and what the Americans, led by Woodrow Wilson, and the British, led by David Lloyd George, did not want. "This was partly a matter of tactics," Keynes argued. "When the final result is expected to be a compromise, it is often prudent to start from an extreme position. . . ." By taking the extreme position, the French got their way at the Treaty of Versailles.*

In many respects the Iraq debt negotiation was similar to Versailles, and I felt that the United States needed to take an extreme position in our own coalition and hold to it if we were to get our way. Because the U.S. responsibility was itself split between State and Treasury, one can expand on Keynes and say that this was really a "triple process of compromise." The U.S. government would first negotiate an interagency position, then negotiate with its coalition partners, and finally negotiate with the French, Germans, and Russians. Hence, I felt it was also necessary for me to take an extreme position within our government to prevent us from "negotiating with ourselves." On several occasions, State, NSC, and even my own Treasury staff would think that I was too uncompromising, but I did so to get us where I wanted us to be.

DIPLOMATIC PRELIMINARIES

Our strategy for debt relief for Iraq would require that we work with the French, and that meant engaging in financial diplomacy with them as soon as possible, preferably at the time of the IMF/World Bank meetings in April 2003. A huge diplomatic rift existed between the French and the United States, brought about by differences about how to handle Saddam Hussein's violation of UN Security Council resolutions.

The regular spring meetings of the G7 finance ministers and central bank governors were scheduled for the weekend of April 11–12, just before the IMF and World Bank spring meetings. Some speculated that the tense relationships over Iraq within members of the G7—France and Germany on one side and the United States and Great Britain on the other—were going to spill over into the

*John Maynard Keynes, *The Economic Consequences of Peace* (New York: Harcourt Brace and Howe, 1920), p. 28.

finance areas. Any new public dispute between the two sides, especially in the finance area, would make it difficult for us to carry out our strategy and accomplish our debt reduction goals. The heavy media attention at these meetings could both catalyze and propagate disputes, making the negotiations that much riskier.

To reduce friction and start a dialogue, John Snow decided to invite the French finance minister, Francis Mer, and his team to lunch in the Treasury Diplomatic Room on Friday, April 11. The atmosphere was tense at the start, but John Snow proved a remarkably cordial and gracious host, even thinking to serve French wines, and soon Francis Mer and his team were at ease, making toasts in English and in French to good Treasury-to-Trésor relations. Although too early to get into substance about Iraq's debt, the lunch was a necessary first step in creating a collegial atmosphere for the French and the Americans to work together over the weekend.

The next step involved bringing the Germans into the discussion along with the French and the rest of the G7. After I checked with John Snow on Friday afternoon, I suggested a special early Saturday morning breakfast meeting of the G7 finance ministers and their international deputies at Blair House, the residence across the street from the White House where foreign dignitaries stay. I quietly sounded out all my G7 counterparts individually, starting with my German counterpart Caio Koch-Weser. I explained that the topic would be Iraq, but we would not get into substance, not even try to reach agreement on a debt holiday, at this meeting. Caio was looking for a way to move the discussions on this sensitive topic forward more rationally, so the Germans readily agreed, and then so did everyone else. We decided on an early time, 7:15 a.m., so as not to publicize the meeting.

As is customary with G7 meetings held in Washington, the breakfast was formally hosted and chaired by the Treasury Secretary. And as with the bilateral lunch with the French the day before, the multilateral breakfast was tense at the beginning. Soon people loosened up, and by the end there was agreement that if the United States said something about working with the Paris Club, the French would say something about cooperating on Iraq debt. The breakfast ended with agreement that my counterparts and I would draft language for a joint press statement, to be released to the public later in the day. After a few more negotiations during the day, the joint statement finally read: "We recognize the need for a multilateral effort to help Iraq. . . . It is important to address the debt issue and we are looking forward to the early engagement of the Paris Club." We had made significant progress in initiating our diplomatic strategy, the French and the Germans were talking about helping Iraq, and we had identified the Paris Club as the venue. The outcome was especially gratifying given the very real risks that the meetings might have blown up in acrimonious debate and further intransigence.

Testing the Waters About a Moratorium

Our next goal was agreement on the debt holiday. On May 1, 2003, I had a speech scheduled on Iraq financial reconstruction at the Center for Strategic and International Studies in Washington. A technical speech, it seemed like a good opportunity to test the waters on the moratorium proposal. A positive reaction would help move the idea ahead with other governments. In the event of a negative reaction, we could adjust and downplay the speech, stressing that it was a technical presentation. The newswire stories that resulted were straightforward and generally positive, just as we had hoped. The one from Agence France-Presse on May 1 read: "'Iraq must be given an 18 month holiday with no payment demands on its crippling external debt,' US Treasury Undersecretary John Taylor said. 'The first thing to do is to make sure that we are not going to start requiring service payments on that debt in, say, the next year and a half,' Taylor told a conference here. 'Certainly for the short term—a year and a half at least—there is really no expectation that payments will be made,' he told the Center for Strategic and International Studies (CSIS)."

We waited a while and did not hear any negative reaction to this speech. In light of this, we figured that at the next G7 meeting in Deauville, France, on May 17, we could reach an agreement on the debt moratorium. At that meeting, Secretary Snow said: "I believe that no one should expect Iraq to begin to make debt payments for some time," and all the G7 plus Russia agreed not to expect any debt payments from Iraq before the end of 2004. This gave us the needed time to negotiate.

I updated President Bush and the NSC on the debt strategy at the same meeting, on May 9, in which I discussed the currency plan for Iraq. Using the usual PowerPoint briefing slides, I reviewed our preliminary estimates of the total size of the debt, which was $80 billion to $130 billion. I recommended that our government "should make clear no debt service payments are expected at least through 2004," and that we begin working through the Paris Club and with the Iraqis in Baghdad on the debt records. This would take a number of months. Multilateral negotiations with the Paris Club would begin as soon as possible.

Following the agreement on a moratorium through the end of 2004, we needed to forge one further agreement before the negotiations could begin. We had to establish a deadline for the G7 to finish the negotiations. After months of discussion, agreement was reached on September 20, 2003, when we released a G7 communiqué stating: "We call upon the Paris Club to make its best efforts to complete the restructuring of Iraq's debts before the end of 2004." Everything appeared to be on track.

THE BAKER MISSIONS

On December 5, the President appointed former Secretary of State and Treasury James Baker III to the position of special envoy on the Iraq debt. Appointing a special envoy would create a dialogue at the highest levels of government and demonstrate President Bush's personal involvement and commitment to Iraq's debt reduction. I first met with Secretary Baker on this issue along with Condi Rice and Gary Edson in Rice's White House office on November 11, and I provided him with data on the amount of debt held by the main creditors and briefed him on our overall strategy to that date.

James Baker's appointment generated a lot of good press and did much to demonstrate the President's commitment. In the next few weeks, Baker would travel to Paris, Moscow, Berlin, London, Rome, Japan, and China. The Baker missions did not deal explicitly in percentage terms for the debt reduction (such as 50 percent or 90 percent). The timing of the mission was too early for numbers, given that the IMF's debt-sustainability work had not been finished. Instead, Baker decided to focus on obtaining general commitments, ranging from "reducing the debt substantially" (as in the case of France) or "writing off the vast majority of the debt" (Japan). I believe that this was the correct diplomatic decision. By staying away from the numbers, the Baker missions generated a lot of good news that the United States was working toward a solution with France and Germany. A focus on numbers at this time may have resulted in more news about disagreements and set the negotiations back.

Another important diplomatic component of the Baker missions was his communication with the managing director of the IMF, Horst Kohler, on the importance of the IMF's completing a professional debt-sustainability analysis that incorporated large debt reduction as an option. Anticipating the importance of our having to adopt a very tough negotiating position later, I suggested to Baker, in a meeting right before his visit with Kohler, that he specifically ask the IMF to run calculations with a 95 percent debt reduction. He did ask and the IMF included those runs in its analysis. This ensured that it would have the most extreme position.

The Debt-Sustainability Analysis

Early on, I had asked our staff to build their own economic model to estimate Iraq's debt sustainability under various debt reduction alternatives. Although I knew that building such a model would ultimately be the responsibility of the IMF—that was the heart of the Evian approach—I wanted to be sure that we could critique the IMF if necessary. "It takes a model to beat a model," was one of my refrains as an academic and it certainly applied here. If we did not like the IMF's analysis and did not have our own analysis, we would not have a very strong critique. Moreover, although there would not be a transfer of sovereignty to Iraq until the summer of 2004, the Iraqis would need to have their own calculations as they negotiated with the IMF. The early work by Treasury might therefore come in very useful to the Iraqis. As in so many other stories in this book, the Iraq debt team in Treasury rose to the occasion, producing an impressive piece of work showing that very deep debt reduction was needed.

During the first quarter of 2004, we started to share our debt-sustainability analysis with the IMF team and they began their own work in earnest. I recall my first meeting with the IMF staff at which we shared Treasury's analysis. I was joined by Al Larson of State and the technical staff at Treasury who did our analysis. It would be the first of many meetings either in person or on the phone with the IMF staff and management on the debt-sustainability analysis. Naturally the IMF was cautious, not wanting to appear pressured by the United States, but the staff were not standoffish and benefited from our work.

By May 24, the IMF team had completed their debt-sustainability analysis and shared it with the Paris Club creditors. The Iraqis and our team had worked very hard to gather all the necessary data and assumptions. The IMF team assumed a rapid recovery in Iraq, with real GDP growth averaging over 10 percent for the remainder of the decade. They made assumptions about the recovery of oil production and the price of oil. And they ran sensitivity analyses in which they varied these assumptions. The IMF's official Debt Sustainability Analysis included five debt reduction scenarios: 50 percent, 67 percent, 80 percent, 90 percent, and 95 percent. For each of these scenarios the IMF computed the level of service payments on that debt as a percentage of GDP. The analysis suggested that a debt reduction on the order of 90 to 95 percent was needed to reduce the debt to a level that would be safe as far as debt sustainability goes. We had the IMF analytics on our side.

A BACK-OF-THE-ENVELOPE MODEL

Though I have a deep personal interest in the complex quantitative models that our staff and the IMF used for debt-sustainability analysis, I did my best not to interfere with the details of their work. I did, however, create my own little model that had some of the features of the complex models, and I used this to explain the more complex models to people who were not debt experts. I would also use my simple calculations as a rough cross-check on the complex models.

At their heart, debt-sustainability models determine whether a country's debt is too high relative to the country's capability of making interest and principal payments on the debt. A country's overall production, GDP, is a good measure of its capability of paying, so a common criterion is the ratio of the debt to GDP. If that number is too high—say 50 percent or more—then the country is likely to have problems. Though there are other factors, such as the interest rates on the debt and the payment schedule, the debt-to-GDP ratio is a basic measure frequently used, and I used it in my back-of-the-envelope model as follows:

Iraq's debt was about $125 billion. The GDP of Iraq is about $25 billion. So their debt-to-GDP ratio was way over 50 percent. It was 500 percent! If they cut their debt by 90 percent they would have 10 percent of that $125 billion, or $12.5 billion of debt, left to pay off. That would be a debt-to-GDP ratio of 50 percent—12.5 divided by 25 gives 50—which is still a large amount of debt and higher than is usually considered sustainable in emerging market economies.

It seemed to me, therefore, that debt reduction in the 90 percent plus range was needed, and I found the IMF analysis to be quite reasonable. My own back-of-the-envelope calculations confirmed the complex calculations.

THE SEA ISLAND SUMMIT AND PRESIDENT CHIRAC'S MESSAGE

In a crucial next step, the IMF's work was endorsed by the heads of G8 governments at the June 9, 2004, Economic Summit held at Sea Island, Georgia. At that meeting, President Bush and his colleagues agreed that "Debt reduction is critical if the Iraqi people are to have the opportunity to build a free and prosperous nation. The reduction should be provided in connection with an IMF program, and sufficient to ensure sustainability taking into account the recent IMF analysis. We will work with each other, within the Paris Club, and with non-Paris Club creditors, to achieve that objective in 2004." Al Larson and Gary Edson, who both attended that summit, deserve a great deal of credit for negotiating communiqué language like this with their counterparts in the French foreign affairs and Elysée Palace staffs.

In the press conference immediately following the summit, however, President Jacques Chirac was much less forthcoming. He made it very clear in his answer to a reporter's question that the French would be tougher on the Iraq debt issue than we had anticipated. The reporter asked: "On the Iraqi debt. We know that the Americans would like it cut by 95 percent, that the IMF has said it should be cut by 80 percent. When France was talking about a substantial reduction, the figure of 50 percent was mentioned. Does France still think 50 percent is the right figure?" And President Chirac answered: "It is absolutely the right one and I'm going to tell you why. Iraq is potentially a rich country, even though she has a substantial debt. How will you explain to the very indebted poor countries or some other countries which are also heavily indebted . . . how will you explain to those people that we're going to do for Iraq in three months more than we've done in ten years for the world's thirty-seven poorest and most indebted countries? That . . . isn't right. This is why, it's true, France—and we aren't alone—has adopted a clear position, a cancellation, yes, a substantial one, yes. What does 'substantial' mean? For us it is indeed around 50 percent."

THE TRANSFER OF SOVEREIGNTY

Soon after the summit, on June 28, 2004, sovereignty in Iraq was formally transferred from the Coalition Provisional Authority to the Iraq Interim Government, which would then be in place until the elections, planned for early 2005. President Bush had made the decision to transfer authority back in November 2003, an ambitious plan that had succeeded. The transfer of sovereignty had an important implication for the debt negotiations: The Iraqi government could now begin making requests for debt reduction on its own behalf. The new government would be in place long enough to complete the debt deal according to our timeline.

The transfer of sovereignty also meant that we would change our personnel in Iraq. Our financial coordinator, who was then Olin Wethington, would come back to Washington as the CPA was dissolved. In place of a financial coordinator, we would appoint a financial attaché, Kevin Taecker, who would work in the newly established American Embassy in Iraq and report to the new ambassador, John Negroponte. Back in Washington, Olin would become our point person on the Iraq debt negotiations, and he worked relentlessly for the next six months to achieve that goal. Olin had served as Assistant Secretary of International Affairs and on the staff of the National Security Council during the first Bush administration, so he had years of experience with the interagency process. He also had developed a great sense of trust with the Iraqis while serving in Iraq. This trust would prove very useful as the new government came into power.

The new finance minister of the interim Iraq government, Adil Abdul al-Mahdi, was a former exile who had escaped Iraq for France in 1969 after being arrested, tortured, and sentenced to death by the Baath Party for his political activities. Along with the central bank governor Sinan Shabibi, he would take responsibility for Iraq's debt reduction on a day-to-day basis. By this time I knew Shabibi very well, and I would work closely with him and Mahdi over the next five months.

To take advantage of the transfer of sovereignty, I suggested that Mahdi, on behalf of the new Iraq Interim Government, send a formal written request for a large reduction in its debt to its major creditors in the Paris Club. I wanted this to be done immediately. We only had six months to finish the deal and I planned to discuss the Iraqis' request with my G7 counterparts at a retreat that I would host in California in late July.

An important tactical question concerned how aggressive the

Iraqis' first letter should be. Of course, because they had just come into power, our advice to them would matter tremendously. I thought they would have to take a tough position if we were ever going to approach 80 percent debt reduction. This was especially true after President Chirac's hard-line 50 percent figure, announced just a few weeks earlier, at Sea Island. I was still concerned about negotiating with ourselves. At several points, our staff asked me if I could move off the 95 percent position. One day, Olin Wethington and Randy Quarles requested a special meeting with me and most of our Iraq debt team to say it was fruitless to ask for such high numbers. I was not about to give in. I explained, somewhat emotionally, that the foreign governments who were now asking for more payments from Iraq would never have gotten anything if it had not been for our troops, who had made great sacrifices. I mentioned that I had discussed the issue with Secretary Snow and he was comfortable with our position. At one point our debt team had devised a clever interactive analysis of the debt so that the Iraqis could see the effect of different debt reduction scenarios and even ask for other scenarios. To their disappointment, I insisted that we only show people runs in the 90 to 95 percent category, so as to be more convincing that we had absolutely no intentions of compromising.

On July 12, Finance Minister Mahdi sent a formal letter to the major Paris Club creditors. The letter asked for a reduction in the face value of the debt by 95 percent, along with a rescheduling of the remaining principal over a twenty-three-year period. Included in the letter was the economic rationale for this request. For the first time, the Iraqis themselves were asking for this debt relief and they were making it on solid economic grounds.

As planned, the governments of the United States, the United Kingdom, and Canada all indicated support for this initial request, even though it was very large. On July 19, 2004, at my G7 retreat in California I reported that the U.S. government fully supported this request, and so did the United Kingdom and Canada. Japan had not yet agreed to this amount, and clearly the French and the Germans were not about to go beyond their 50 percent at this time. Nevertheless, the message was beginning to sink in that we were serious.

On an August 4 call with President Jouyet of the Paris Club, I reiterated our position. Jean-Pierre was disappointed. He was trying to bring the two sides together, but with the big gap between 50 percent and 95 percent, things seemed pretty hopeless. He asked that we put the U.S. position down in writing, perhaps hoping that the act of writing it down would force people in the U.S. government to start negotiating with themselves. We didn't. I sent him a one-page paper summarizing our position on the Iraqis' request. The one-pager was vetted by the interagency team so it accurately represented the U.S. position. Here is an excerpt:

> . . . *The specific request from Minister Mahdi and Governor Shabibi is for an upfront 95 percent face value reduction on the stock of Iraq's external debt. . . . The U.S. is fully supportive of Iraq's request. The growth of the Iraqi economy is pivotal to a stable and prosperous Iraq and is highly important for global stability. The G-7 and other creditors of Iraq have a shared interest in meeting Iraq's request, so that the Iraqi people are not left with a debt overhang that stymies the internal and foreign investment needed for this economic growth.*
>
> *The debt sustainability analysis completed by the IMF provides a financial basis for this position. That analysis shows that a debt reduction of the size requested by the Iraqis is needed to restore sustainability. According to the IMF's analysis, any reduction in face value less than 95 percent would result in large financing gaps. Moreover, some of the assumptions used in the IMF's analysis are very optimistic, suggesting that 95 percent is by no means an overestimate of what is needed. For example, the IMF's baseline scenario assumes a near doubling of Iraq's oil output by 2010, an ambitious target given the poor state of Iraq's oil infrastructure, the continued security threats, and the huge investment that will be needed.*

On September 29, I met in my office with the whole interagency team, Mahdi, and Shabibi. We reviewed the positions that we were going to take in the next few weeks. Again we talked big, stressing the need to stick together and that there would be time to compromise later. The Paris Club met in October to hold technical discussions and decided, as planned, to invite the Iraqis to the November meeting. Again, all was on track.

COMPROMISE I

While four of the G7 members agreed to support the Iraqi position, Japan would have to join us if we were going to go any further. I had asked my counterpart, Hiroshi Watanabe, several times to come on board. I even met with the finance minister, Sadakazu Tanagaki, early in September in Santiago, Chile. John Snow talked to Tanagaki on the telephone as well. We stressed that this was a tactical issue and that in the end we would probably have to compromise, perhaps to 80 percent. But if we started with 80 percent now, we would never get to 80 percent in the end. The Japanese are very good allies and friends, but the 90-plus numbers were simply too high for them.

It was now time to bring our side of the coalition together, including the Japanese. Another complication, which reinforced the need to move now, was the increase in the price of oil. Other things being equal, this would make the case less favorable for substantial debt reduction if the IMF was asked to do the analysis again. For the first time, I agreed to compromise our position internally, and decided to go below the 90–95 percent range. We said that we could consider a debt reduction of 89.5 percent. I know it sounds like pricing gasoline, but moving out of the 90-something range could make a difference to the Japanese. We again contacted our coalition members to see if they approved. Those already on board with the higher numbers naturally agreed to the new numbers. Importantly, the Japanese now indicated a willingness to go along.

Based on this favorable response, on November 8 we circulated a paper to the G7 members, which showed how the IMF's analysis demonstrated the need for the higher level of debt reduction, but in the interest of moving the negotiations along we were ready to compromise at 89.5 percent. I scheduled a call to my G7 counterparts for Wednesday, November 17. As planned, five of the G7 expressed support, leaving the French and the Germans, still arguing for the 50 percent figure, isolated from the five. With this new show of unity on one side, it looked like we were going to get some movement. Over the weekend, the finance ministers would be attending a meeting of the G20 in Berlin. The G20 includes the G7 plus emerging market economies such as China, India, Brazil, Russia, and South Africa.

COMPROMISE II

I sat next to Caio Koch-Weser at dinner in Berlin the night before the weekend meeting. The Germans were still in lockstep with the French, but might be attracted to striking a deal while the finance ministers were meeting in Berlin. We had to come to an agreement by the end of the year anyway, and settling in Berlin would bring favorable publicity to our German hosts. Caio indicated that the Germans could allow 80 percent as a contingency in the event that oil prices fell substantially, but otherwise would have to insist on a much lower percentage. I said that we would have to hold to the high 80s, but given the increase in oil prices, such high levels were not as necessary as before. We could live with 80 if oil prices stayed high, though we would need a contingency, a higher percentage, if oil prices fell. The Germans and the Americans were now very close. We wanted 80 percent as a guaranteed minimum and a higher percentage if oil prices were lower. They wanted 80 percent as a maximum, but only if oil prices were lower and not as a guarantee. We would have an agreement if the United States gave up on having a number above 80 if oil prices were lower and the Germans would guarantee 80. Caio and I agreed that we should address the issue in a meeting with John Snow and the German finance minister, Hans Eichel, scheduled for the next morning.

Before the meeting, John Snow and I agreed that if the Germans offered a guaranteed 80 percent, we would agree with 80 and would not insist on a contingency in which the number could be higher. The meeting consisted of just five people: Snow, Eichel, Koch-Weser, myself, and a translator. Given the great interest and significance to this meeting, many others would have liked to have been in the room.

Right at the start, Eichel made the 80 percent offer without contingencies, and Snow immediately agreed. It was a matter of minutes and we were done. We then exchanged a few pleasantries about the Germans being excellent hosts and we all left the room beaming, with me debriefing our team waiting outside the door. As the French and the Russians were still not on board, we were reluctant to say anything to the press, but Eichel did so, saying things were essentially wrapped up. He was quoted by the Associated Press on November 21 as saying: "We agreed that there should be a write-off of debts in several stages amounting to 80% in total." A BBC report* then stated that "Germany and the US agreed to a deal on the sidelines of the G20 summit of rich and developing nations meeting in Berlin. . . . The breakthrough came in talks between German Finance Minister Hans Eichel and US Treasury Secretary John Snow on the fringes of the G20 meeting to discuss the world economy."

The Russians, the French, and the Deal Is Done

These early press statements confused things quite a bit, and for a while I thought they would derail the agreement. The French were very surprised by the German "defection" and did not want to go along. I immediately spoke with my counterpart Sergei Storchak from Russia, who was in Berlin, and told him about the German decision. He was surprised and called the Russian finance minister, Alexei Kudrin, in Moscow, who then decided to defer to President Putin, who was in Chile meeting with President Bush. In the end, Putin agreed; Kudrin informed my counterpart, who then called his Paris Club representative in Paris. Things started moving to completion immediately. Of course, now it was everyone in the G8 except the French, so they had to come around too, and the deal was done.

*BBC News, "Deal Nears on Iraq Debt Write-Off," November 21, 2004.

There was joy, thanks, and congratulations in the Iraqi and the American camps that night. John Snow kindly congratulated me and he was able to get on the phone to thank and congratulate Olin Wethington, who was in Paris working with the Iraqis. I talked to Minister Mahdi on the phone in Paris, who was ecstatic and grateful. So was Governor Shabibi.

CHAPTER TEN

Exchange Rate Diplomacy

◆

I n the hours immediately following the 9/11 attacks, I called my
counterparts in the G7. When I reached Haruhiko Kuroda of
Japan, he first expressed his condolences and then got right down
to business. He suggested that Japan and the United States should
buy dollars in the foreign exchange markets to prop up the value of
the dollar. I said that it was best to let the exchange markets adjust
to the new information on their own, without government intervention. I would never completely rule out foreign exchange market
intervention, but I had followed the markets closely for years and
had spent time on trading floors in New York and Tokyo. My experience made me reluctant to intervene, and that was a policy position
held throughout the Bush administration.

In fact, the United States did not intervene in the currency markets during my tenure at Treasury. This set a new record, and it was
a big change from past administrations. The Clinton administration
intervened twenty times in the foreign exchange markets, the last
time just before the 2000 presidential election. Kuroda had worked
with the U.S. Treasury during that intervention, so it was not surprising that he would ask the United States to intervene just one year

later. The first Bush administration also intervened in the foreign currency markets, as did the Reagan administration, the Carter administration, and so on. However, I believe that adopting a policy of non-intervention was for the better. Traders soon adjusted their expectations to the absence of the U.S. government in the markets, and as a result the markets have worked more smoothly and with less volatility.

My Japanese counterparts frequently intervened in the markets, and the markets in turn gave them a nickname. Haruhiko Kuroda's predecessor, the gregarious Eisuke Sakakibara, was called "Mr. Yen," because he frequently talked about whether the yen was too high or too low, and he moved markets whenever he did. Kuroda, quieter and more reserved than Sakakibara, also intervened and was dubbed "Mr. Asian Currency" because of his long-term vision of a single Asian currency like the euro. Kuroda's successor, Zembei Mizoguchi, was called "Mr. Dollar" because he spent record sums of yen buying up dollar assets like Treasury Bills.

Japan was not the only country to intervene heavily in the currency markets during this period. The Chinese intervened in even larger amounts. The Chinese were more secretive about their intervention than the Japanese, who regularly informed me of their interventions, a common practice in the G7. In contrast, the Chinese did not inform me of their interventions on a daily basis, but their purpose was no secret. They wanted to prevent the Chinese currency, the yuan, from rising in price against the dollar. The appreciation of the yuan would make Chinese exports more expensive abroad. The Chinese currency became a growing issue for the United States in 2004 and 2005.

The Largest Market in the World

The foreign exchange market is the largest market in the world. An astounding $2 trillion worth of currency is bought and sold daily. It is a global, twenty-four-hour market, with the majority of trading done in London, New York, and Tokyo.

Like most markets, seeing the foreign exchange market in operation is the best way to appreciate how it works. From a distance, a trading floor looks like a vast sea with wave after wave of computers. It is on these trading floors that the exchange rate—the price of dollars in terms of yen or euros or any other major currency—is determined as the traders compete with each other to get the best price, shouting information across the room and into the phone to customers and traders on other trading floors around the world. A very quick moving market, any news that affects the price of dollars, such as a remark by a financial official, or a release of data on the unemployment rate, spreads instantaneously around the world as traders' computer screens flicker with the news and they quickly decide whether to buy or sell.

Economists debate whether it is an efficient market, or whether it overshoots or reacts to extraneous information. In my view, it is a remarkably efficient market that usually incorporates news sensibly and quickly, governed by the basic laws of supply and demand. If the news is that the Fed is more likely to increase interest rates, then the dollar generally rises because more people want to hold dollars to get the higher interest rate. If the news is a higher-than-expected unemployment rate, then the dollar usually falls because traders reason, correctly, that the Fed will be more likely to lower interest rates, or at least keep them where they are. Large purchases and sales can also move the markets. If the Japanese intervene by buying a huge amount of dollars with yen, they can usually increase the price of the dollar relative to the yen. But the impacts of such interventions are temporary and their size is hard to predict because the volume of trading in the market is many times larger than even the largest interventions.

I know, however, of cases where the market has reacted to news that any person with common sense would know was completely bogus or irrelevant. Early one morning I was in midtown Manhattan doing a live TV interview and someone asked me about the dollar. As usual I said nothing of consequence, but later that morning when I was on the trading floor of Merrill Lynch, one of the traders offered to show me how he made money on that innocuous remark. Sure enough the dollar moved on my statement, but whatever that trader made, another trader lost. The more savvy traders gained from the extra volatility in the market, but it was not a healthy thing for the economy, because volatility makes it more expensive to hedge against risks.

Aware that volatility or turbulence could swell up at any time, I followed the markets closely. I set up five video screens at my Treasury desk—I usually had two live Bloomberg and Reuters screens as well as a TV, and could switch back and forth between the screens and onto the Internet quickly if needed. I had a direct connection to the markets through Dino Kos, the head of the trading desk at the New York Fed, and he would call me whenever he saw unusual price movements, and I called him a lot too when I was concerned about a market move. When I arrived at Treasury in 2001 there was a "market room" where a staff would watch the currency markets, but we found that distributing the Bloomberg and Reuters terminals around Treasury provided us with more immediately useful information, and I closed the room, collaborating with my Treasury colleague Peter Fisher, who had preceded Dino Kos in New York. Our financial attachés in Frankfurt and Tokyo could contact me with market developments when I was traveling in different time zones.

I carefully considered the market impact of congressional testimony by the Treasury Secretary, and we all worked to make sure the language would not inadvertently rile the markets. I also considered the impact on markets of other influential people, and worried when they made alarmist-sounding remarks that could impact the stability of the dollar. On January 5, 2004, for example, former Secretary of the Treasury Robert Rubin warned that the growing U.S. trade deficit could cause a dollar crisis, risking a "loss of investor and creditor confidence" and "disruptions to financial markets." Two days later, the IMF released a technical report stressing similar themes. And the next day, January 8, the *New York Times* featured the IMF study on the front page above the fold with the headline: IMF SAYS RISE IN US DEBTS IS THREAT TO WORLD'S ECONOMY. Throughout the rest of the year, currency traders reacted more strongly than ever to the monthly release of the trade deficit and sold dollars whenever the deficit was larger than expected.

The Bush administration was quite aware of the trade deficit, which had grown steadily since the early 1990s, and agreed with economists that the deficit resulted from the imbalance between saving and investment in the U.S. economy. In a meeting in the Oval Office on October 15, 2003, the President and his advisers discussed this phenomenon. President Bush asked about policies that would reduce the trade deficit. I reviewed how the deficit emerged from the gap between saving and investment, holding my investment hand above my saving hand to illustrate the difference. The United States remained an attractive place to invest, but Americans were not saving very much, leaving it to foreigners to fill in the difference. The only real remedy to the problem was for the United States to save more and for other countries to invest more in their own countries. It would be irresponsible to take action to slow down the U.S. economy, which was performing better and better each year since 9/11. "So increasing saving will lower the trade deficit," the President said, and all agreed. That idea became a key element in U.S. policy toward the trade deficit—a policy that consisted of cutting down the budget deficit gradually as a share of GDP and reducing disincentives for Americans to save. If increasing savings was to bring about a smooth adjustment in the trade deficit, I knew that exchange markets would have to adjust efficiently as well. That fact placed increased importance on a results-oriented management of our exchange rate policy.

BASIC POLICY PRINCIPLES

In exchange rate policy, as in all areas of economic policymaking, it is important to keep certain basic principles in mind. This is even more true in the case of foreign exchange policy, where you have to be ready to make on-the-spot decisions and the seemingly important issues of the moment may pull you away from the principle.

The "Field of Dreams" principle: The most important principle is also the simplest—a good exchange rate policy must be supported by sound domestic economic policies. Monetary policy should
focus on maintaining the purchasing power of the dollar; countries
that let inflation get out of hand always suffer from unstable depreciating currencies. Fiscal policy should keep the federal debt from
rising beyond our ability to service it. Tax policy should minimize
distortions and provide incentives for people to invest. Regulatory
policy should provide both the credibility and the flexibility that
make the United States an attractive place to invest. Confidently
build a playing field with good domestic economic policy and a good
exchange rate policy will come.

Avoiding currency market intervention: Policymakers should
also rely on the markets to determine the exchange rate with a minimum of intervention, or direct buying and selling currency in the
market, and they should communicate this policy as clearly as possible to the markets. However, it is also unwise to say dogmatically
that you would never intervene. It is important to stress that the
exchange rate is not considered a separate instrument of policy;
rather, it is the market's reflection of economic policy and a host of
other factors.

Being cautious about government intervention in the foreign
exchange markets does not imply that you should ignore developments in the exchange markets. A sharply depreciating exchange rate
could reflect a lack of confidence in other policies. Moreover, even if
the United States does not intervene, other countries do, and this
can affect the exchange rate.

Avoiding verbal intervention: Government officials also should
minimize verbal intervention. The markets pay close attention to
what senior government officials say about the exchange markets. In
particular, trying to "talk down the dollar" by saying, for example,
that it is overvalued is bad because it conjures up all the terrible policies that are associated with weak currencies, including an inflation-

prone monetary policy. Moreover, for verbal intervention to appear credible it must be backed up by action, at least occasionally, so verbal intervention leads to actual intervention. Many traders like officials to comment, and it is sometimes difficult not to do so; for Treasury officials who have responsibility for exchange rate policy it is especially difficult. By their nature, comments cause volatility, and for this reason, we adopted a policy that the Treasury Secretary makes all comments about the dollar and that those comments should be few and far between. There was no reason for the chairman of the Fed, or the Secretary of Commerce, or anyone else to comment. Of course, the policy of not commenting applied to me, too, but I did find it frustrating not to be able to say anything about the currency when, as an economist, I had so much to say. In late 2004 and 2005, when exchange market volatility was very low, traders begged me, half in jest, to say something, anything, about the markets to introduce some volatility so they could make some money.

The Bush administration inherited from the Clinton administration a particular way to talk about the dollar, called the "strong dollar" line. The idea was for the Treasury Secretary to simply say, "A strong dollar is in the interest of the United States," whenever a news reporter asked a question about the dollar. They would then repeat the same words again and again if asked more than once. This was a difficult legacy because by all accounts the dollar was very strong in 2001 and 2002, and saying "strong dollar" sounded like you wanted the dollar to get even stronger, which looked downright silly. "Strong dollar" talk also brought the wrath of all the U.S. manufacturing exporters, who thought that the dollar was way too strong and hurting their business. In February 2001, Paul O'Neill inadvertently strayed from the strong dollar line and the markets tanked.* Reuters wire service reported that, in an interview on February 16, 2001, with *Frankfurter Allgemeine Zeitung*, he said: "We are not pursuing, as it is often said, a policy of a strong dollar. In my opinion, a strong

---

*Swaha Pattanaik, "O'Neill Remark Confuses Financial Markets," Reuters, February 16, 2001.

dollar is the result of a strong economy." The next day he then had to reassert the "strong dollar" mantra, saying: "I made a mistake of assuming it was okay to talk about the intellectual fabric around that subject." Since the room for misinterpretation is so huge, he said that he would restrict himself in the future to simple words. "I believe in a strong dollar . . . if in the future, I should ever decide . . . that I should change my stance . . . I will hire Yankee Stadium and I will get the most rousing brass bands I can find . . . and I will announce to you that we have decided to change our policy."

During the preparations for John Snow's Senate confirmation hearing in 2003, we tried all sorts of ways to adjust the strong dollar language, so as to avoid the impression that he was trying to verbally drive the dollar up. We tried to define what the "strong dollar" language meant, anticipating follow-up questions like, "What do you mean by strong dollar?" After much debate we concluded that it was best to keep using the same language. I sympathize with any Treasury Secretary who has to comment on the dollar in response to questions from the press, but does not want to inadvertently move the market and perhaps cause a crash. Over time the policy of saying the same thing over and over again, and not intervening, verbally or otherwise, led the press to ask less and less about the dollar.

It takes two (or more) to tango: An exchange rate policy is not solely the decision of one country. The exchange rate between the dollar and the yen or between the dollar and the yuan depends not only on whether the United States decides to follow the three principles that I just outlined, but also on whether Japan and China decide to follow those principles. As sovereign governments, Japan and China must decide for themselves. It is here that financial diplomacy comes into play. If the United States thinks Japan or China should stop intervening, then it must develop a diplomatic strategy to bring this change about. As with all diplomatic strategies, one has to determine whether bilateral or multilateral approaches will work, whether a new coalition is needed, or whether an international institution like the IMF should be brought into play.

Facing up to broader ramifications: Policymakers must also recognize that the exchange rate influences international political and security concerns. The currency is so important to the health of the economy that economists and finance experts naturally argue that policy decisions should be left to the experts. They are tempted to ignore the non-economic ramifications, but such a head-in-the-sand approach is a mistake. An increase in the price of the dollar makes U.S. exports less attractive, and thereby makes U.S. exporting firms and their employees very unhappy. Their unhappiness influences election outcomes in swing states and creates pressure on Congress to enact protectionist legislation. Exchange rate issues also relate to national security. Some warn, for example, that China's huge accumulation of dollars has given the country leverage over the United States. Spinning a Clancy-esque tale, they outline a scenario in which the Chinese government suddenly dumps hundreds of billions of dollars onto the market, causing the dollar to collapse and creating financial chaos in the United States and around the world.

For these reasons, we must face up to reality and develop a process for systematically addressing these other concerns. A good exchange rate policy requires reaching a delicate balance between the three separate forces of finance, politics, and security. It is no surprise, then, that the White House and the National Security Council are interested in exchange rate policy. Steve Friedman, former chairman of Goldman Sachs and the White House economic adviser during 2003 and 2004, took a great deal of interest in currency matters, as did the top international economics person at the NSC, Faryar Shirzad. Perhaps most important, the President also took a keen interest in currency matters.

But Who's in Charge?

In the United States and most other countries, the central bank and the Treasury divide responsibility on monetary matters. The Fed has responsibility for domestic monetary policy, which primarily concerns setting the short-term interest rate and the U.S. money supply. The Treasury has responsibility for exchange rate policy, which includes decisions about U.S. intervention in the foreign exchange market and decisions about whether to engage with other countries about their intervention.

For example, in the hours immediately following 9/11, when U.S. banks and other financial institutions faced a sudden shortage of money to make payments, the Fed had responsibility for providing enough money to prevent a severe payments disruption. Fed Vice Chairman Roger Ferguson made the calls, since Chairman Alan Greenspan was still flying back from Europe, and successfully averted such a disruption.

As with all policy matters, exchange rate decisions may or may not travel all the way up the financial chain of command to the President. My refusing a request from Haruhiko Kuroda to intervene in the currency markets after 9/11 when it is the administration's general policy not to intervene would not require the President's attention. Designing a diplomatic strategy to deal with Japan or China on their exchange rate policy, however, would be something that the President should be involved in, and in fact was involved in.

No clear-cut way exists to determine what issues merit passing along the chain of command, and this makes it difficult for outsiders to determine who is in charge of exchange rate policy. In my view, it is always a good idea to err on the side of passing information up, and I asked people who worked for me to do the same. People on the outside, especially the press, are always on the lookout for apparent defects in the decision-making process. For example, in mid-April 2005, I recommended on an interagency conference call that we ratchet up to the next phase of our diplomatic engagement with the Chinese on the currency policy. Anyone in the loop would know that this particular recommendation originated in Treasury. But somehow Andrew Balls, a reporter for the *Financial Times*, wrote the exact opposite: that the White House had told Treasury to ratchet things up. On April 22, he published a story with the headline: "Treasury Feels White House Heat on Policy: About-Turn on China Currency Signals Economic Strategy Is to Be Firmly Led by the President's Inner Circle."

Despite the formal division of responsibility, the Treasury and the Fed cooperate closely on exchange rate issues. I made sure to involve Alan Greenspan in all major exchange rate issues that we dealt with during my tenure, and we had a number of meetings with him both in the Treasury and the White House on the exchange rate. In addition, if there were an intervention, the Fed and the Treasury would traditionally intervene together, with the Fed using some of its foreign exchange and the Treasury using some of its foreign exchange, which was stashed away in the Exchange Stabilization Fund. The Fed also acts as the fiscal agent of the Treasury, and in the case of an intervention Dino Kos would actually execute the buying or selling of currencies in the New York market on our behalf, even though I never had to ask for his services.

Other countries have similar divisions of responsibility. In Japan, the Ministry of Finance is responsible for exchange rate policy and the Bank of Japan handles domestic monetary policy. With the creation of the euro, governance of exchange rate policy in Europe has become more complex. While the European Central Bank (ECB) sets the interest rate, it shares responsibility for the exchange rate with a group of finance ministers called the Euro Group. Hence, the ECB has more responsibility for the exchange rate than either the Fed or the Bank of Japan.

JAPAN: THE EXCHANGE RATE AND THE END OF THE "LOST DECADE"

Deciding on a strategy for dealing with the Japanese intervention in the markets was one of the first diplomatic issues we faced in the currency area. Economic growth in Japan had hovered near zero for much of the 1990s—a period many call the "lost decade." Japan was experiencing a deflation, which was holding back economic growth because consumers and businesses curtailed their spending plans, anticipating lower prices in the future. The deflation and lack of growth made it difficult for people to pay interest on, or even pay back, their bank loans. Hence, the banks found themselves with many non-performing loans on which payments were not being made, an obvious threat to the banks and the whole banking system.

Economic stagnation in Japan was clearly not in the best interests of the United States. A stronger Japanese economy would provide the resources to help Japan play a key role with the United States and other allies in providing security and development assistance to poor countries. Two developments presented an opportunity for the United States to help Japan change direction.

In March 2001, the Bank of Japan announced that it would follow a new type of monetary policy called "quantitative easing," under which it would pump up the money supply in Japan until the deflation ended. I was ecstatic when I heard this announcement. Since 1994 I had been an adviser to the Bank of Japan, a post I had to resign when I joined the Bush administration. I had recommended many times that the Bank of Japan focus on increasing the money supply as a means to end their deflation, and many other economists had recommended the same thing. The Japanese never took that advice in the 1990s, but they took it now, and it became the policy of the Bush administration to support this in Japan.

In April 2001, a reform-minded politician, Junichiro Koizumi, was elected prime minister of Japan. When President Bush met with Prime Minister Koizumi at Camp David in June 2001, he strongly supported the prime minister's reforms, saying to the press afterwards, "I have no reservations about the economic reform agenda that the Prime Minister is advancing. He talks about tackling difficult issues that some leaders in the past refused to address." Their friendship and mutual respect—which set the tone for discussions at all levels—was symbolized by the prime minister's frequent references to his favorite movie, *High Noon*, and how it reminded him of President Bush's determination and leadership. They discussed the economic issues too—including the problems in the Japanese banking system. In this way, President Bush and his team developed a new approach to U.S. economic relations with Japan. There would be no more "Japan-bashing." The President wanted to base our relations with Japan on mutual respect and cooperation, not antagonism. Lectures from the U.S. government had proven ill-suited to advancing Japanese prosperity. The title of a 1999 Brookings Institution book, *Troubled Times: U.S.-Japan Trade Relations in the 1990s*, captured the problematic nature of the relationship. The President called for a very free and frank exchange of views, but no lectures.

THE GREAT INTERVENTION

Our policy toward exchange rate intervention in Japan was part of our effort to be supportive of quantitative easing. By not registering strong objections to the intervention, effectively allowing it to happen, we made it easier for the Japanese to pump up their money supply. The strategy worked this way: When the Bank of Japan intervenes and buys dollars in the currency markets at the instruction of the finance ministry, it pays for the dollars with yen. For every 10 billion of U.S. dollars they purchase, they pay out over 1 trillion yen; in other words, they increase the Japanese money supply by over 1 trillion yen. Unless the Bank of Japan offsets—"sterilizes" is the technical term—this increase in yen by buying other assets, such as Japanese government bonds, the Japanese money supply increases. In the past, U.S. administrations had leaned heavily against the Japanese intervening in the markets to drive down the yen. By adopting a more tolerant position toward intervention—especially if it went unsterilized—we could help to increase the money supply in Japan. When Zembei Mizoguchi was chosen to replace Kuroda at the end of 2002, as part of the transition they both informed me that currency intervention was going to increase. I did not object, as Treasury might have in the past, but I repeated our own views about the merits of keeping intervention to a minimum. True to their word, intervention did increase; eventually it increased to unprecedented magnitudes, to $320 billion!

After a few months into 2003, the unprecedented nature of the intervention was becoming clear to everyone. The Japanese would not publicly announce their daily interventions, but the markets began to sense it, and at the end of each month Japan would report on the monthly totals. I had arranged for the Japanese to e-mail me personally whenever they intervened in the market, and to call me about very large interventions. When I read e-mail on my Black-

Berry in the early morning I would frequently find messages from Tokyo such as, "Small intervention during Tokyo trading hours; 1.2 billion dollars purchased," and I was awakened by quite a few late night or very early morning calls from Tokyo, too.

By the summer of 2003, the data began to show that the Japanese economy was finally turning the corner. Though it was too early to be sure about the recovery, it seemed to me that the Japanese could soon begin to exit from their unusual exchange rate policy of massive intervention, and they could call it a success.

A "G3" GROUP

Many international policy discussions about exchange rates occur bilaterally, as my conversations with Kuroda and Mizoguchi exemplify. Multilateral discussions are needed, too. The IMF used to be a forum to discuss and comment on exchange rates policies, but that role seemed to atrophy with the end of Bretton Woods in the early 1970s. The G7 soon picked up much of the multilateral action on exchange rates and became a natural forum for the United States to discuss exchange rate policy with other countries. Issuing communiqués about the exchange rate remains an important task of the G7, but the creation of the euro brought the need for another grouping to discuss such issues. For certain issues the G7 was too large, and three of the countries (Germany, France, and Italy) now had the same currency. After discussing this with the Europeans and the Japanese, I decided that a "G3" group representing the three major currencies—the dollar, the euro, and the yen—made the most sense. Caio Koch-Weser, chair of the Economic and Finance Committee that represents the Euro Group, Zembei Mizoguchi of Japan, and I then worked to establish such a regular consultation process.

We held the first "G3" meeting on July 9, 2003, at the same time I hosted a summer retreat for my G7 counterparts in Stanford, California. I thought carefully about the best venue for this first meeting. To avoid publicity, it would have to take place away from the Stanford campus and the hotel where our other colleagues were staying.

I decided it would be best if the location was a memorable place with a "dealmaking" atmosphere. I chose a restaurant called "Bucks of Woodside," located in a small village in a woodsy area a few miles from the Stanford campus. "Bucks" had earned a reputation as the place where Silicon Valley venture capitalists and entrepreneurs go to make deals and start companies. It had the right atmosphere, then, though I doubt previous deals made there came close to the hundreds-of-billions-of-dollars magnitude that we would be talking about.

Bucks is memorable in other ways, especially if you regularly dine in the best restaurants in Europe and Japan as my two G3 counterparts did. When you walk through the front door, a miniature Statue of Liberty greets you. Model airplanes and cowboy boots dangle from the ceiling. A giant ketchup bottle stands next to the cash register. Paintings of cowboys on bucking broncos line the walls along with rattlesnake skins. The morning we visited, most of the cars in the parking lot were German or Japanese, mainly BMWs, Porsches, Lexuses, Infinitis, which I'm sure made Caio and Zembei feel at home and reminded them that the U.S. economy was strong and recovering quickly.

We sat in a booth and laid out the charts we had brought on the table. For a while Caio and Zembei kept looking around at the strange decorations, but soon we were all staring intently at the charts. One of Zembei's was a line graph showing the dollar/yen exchange rate since January 2003; the line fluctuated but seemed to always turn up when it got close to 116 yen per dollar.

Whenever the line approached 116, an oval revealed the amount of dollars Japan bought in an effort to make the dollar turn back up, or equivalently make the yen turn down. "Zembei," I said. "Let's take a look at your chart. The dollar hasn't gone below 116 yen all year, and just as it starts to get close to that level the chart shows interventions to drive the yen exchange rate back up. How can one say this is merely smoothing out fluctuations, when the interventions seem so one-sided?" Caio asked a similar question, and before Zembei could answer, a familiar voice called out: "John, how are you?" I

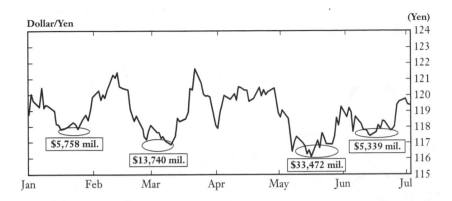

looked up and saw Tad Taube, an old friend and highly successful real estate investor. Reflexively, Caio and Zembei turned over their papers and I introduced everyone. Tad was pleased to hear that I was working on some great international finance deal, whatever it was, and he wished me luck, mentioning that he had done a few closings at Bucks himself.

After Tad left, Zembei replied that he was merely trying to prevent overshooting of the value of the dollar, rather than trying to hold it to a particular level. The semantic distinction was subtle but I concluded that Zembei agreed in substance with our point. Zembei then went on to discuss the possibility that the United States, Europe, and Japan might reach a common understanding on "reference rates," or a permissive range of exchange rates, within which the dollar, the yen, and the euro would fluctuate—an agreement like the famous Louvre Accord of 1987, in which the United States, Japan, and other countries agreed to jointly intervene in the markets to stabilize currencies. He sketched on a piece of notepaper (shown on the next page) how such a system might work to keep the euro and the yen from fluctuating too far from the reference rate. The idea was that intervention would occur if the exchange rate deviated by more than ZZ or MM from the reference rate; XX or YY would be okay. A similar concept would work for the yen/dollar rate and for the dollar/euro rate.

Caio and I made it clear that neither the United States nor

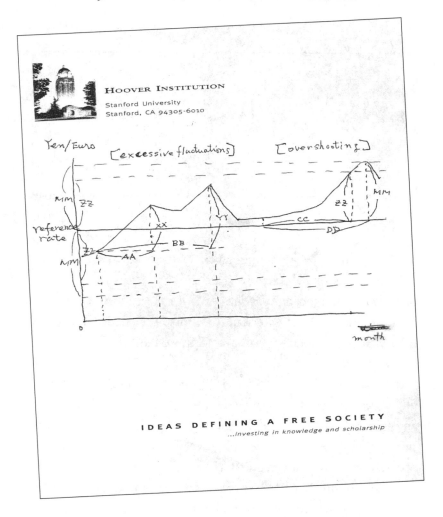

Europe would agree to such an arrangement. I was happy to hear the Europeans' view—a "Bucks accord" was the last thing I was looking for. The meeting demonstrated that it was useful to air views held by Europe, Japan, and the United States in the context of a civil, technical discussion. After that meeting, it was clear that a new system of reference rates, or nearly fixed exchange rates, was simply not in the cards.

This would mark the first of many G3 meetings, most of which occurred by phone. We did modify the process to include a representative from the European Central Bank because of its explicit shared responsibility for the euro exchange rate. Tommaso Padoa-Schioppa, the international representative of the ECB, participated in many future meetings.

At that first G3 meeting, I first began to discuss the need for an exit strategy from the Great Intervention, referring to the evidence of recovery in Japan. On September 9, at the next G3 meeting, in Paris, I gave Zembei another reason—a multilateral reason—to exit soon. We had started to prepare for the upcoming G7 meeting later that month in Dubai, and we wanted to issue a multilateral statement calling on the Chinese to move to a flexible exchange rate. That would prove a difficult sell if the Japanese continued to intervene heavily.

THE EXIT STRATEGY

Soon after I got back to Washington from Paris, on September 12, I received an important call from Mizoguchi. He said they would ease up on the intervention as part of an informal understanding. The proposal was that (1) Secretary Snow would stop saying, "Japan should keep intervention to a minimum," which Zembei felt required them to intervene even more; (2) Japan would let the yen move more flexibly, though there will still be a need to intervene when there is excess volatility and overshooting in the markets; and (3) if the dollar fell below 110 yen, the United States would be willing to engage in consultation on a possible action. I said I would have to check with John Snow, but that I knew we could not commit to item (3) or any particular action regarding a reference rate in advance. John Snow readily agreed with items (1) and (2), and I also confirmed that plan with Steve Friedman and Alan Greenspan, who both agreed. I then confirmed the agreement with Mizoguchi.

True to their word, the Japanese did begin to reduce their interventions. For a whole week starting on September 12, they did nothing, even though the dollar dropped below 116. In fact, it fell rather sharply: from 117.4 on September 12 to 114.0 on September 19. It was a sudden movement that surprised the markets and gave us all pause. Exiting from this heavy intervention strategy might be more difficult than we anticipated. The turbulence continued for a few more days, and on September 20, at the time of the G7 meeting in Dubai, the dollar also depreciated sharply following release of the G7 statement on the currencies. After talking to Dino Kos in New York, I suggested to John Snow that he give the "strong dollar" line in his post-meeting press conference and he did so, which was enough to offset the dollar's weakness.

During the fall and winter, evidence of a sustainable recovery in Japan mounted, and I thought that the sooner the recovery became clear, the sooner Japan could exit from its intervention. On December 5, 2003, I gave a speech in New York asserting that Japan was on the road to recovery. It was still a little risky to declare victory that early, but fortunately I was right and the economy had indeed turned the corner. Michael Phillips of *The Wall Street Journal* wrote a piece entitled "U.S. Sees Reason to Be Optimistic on Japan Growth" on the morning of my talk, saying: "The Bush Administration believes the Japanese economy may finally have turned the corner after more than a decade of little or no growth. In a speech to be delivered today, the Treasury Department's top international official, John Taylor, will credit the Koizumi government's market changes and the Bank of Japan's accommodating monetary policy for giving impetus to the country's laggard economy. . . . The upbeat comments from the undersecretary of the Treasury for international affairs represent a sharp shift in Washington's long pessimistic view of Japan's fortunes."

For the next few months we continued to work with the Japanese on an exit strategy. By early February 2004, the Japanese decided to complete the exit and Zembei reached me in the United Arab Emirates to tell me the news. I was in Dubai again, but this time only changing planes on my way from Kabul to Baghdad. Zembei said they had decided to end the massive intervention and outlined their exit strategy. They might intervene even more heavily in the next month, but they would then stop. The Japanese had never tried to mislead me, so I knew that this was indeed their strategy.

On March 2, Alan Greenspan spoke in New York, explaining how the overall intervention strategy had worked, but that it was now time to stop. He used the somewhat technical language of a central banker, but the message was clear: " . . . partially unsterilized intervention is perceived as a means of expanding the monetary base of Japan, a basic element of monetary policy. In time, however, as the present deflationary situation abates, the monetary consequences of continued intervention could become problematic. The current performance of the Japanese economy suggests that we are getting closer to the point where continued intervention at the present scale will no longer meet the monetary policy needs of Japan."

Friday, March 5, 2004, marked the start of what I would later call the real end of the intervention. At eight-thirty that morning Washington time, the U.S. Labor Department released its monthly employment report. Employment for the month of February was up by only 21,000 jobs, much less than we or the market had anticipated. News like this would normally have a negative impact on the dollar because weaker jobs data would lower the chances of an interest rate increase by the Fed, thereby making the dollar slightly less attractive to investors seeking higher interest rates. But the dollar did not weaken, and that same day—March 5—the Japanese had purchased $11.2 billion, which made the dollar appreciate rather than depreciate as one would expect. Zembei had told me they might do more intervention before they did less, but this was simply excessive, and I called him over the weekend to complain, being as forceful as a friend and ally could be. Zembei acknowledged that they were still intervening heavily now, but the March 5 dollar buy was part of the exit plan.

Zembei did soon stop intervening, after another week of heavy dollar purchases, but nothing that equaled March 5. The last purchase of dollars occurred on March 16 when the Japanese bought "only" $615 million. On the 17th, my BlackBerry reported no intervention, and again on the 18th. There was no intervention for the rest of March, or for the rest of 2004, and all the way through 2005. Eventually I stopped checking my BlackBerry for reports of Japanese intervention. The yen did not strengthen much after the intervention ended March 5. Everyone recognized that the Japanese recovery was solid and that the lost decade was a thing of the past.

BusinessWeek wrote this about Zembei Mizoguchi on March 22, 2004: "In Tokyo, he's a faceless bureaucrat in a town full of them. But in trading pits in London and New York, and among chief financial officers from Detroit to Stuttgart, Vice-Minister of International Affairs at Japan's Ministry of Finance Zembei Mizoguchi enjoys celebrity status. And with good reason: This financial diplomat—call him Mr. Dollar—is the architect of perhaps the biggest single-handed currency intervention since World War II."

CHINA: TOWARD THE END OF THE PEG

China had also been intervening in the currency markets during this period, but the situation there differed greatly from Japan. China maintained a completely fixed exchange rate; by intervening in the currency market, the Central Bank of China pegged the currency at 8.28 yuan per dollar. It had done so for ten years. Moreover, the Chinese economy did not experience a lost decade in the 1990s from which it had to recover. China had suffered a setback from the global downturn of 2001 and the economy was further damaged by the SARS virus, which caused businesses to close and tourists to go elsewhere. By the summer of 2003, however, the Chinese economy was clearly booming again and U.S. policy began to focus on Chinese exchange market intervention and its currency peg.

The Chinese policy led to a situation analogous to the state of the world near the end of the Bretton Woods fixed exchange rate system in 1971. At that time, most countries were pegging their exchange rate to the dollar. The lack of exchange rate flexibility was putting strains on the United States and other economies. Getting out of that fixed exchange rate system required aggressive financial diplomacy by the United States, starting on August 15, 1971, with the imposition of an import tax, which led to considerable turbulence in the financial markets. Some economists had dubbed the decade-long Chinese peg "Bretton Woods II," because other countries in Asia kept their currencies close to the Chinese yuan, effectively tying them to the dollar. In essence we were trying to end Bretton Woods II.

Unlike the exit from Bretton Woods I, we did not want to employ tariff increases to get results and we wanted to avoid financial instability.

In their inside account of policymaking in the 1970s George Shultz and Kenneth Dam write that "A 10 percent import surcharge—an implicit devaluation on the import side, an attention-getter, and a bargaining chip—was therefore introduced in the August 15, [1971] package . . . we regarded the surcharge as a temporary part of our negotiating strategy. It was designed to be a signal that the United States was seeking a fundamental change not only in existing exchange rates but also in the monetary system itself. Secretary [John] Connally flashed the signal in true Texas style, with both guns blazing in the corridors of international finance."[*]

However successful the tariff had been as a bargaining chip in 1971, I wanted to avoid a tariff now. In fact, at the time, we were trying very hard to avoid a 27 percent tariff increase proposed by Senator Charles Schumer of New York. I wanted to avoid the kind of turmoil in the financial markets that resulted from the end of Bretton Woods I. There was no reason to pursue a more timid financial diplomacy than the one employed by John Connally, but by avoiding the threat of a tariff we would have a much better chance of market stability.

The Diplomatic Strategy

We developed our strategy for the Chinese exchange rate with deliberation and, as with Japan, under the leadership of President Bush. The strategy had four main elements.

First, we emphasized that increased exchange rate flexibility was in the interest of China, as well as the United States. In China, a new exchange rate regime would enable the central bank to conduct monetary policy much like successful central banks in large developed economies, including the Federal Reserve. Free from the constraints

[*]Shultz and Dam, *Economic Policy Behind the Headlines*, p. 115.

of a rigid exchange rate, the Central Bank of China could adjust its interest rate by enough to achieve price stability.

Second, we recognized that in order for China to move to a flexible exchange rate, it would have to create a modern exchange rate market with both spot and futures trading. We decided that the United States would offer technical assistance to the Chinese to help create these markets.

Third, we used a multilateral approach. Chinese intervention in the markets was not simply an issue for the United States, but rather for Europe and Japan as well. A more flexible exchange rate would help in the adjustment of trade imbalances by facilitating appropriate changes in the price of exports and imports. This benefit would increase if other central banks in Asia also allowed greater exchange rate flexibility.

Fourth, we explained the strategy carefully both to the Congress, in order to prevent protectionist legislation, and to the markets, in order to prevent sharp movements and volatility.

The rollout of the new strategy would commence with Secretary Snow's trip to China on September 2, 2003. Over the course of a number of NSC meetings, we finalized our plan. The most significant of these meetings, in my view, occurred on August 26. I was in the White House Sit Room with John Snow; the President was on the video from Crawford, Texas. "This is a very important trip," President Bush said. He then reminded us of John Connally's diplomatic approach in 1971 and said, "It is appealing," to make sure we knew that he wanted a tough financial diplomacy strategy. He spoke about the communications element of the strategy. "Our message is: 'We support trade, but we want trade to be fair. We expect China to be open to our products. Part of that is the exchange rate.' Our people need to hear that we are creating jobs by being free traders." He also wanted us to keep the message simple. "Remember, most people out there do not know anything about floating currencies. . . . Explain the reality on the ground." Finally, the President stressed the differences between Japan and China, acknowledging the economic difficulties that Japan had experienced and that we were trying to help them overcome these difficulties. "This is China, not Japan. Be sensitive with Japan," he advised.

John Snow's trip to China was a success. He not only delivered his message about the need for exchange rate flexibility with forcefulness and candor, he also impressed the Chinese with his substantive knowledge of the issue. They listened to him when he said that a flexible exchange rate was in their interest.

THE BOCA RATON LANGUAGE

The multilateral element of our strategy took shape at the September 20, 2003, G7 meeting in Dubai. From the time of the G3 meeting at Bucks, I had been working with Caio and Zembei on possible language on exchange rate flexibility for the G7 meeting. We had considered option after option and in the end only settled on the actual wording on the morning of the meeting. John Snow, Alan Greenspan, and others in our government were also comfortable with the language, but you never know what to expect once everyone is in the room. The G7 discussion proved contentious, mainly due to the fact that the European central bankers felt they had not received an adequate briefing and had not had time to study the wording. At one point the meeting almost ended with no agreement to call for a flexible exchange rate, which would have been a severe blow to our diplomatic strategy. The day was saved when the president of the ECB, Wim Duisenberg, suggested changing the phrase "a flexible exchange rate" to "more flexibility in exchange rates." I was worried that the markets would misinterpret this statement and think that it applied to Europe rather than China, but the new wording was the only way we could come to an agreement. In the end, the statement read: "We emphasize that more flexibility in exchange rates is desirable for major countries or economic areas to promote smooth and widespread adjustments in the international financial system, based on market mechanisms." It hewed close to the multilateral message we wanted to give to China, but it did leave some ambiguity.

It would take until the next G7 meeting in Boca Raton, Florida, in February 2004 to clear everything up. The exchange rate language produced tension during the fall of 2003 that lasted right up until the time we all arrived at the resort hotel in Boca Raton. The Europeans felt that the Dubai language was causing the dollar to depreciate against the euro and they wanted either to throw it out or to radically change it. We wanted to keep it unchanged. To resolve the differences, John Snow suggested that Alan Greenspan, Mervyn King of the Bank of England, Jean-Paul Trichet, who had replaced Duisenberg at the ECB, and I meet together in a separate room and then report back to the full G7. But after nearly an hour and a half we had failed to find a solution, and I went back to negotiating with Koch-Weser, Mizoguchi, and our other colleagues. With the negotiations stalled, John Snow called me out of the room to offer the key suggestion, which was to add "in countries that do not have flexible exchange rates" after "more flexibility." That did the trick. No longer could the language by interpreted as pointing to Europe. It was unambiguously pointing to China.

Soon after the Dubai meetings, on October 15, we met with the President in the Oval Office to review the state of play and to get his approval not to identify China as a manipulator in the currency markets. The President agreed with the decision not to designate China as a technical matter, but said he wanted continued strong action. It was at that meeting that we discussed the trade deficit and its link to the imbalance between saving and investment, referred to at the start of this chapter.

GUESS WHO CAME TO DINNER

The Dubai meetings also marked the start of my efforts to bring the Chinese into the G7 process to discuss the exchange rate. Zembei Mizoguchi and our G7 counterparts and I invited China's two top "financial diplomats" to meet with us for the first time in Dubai: Li Rougu from the central bank and Li Yong from the finance ministry. For some reason the two Li's insisted on treating us at a dinner meeting, and they chose an elegant Chinese restaurant in Dubai. Our aim was to have a candid discussion of the just-finished G7 statement on exchange rates and to lay the groundwork for the Chinese finance minister and central bank governor to attend a G7 ministerial meeting within the year.

We met quietly with our two Chinese counterparts again three more times during the following year, in Rome, Paris, and Washington. My Italian and French colleagues contributed to the quiet diplomatic effort by hosting elegant dinners featuring their countries' cuisines, while in Washington, with our tight budgets, we settled for an American breakfast in my Treasury office. Though we discussed many topics of mutual interest, the discussions always centered on the Chinese exchange rate. We always stressed the advantage of a flexible exchange rate for the Chinese economy and for the broader international financial system.

This quiet approach paid off when the Chinese agreed that Finance Minister Jin Renging and the central bank governor, Zhou Xiaochuan, would attend a dinner on October 1, 2004, and that the exchange rate, among other things, would be the key topic. The dinner was held in the historic Treasury Cash Room. An historic first meeting, the press covered the event closely. The *New York Times* previewed the meeting with a story on September 23 headlined: GUESS WHO IS INVITED TO DINNER? Fortunately, the newspapers did not report on how the Secret Service at first refused to allow the Chinese finance minister, Jin, into the Treasury Building. It was one of those diplomatic screw-ups that always seem to happen at the worst time, and that could upset all the careful planning. The meeting started off on an awkward note, but fortunately had no lasting impact.

People often asked me what that first meeting was like and I would say it was amazingly candid and free-flowing, which it was. Jin explained that "a flexible rate that reflects supply and demand is our clear goal; it is part of a larger reform effort." He said that they appreciated the technical assistance the U.S. Treasury was providing to help them achieve that goal. The Canadian finance minister, Ralph Goodale, then asked the crucial question: "Do you have a timeline or signposts?"

"That is a difficult question," Zhou answered. "We don't have a timetable. There is an old Chinese story about crossing a stream by walking from stone to stone. You can't set a timeline because you don't know which stones will be secure enough to step on. But please believe me when I say that China is going to do this." Mervyn King of the Bank of England asked them why foreign reserves were rising so rapidly at the Central Bank of China, and Zhou explained that it was a necessary implication of holding the peg in the face of upward pressures. They had to buy dollars to prevent its value from rising against the yuan. There was no disagreement on the technical issues at that meeting, a sign that some progress was near.

CHINA STARTS TO MOVE

After the dinner we moved to a purposefully quieter time in our strategy, but by early 2005 it became clear to us that the necessary prior steps to remove the peg had been taken in China. The spot market was ready for more flexibility, and it was time to start the exit. John Snow and I began to say this explicitly and publicly.

On July 21, 2005, the Chinese officially abandoned their peg, and then gradually allowed for more flexibility. They let the exchange rate depreciate by a small 2.1 percent, and said they would then allow a 0.3 percent limit on daily currency changes. Governor Zhou took the first step across the proverbial Chinese stream. Since then, the yuan has been moving up slowly against the dollar. And with the increased flexibility, the spot and futures currency markets have been developing further, which will in turn permit the Chinese to have more flexibility in the exchange rate. China had successfully exited from its decade-long peg and had done so with remarkably little turbulence in the financial markets. Bretton Woods II was ending, with little of the turbulence seen when Bretton Woods I ended. It was a first step, but the exchange rate diplomacy of the United States and the rest of the G7 countries was finally paying off.

Epilogue

My last day as a global financial warrior began in the White House Situation Room in a meeting with President Bush and his national security team. It was Friday morning, April 22, 2005. I was there to report on the financial situation in Iraq. The meeting began with political and security briefings, after which President Bush called on me. I reported that financial conditions remained good. "We were concerned about an up tick in inflation late last year, but we worked with the Central Bank and that episode now seems behind us for the time being. The new Iraqi currency remains strong and stable. We need to work on helping the Iraqis install an electronic payments system, which will facilitate paying the newly trained Iraqi security forces. We also need to make sure Iraq stays committed to the IMF program, so the Iraqi people can get the nearly $100 billion in debt relief that we negotiated."

The President listened and then commented that things had worked out pretty well in the finance area. Steve Hadley, who had replaced Condi Rice as National Security Adviser, then reminded people of the international fund-raising effort that Al Larson, Dov

Zakheim, and I had initiated, and he advised that we needed to maintain that kind of effort. Condi Rice, now Secretary of State, agreed and mentioned that the next donors' conference in June would be an opportunity to do so.

As the meeting broke up, President Bush thanked me for serving on his team and for what we accomplished. He offered to have my family come around to visit him again in the Oval Office, but I said he already had done enough. He then asked, "Have you decided what's next?"

"I'm going back to Stanford," I said. "In fact, I'll be giving a lecture at the Hoover Institution on Monday on what we've accomplished here." It was at Stanford exactly seven years earlier, in April 1998, that I first met President Bush—then Governor Bush—as he was considering a run for the presidency. We met at George Shultz's house across the street from mine on the Stanford campus. Condi Rice and several other Stanford colleagues were there. We discussed foreign policy and economic policy; we then worked for the next two plus years on the 2000 presidential campaign. After the election, Condi and I came into government. We brought ideas with us, developed new ideas after 9/11, and implemented those ideas, all as part of a team led by the President and, in my case, driven by our dedicated financial warriors in the Treasury. Now I was leaving government, saying good-bye to the President and the team, going back to the world of ideas.

Yet it was Steve Hadley's forward-looking comment about maintaining the effort that really got me thinking. Steve's comment applied to everything that had been accomplished—disrupting the financing of terror, the financial reconstruction in Afghanistan and Iraq, stopping global contagion of financial crises, the new reforms at the IMF and the World Bank, and the resulting greatly improved performance of the global economy. But it also applied to what had not yet been accomplished, most important, finishing the global war on terror, which would likely take many more years, well beyond the Bush presidency. As the impetus from 9/11 receded further into the past, it would be more difficult to maintain this record of accomplishment. What factors led to the successes? What are the lessons learned from the stories—the case studies—in this book that might be applied in the future? Of the myriad of possible answers, two factors above all made things work, in my view: establishing clear, understandable missions and creating specialized teams of people committed to those missions.

ESTABLISHING CLEAR, UNDERSTANDABLE MISSIONS

A frequently stated, but often ignored, lesson from anyone who has served in a position of leadership is to establish a clear set of principles. Every successful operation I describe in this book had a clear, understandable mission. Whether we outlined the mission as a set of principles, or goals, or objectives, or rules, we chose the mission and stuck with it as each decision was made. Principles provide an anchor or a guide, which is especially useful when you can be thrown off track by pressures of time and overcommitment, worries of financial calamity, lack of sleep, criticism in the press, turf battles, personality conflicts, doubts from above, doubts from below, and inevitable setbacks. The more confidence you have in the principles, the better.

Principles can be set at all levels of government. At the highest level, the President of the United States sets the principles. The stories in this book give one example after another of how President Bush set principles in the international finance area. Starting with the premise in the epigraph to this book that international finance will be a front in the war on terror, he established the principles:

- that freezing terrorist assets should be the first shot in the war;
- that measurable results and revenue accountability are essential to financial reconstruction in Afghanistan;
- that financial stability in Iraq should be the key goal of financial reconstruction;
- that currency flexibility in China should be the objective of our financial diplomacy;

- that a new type of economic relationship was needed with Japan to help the Japanese people emerge from the lost decade;

and many others found in this book.

I used this principles concept relentlessly in the international affairs division at Treasury. At the going-away party my staff threw for me, they presented me with a plaque that set out the ten broad principles they remembered me espousing most often. They called them the ten "Taylor Rules," an extension of the Taylor Rule I had developed for monetary policy years earlier, though I had never written these rules down. The plaque reads:

1. Economic policy should aim to increase economic stability and economic growth.

2. Official finance should support good economic policy with strong ownership. It cannot substitute for bad economic policy.

3. Raising productivity growth is essential for reducing poverty. This requires economic freedom that eliminates impediments to efficient allocation of capital and labor and to the spread of technology.

4. The private sector—not the government—is the engine of economic growth.

5. The international financial system works better when official lending decisions and sovereign debt restructuring processes are predictable. This encourages more efficient movement of capital and a lower cost of capital.

6. Contagion is not automatic. It can be contained by good policy, by the dissemination of information, and greater predictability in the international financial system.

7. Loans should not be made when there is a high probability that they will be forgiven. Assistance for the poorest countries should be in the form of grants, not loans.

8. Development assistance must produce measurable results. All donors should set clear goals and guidelines. Success should be measured by whether these goals and timelines are met, not by the volume of disbursements.

9. Monetary policy should focus on price stability. Sound exchange rate policies support this objective, prevent crises, and allow adjustment throughout the global financial system.

10. Tax systems with broad bases, efficient administration, and low marginal tax rates are best to encourage both growth and sustainable public finances.

The concept of principles applies both broadly and to specific initiatives. We applied No. 1 to everything we did. We applied No. 5 to the IMF reform initiative. We applied No. 6 to the Argentine financial crisis. We applied Nos. 7 and 8 to the World Bank reform initiative. In the case of forming an international coalition to freeze terrorist assets, we stipulated two other overriding principles: that the freeze should be *simultaneous* and that it should be *global*. In the case of the reduction of Iraq's debt, our principle was the greatest possible debt reduction for the Iraqi people. And so on.

Of course, you have to have the right set of principles, and choosing the right principles is as essential as following the principles. In the case of World Bank reform, we chose not to try to reform the whole Bank; our reform principles focused on the part that dealt with the poorest countries. In the case of IMF reform, we decided that decentralized "collective action clauses" was the right principle rather than a centralized world bankruptcy court. In the case of China, the principle was a flexible exchange rate, not a revaluation of the exchange rate by a certain amount.

Each year I gave a speech that reiterated our goals and assessed progress, asking the question, "How are we doing?" In November 2001, I gave a speech at Harvard explaining the administration's international financial agenda following 9/11. In 2002, I gave a follow-up speech, reporting that recovery from the global slump of

2000–01 and the terrorist attacks was well underway, but we still had more to do. By 2004, three years had passed since the first policy speech at Harvard, and the answer to "How are we doing?" was unequivocal. Economic times were good. Global growth in 2004 was turning out to be the highest in three decades. There were no crises anywhere. There were no recessions anywhere. Interest rates in emerging markets were very low.

CREATING SPECIALIZED TEAMS OF PEOPLE COMMITTED TO THE MISSION

Every successful initiative in this book was carried out by a specially designated team of people dedicated to that initiative, from chapter 1's high-spirited War Room, aka Task Force on Terrorist Financing, created just after 9/11, to chapter 10's Chinese currency team. The Argentine team of chapter 3 consisted of financial market experts, monetary experts, sovereign debt experts, and legal experts focused on that crisis in 2001. I told the stories of "Team Turkey" in chapter 7 and the Iraq debt team in chapter 9. Sometimes there were two teams working in tandem, such as the team deployed forward in Iraq and the "reach-back" team in Washington described in chapters 7 and 8. Hugh Tant's motto "Teamwork That Works," for the currency war room in Baghdad, could apply to every team we created. Of course, most of the teamwork described in the ten chapters of this book was going on simultaneously, as was the work of teams that I could not, for lack of space, include: teams for financial reconstruction in Liberia; for measuring results of aid to Haiti; for fund-raising for Bolivia; for negotiating free trade agreements with Chile and Singapore; for developing the economic components of the new Millennium Challenge Account; for the broader Middle East and North Africa initiative; and for the Africa mortgage markets initiative.

Not everyone in Treasury international affairs was assigned to specialized teams. There were essential ongoing jobs, such as accounting, budgeting, and monitoring the state of the global economy. But here I found the focused mission concept useful too. I created a new "business office," the name conjuring up its main budgeting and accounting mission. I created a monthly "blue chip economic indicator," in which people who followed different countries in different parts of Treasury could pool their information in a teamlike fashion. Similarly, I created a weekly "hot spots" report to make sure we were on top of any development around the world that could affect financial markets.

The lessons learned from the stories in this book are that to be effective, a team must have four essential characteristics:

The team must have a strong leader and people with the requisite expertise and experience—in our case, in the areas of financial markets, international institutions, international law, logistics, and financial diplomacy.

The team must be accountable, with performance benchmarks and timelines, and must report up the chain of command regularly, an antidote to micromanaging. The situation reports from our teams in Baghdad or Kabul prevented mistakes and allowed for smooth adjustments in plans when necessary. Ideally, the team would report directly to me or at least to someone who directly reported to me so that it would not get lost in the bureaucracy.

The team must have enough autonomy to implement its mission. Autonomy does not mean preventing others from getting on your turf, or not coordinating with other agencies of foreign policy. But it does mean keeping operational responsibility close to the people who know the operations. Indeed, I encouraged other agencies, including State, USAID, and the Fed, to detail people to our task forces, and I asked that they regularly report back to their own supervisors so that no one was left out of the loop. I often repeated my motto for preventing turf battles: "Convey information, don't contain information."

Most important, the team must have a sense of the mission. When the mission was completed, the team would be dissolved and people returned to their usual places in the organization. How do you convey a sense of mission? Forming the team itself helps, and is one of the most important advantages of teams. As with a football or baseball team, people on an international finance team quickly come to know the importance of their role. One of the first Treasury people I assigned to the War Room on terrorist finance was previously in a job where he was losing interest, lacked motivation, seemed down in the dumps. Once he joined the War Room, his personality changed overnight; suddenly he was enthusiastic about what he was doing. He could understand the mission and he was soon one of the most effective members of the team.

I interviewed everyone we sent to Iraq to tell them how much we appreciated what they were doing and to explain how essential they were to the success of the mission. We assigned them clear tasks—such as the terms of reference for David Nummy that describe in chapter 7. Repeating the principles often, in special memorable ways, also helps. That my staff chose to give me a framed plaque with our ten top principles conveyed to me that they indeed had a sense of those principles.

In my experience, President Bush was highly effective in giving people on his team a sense of the mission, and I give plenty of examples in this book: his tasking me in the Oval Office, in front of the president of the World Bank, that he would insist on measurable results there; his moving statement of resolve in the NSC meeting following the bombing of the UN office in Baghdad; his small talk with President Musharraf and me outside the Oval Office on a financial assistance package for Pakistan; his comments to President Duarte of Paraguay on supporting IMF assistance to countries who help themselves. In my experience, this leadership approach goes back to the 2000 presidential campaign, when he insisted on the principle of low marginal tax rates across the board and we all worked to come up with specific proposals to deliver on his principle.

To help instill a sense of the mission, I tried to follow the management guideline that you should tell people the goal or task rather than how to do it. Before I came to Treasury, I ran two centers at Stanford. One was dedicated to the goal of excellence in economic research, the other to the goal of excellence in economics teaching. In both centers I learned that micromanaging people—perhaps especially professors—was a ludicrous way to achieve a goal. You are much better off telling people about the goals and the tasks rather than telling them how to do them.

There are other things that I found useful for bolstering morale: making visits to the front line, giving others credit, having an open door policy where any staff member could come in and raise any issue, holding occasional "all-hands" staff meetings where teams could explain to others what they were accomplishing. I even encouraged the creation of a Treasury singing group—called the "Treasury Notes"—by asking them to sing at staff meetings.

Because there were so many initiatives going on at the same time, my immediate senior advisers devoted a great deal of time to keeping track of them and pushing them along when necessary. I was fortunate to have three extraordinary senior advisers while I was at Treasury: Ramin Toloui, Alpita Shah, and Sonja Renander. They helped me keep a list—which I called "plans and priorities"—that tracked progress on all our initiatives. The plans and priorities list was my own measure of accountability. My view is that everyone should be accountable, and I would update and review the list regularly with the Secretary of the Treasury.

Why were we doing so many things in the international finance area? One reason was that the global slump in financial markets in 2000–01 and the 9/11 terrorist attacks created a huge agenda that was added to the reform agenda we already hoped to pursue upon entering government. International cooperation between the United States and other countries in the finance area has been unprecedented in the post-9/11 world. But more fundamentally, in my view, the answer relates to America's large role in the world.

It goes without saying that the United States is the only global superpower. Because of this, and also because the United States is the world's largest economy, we are frequently put, whether we like it or not, in the position of global financial leadership. Take a simple example. After a year and a half on the job, I began to notice that the World Bank's operating budget was growing very rapidly, and I raised my concerns with my G7 finance colleagues. Of course, as good allies they agreed to help and support me, but their reaction was telling: "It's about time you raised this. We always expect the United States to watch over operations like this." Until these circumstances change, the United States will continue to be at the demanding center of global financial policymaking, and the dedicated work of the global financial warriors at the U.S. Treasury will remain crucial to global stability.

Acknowledgments

I first began telling the stories in this book orally soon after they happened in the days and months after 9/11. I found that people always seemed to react the same way: "That's amazing. I never heard anything like that before. You don't see that in the press," and then advised, "You've got to write it down. Do a book or something." I first want to acknowledge one person in particular who listened to those stories, who gave that advice, and who, because of his policy experience holding four cabinet posts, was more convincing than anyone else that a book of these stories would be a contribution to the history of international finance worth writing. So I dedicate this book to George Shultz, grand master of finance and foreign policy, who not only advised me to write the book but also to take the job that the book is about.

Deciding to write a book is nothing compared with actually sitting down and writing it. For support and encouragement I thank my wife, Allyn, who put it simply: "You've got a new job now, John, writing that book," as well as my children, Jennifer, John, and Josh, and my parents, John and Lorraine, who were equally supportive, and, who along with Allyn, George, John Cogan, and Martin and Annelise Anderson, read many early drafts and gave me valuable comments.

I want to thank Drake McFeely, president of W. W. Norton, for his excellent guidance in this project and for serving as editor simultaneously with his overall leadership responsibilities at Norton. And for day-to-day management of the project—editing, proofing, finding citations, getting permissions—from first draft to a published book, I am grateful to Brendan Curry at W. W. Norton and to my administrative assistant at the Hoover Institution, Marie-Christine Slakey.

Many people read and commented on parts of the book, and I would like to thank specially David Aufhauser, Roger Bezdek, Doug Feith, Tony Fratto, Milton Friedman, Ashraf Ghani, Alan Greenspan, Marc Grossman, Tom Hart, Anna Jewell, David Kennedy, Anne Krueger, Caio Koch-Weser, Alan Larson, John Lipsky, Larry McDonald, Ronald McKinnon, Allan Meltzer, Zembei Mizoguchi, Alan Murray, David Nummy, Michael Phillips, Bobby Pittman, Sonja Renander, Peter Robinson, Larry Seale, Tom Simpson, Faryar Shirzad, T. N. Srinivasan, Hugh Tant, and Ramin Toloui for their comments.

An unexpected and uplifting pleasure from receiving the letters, e-mails, or phone calls with these comments has been reuniting and sharing memories with so many people who worked together during the post-9/11 years. One e-mail, from Brigadier General Hugh Tant, commenting on a paragraph I wrote in an early draft, exemplifies this uplifting spirit, and I want to acknowledge it in particular: "I wept when I read your excerpt. Memories are still overwhelmingly powerful. Thank you for writing this important story and for including the ICE Team's efforts as part of it. . . . I retired from the military on 1 October 2001 after saying goodbye to people I had worked closely with for $5\frac{1}{2}$ years in the Pentagon. Thirty-three of these budget personnel who regularly got me smart to go and brief the Hill perished on 9/11, as well as two of my close friends. I had been a banker with Southcoast Community Bank for only four months when I received the call to serve as Director of the Iraqi Currency Exchange."

Index

Page numbers in *italics* refer to maps and charts.

313